D1351609

THE COLOURED WORKER
IN BRITISH INDUSTRY

The Institute of Race Relations is an unofficial and non-political body, founded in England in 1958 to encourage and facilitate the study of the relations between races everywhere. The Institute is precluded by the Memorandum and Articles of its incorporation from expressing a corporate view. The opinions expressed in this work are those of the author.

The Institute of Race Relations and Dr. Peter Wright make grateful acknowledgement to the Rowntree Memorial Trust for financing the project on which this book is based.

THE COLOURED WORKER
IN BRITISH INDUSTRY

WITH SPECIAL REFERENCE TO THE MIDLANDS
AND NORTH OF ENGLAND

PETER L. WRIGHT

Published for the
Institute of Race Relations, London
OXFORD UNIVERSITY PRESS
LONDON   NEW YORK   TORONTO
1968

QUEEN MARY
COLLEGE
LIBRARY

158160

HD 8398.A2

Oxford University Press, Ely House, London W.1

GLASGOW NEW YORK TORONTO MELBOURNE WELLINGTON
CAPE TOWN SALISBURY IBADAN NAIROBI LUSAKA ADDIS ABABA
BOMBAY CALCUTTA MADRAS KARACHI LAHORE DACCA
KUALA LUMPUR HONG KONG TOKYO

© Institute of Race Relations 1968

PRINTED IN GREAT BRITAIN
BY EBENEZER BAYLIS AND SON, LTD.
THE TRINITY PRESS, WORCESTER, AND LONDON

To My Wife

Contents

List of Tables

List of Figures

Purpose of Research and Field Work Methods

The importance of economic factors in the integration of immigrants was strongly emphasized at the U.N.E.S.C.O. conference on immigration held in Havana in 1956. In one of the conference discussions, economic absorption was succinctly described as a 'way-station to cultural integration'. According to Borrie, 'the Havana conference—not surprisingly—took it as axiomatic that reasonable security of employment was the essential foundation to the long process of cultural integration'.[1]

Until recently, however, research into race relations in Britain has tended to concentrate upon the community rather than the industrial environment. Writing in 1956—the same year as the Havana conference—Janet Reid summarized the situation as follows:

Valuable study has been made of the social aspects of the post-war negro settlement in the United Kingdom, but the industrial picture has not been drawn with any thoroughness. . . . Therefore, there is little general knowledge of the subject and the superficial conclusion voiced in gallup polls and at racial meetings was that the employment of negro immigrants, as opposed to housing and social adjustment, raised no serious problem. But at a time of full employment and housing shortage, it is easy to see how such a verdict is reached.[2]

Soon after this was written, conditions were to change radically. The 1957–8 recession had far reaching effects upon employment prospects for coloured immigrants. Full employment could no longer be taken for granted. In 1955, Senior

[1] W. D. Borrie, *The Cultural Integration of Immigrants*, U.N.E.S.C.O., Paris, 1959.
[2] Janet Reid, 'Employment of Negroes in Manchester', *The Sociological Review*, Vol. 4, 1956.

and Manley[1] stated that West Indian immigrants seldom reported any difficulty in finding a job. By 1958, according to Wickenden,[2] employment rather than housing had become the main problem facing coloured immigrants in this country.

It was to provide the much-needed information concerning the employment aspect of coloured immigration to Britain that the present research was begun in 1961. This is not to say that there was no information whatsoever available concerning the industrial field at that time. Richmond's study of the West Indian technicians and trainees who came to Britain during the Second World War,[3] and community studies such as those of Little,[4] Banton,[5] and Collins[6] had contained sections on the question of employment. In addition, there were shorter articles and papers devoted entirely to employment, such as those of Janet Reid[7] and Stephens.[8] Nevertheless, an over-all picture was lacking. No major research study of race relations in British industry has yet been published, and the three year research project on which the present study is based, was intended to fill this gap.

The research began with a series of interviews with managers of firms in the Midlands employing coloured immigrants. This was intended at first merely as a means of obtaining background data for a more objective study. In all, fourteen firms were visited; in two cases contact was made via the Institute of Race Relations and in the other twelve by means of introductions from Employment Exchange managers. Non-directive interviewing was used in the main. As the intention was to obtain background data, it was felt that it was better to allow the managers to discuss what *they* considered important, rather than to ask specific questions which may not have been relevant.

Often it was possible to elicit most of the information required

[1] C. Senior and D. Manley, *A Report on Jamaican Migration to Great Britain*, Kingston, Jamaica: Government Publications, 1955.

[2] J. Wickenden, *Colour in Britain*, London, 1958.

[3] A. H. Richmond, *Colour Prejudice in Britain*, London, 1954.

[4] K. L. Little, *Negroes in Britain*, London, 1948.

[5] M. P. Banton, *Coloured Quarter*, London, 1955.

[6] S. Collins, *Coloured Minorities in Britain*, London, 1957.

[7] Janet Reid, op. cit.

[8] L. Stephens, 'Employment of Coloured Workers in the Birmingham Area', London: Institute of Personnel Management Occasional Paper, 1956.

simply by asking when the firm had begun to employ coloured workers. The manager would answer this question and then go on to other topics as they occurred to him. Only when the respondent failed to touch upon some general topic which seemed important, such as supervision or labour turnover, were further questions asked. In keeping with the non-directive technique, these questions were only of a general nature, e.g. 'How do you find coloured workers with respect to supervision (or labour turnover, etc.)?' Fairly detailed notes were taken during these interviews, but in no case did this appear to have a detrimental effect on the rapport.

As this stage of the enquiry progressed, it became increasingly apparent that the information gained was much too significant to be used merely as background data, and more time was spent on it than had originally been intended. At the same time, it was equally apparent that a report from management alone was not sufficient to provide a complete picture of race relations in a particular firm.

There seemed to be two obvious ways of rounding out this picture. One was to carry out observational studies of white and coloured workers in the context of both the formal and the informal organization. The other was to carry out interviews with white workers, coloured workers, and supervisors similar to those which had already been carried out with management. In this way it would be possible to obtain opinions from four different viewpoints and thus, it was hoped, to be in a position to build up a composite picture.

The original intention was to utilize both methods. An observation study had already been carried out in one of the firms visited (Bradfield Foundry).[1] Much useful data was obtained, but the main drawback to this method was the fact that it was somewhat time consuming and would permit only a relatively small number of firms to be studied. It was therefore decided to use the interview method and to return to observational techniques in a further two or three firms when this stage had been completed. Unfortunately, by the time the second set of interviews had been carried out and the data analysed, time did not permit further field work and it proved impossible to carry out further observational studies.

[1] The results of this study are described in Chapter Seven.

Pilot interview schedules for the interviews with workers and supervisors were tested in two of the firms already visited in the course of the management interviews (Edge Tools Ltd. and Omega Metals Ltd.). Based on this experience the interview schedules were modified and a further schedule evolved for management representatives. Letters were then sent to some fifty firms in two industrial cities in the North of England, enquiring whether it would be possible to interview a member of management on the question of the employment of coloured workers. Agreement was given in seventeen cases.

All seventeen firms were visited and at least one member of management interviewed. At the end of the interview, the writer asked whether he could carry out further interviews with white workers, coloured workers, and supervisors. Permission to do so was granted in thirteen cases. For a number of reasons, however, it proved impossible to interview a representative sample of white and coloured workers in any of these firms.

Managers naturally wished to disrupt production as little as possible and the number of interviews granted was relatively small, varying from one in one firm to nine in another. In some cases managers stated that it was impossible to take the workers away from their jobs and as a result the interviews had to be carried out at the respondent's place of work which limited their scope considerably. Furthermore, the interviews with Asian (Indian, Pakistani, and Arab) workers were limited by the writer's inability to speak any of their languages and the respondents' lack of facility with English. Respondents had, therefore, to be selected for their ability to speak at least some English, a procedure which introduces a further bias. These difficulties, of necessity, limit the value of the data obtained from the interviews with white and coloured workers. Nevertheless, it is difficult to see how they could have been avoided, and the writer has found the material a useful check on, and often addition to, the data already obtained from management interviews.

Finally, in order to obtain some idea of how representative were the firms visited in the course of the management interviews, a postal questionnaire was sent to 150 firms in the Midlands where coloured workers were known or thought likely to be employed. Fifty completed[1] questionnaires were returned, and in a further thirty-five cases some data concerning either the number of coloured workers employed or the firm's attitude towards the employment of coloured labour were obtained.

For purposes of convenience, the three stages of the present study will be referred to as the non-directive survey, the directive interview survey, and the questionnaire survey respectively. In the chapters which follow, the firms visited in the course of the non-directive and the directive interview surveys are referred to by pseudonyms in order to preserve their anonymity. In footnotes, this procedure was often too unwieldy, especially when a long list of firms was being given, and here they are mainly identified by numbers. These numbers can be related to the relevant pseudonym in the Appendix where a brief description of the firm concerned is also given.

The present study was carried out between 1961 and 1964 whilst the writer was a research worker for the Institute of Race Relations, who generously allowed the same material to be used as the basis of a Ph.D. thesis.[2] It was made possible by a grant to the Institute of Race Relations from the Joseph Rowntree Memorial Trust. The research was supervised by Dr. Michael Banton of the Department of Social Anthropology, and Mr. R. M. McKenzie of the Department of Industry and Commerce, University of Edinburgh, whom the writer would like to thank for all their guidance and criticism.

[1] I.e., 'completed' in the sense that the respondent had answered most of the questions. Often, however, the answers related only to the particular coloured group or groups employed by the firm. Answers to the questionnaire survey are therefore presented as a percentage of the total number of respondents supplying data concerning the group in question.

[2] P. L. Wright, 'The Coloured Worker in British Industry, with special reference to the Midlands and North of England', unpublished Ph.D. thesis, University of Edinburgh, 1965.

CHAPTER ONE

Theoretical Concepts

1. *Introduction*

In as much as coloured immigrants to Britain are both coloured *and* immigrant, the theoretical background to the present research stems from two main sources, race relations and immigration theory. In recent years, both these areas of study have undergone radical changes in orientation and a considerable revision, and in some cases outright rejection, of earlier terminology, concepts, and theories has taken place. In the writer's view, the newer approaches mediate a much better understanding of the pattern of race relations in Britain today. To appreciate their full significance, however, it is necessary to know something of the earlier, either revised or rejected, theories which they are intended to replace. We will begin, therefore, with a brief outline of the major developments in both fields and then, in the final section of the chapter, draw together those elements which have greatest relevance to the main theme of the present study—the coloured immigrant in industry.

2. *Immigration Theory*

In the study of immigration, the main concern has been with what may be termed the process of immigrant-host adjustment, and until recently the main concept which has been used both to denote and explain this process has been that of 'assimilation'. Two main strands of argument are to be found in the work of early assimilation theorists such as Park and Fairchild:[1] firstly, assimilation involves *identity* between immigrant and host, and secondly, it is a *one-way* process (that is, whatever changes are necessary to produce this identity take place in the way of life of the immigrant group, but not in the host society).

[1] H. P. Fairchild, *Immigration*, New York, 1924.

Both these theses are well illustrated in Fairchild's[1] analogy between the assimilation of immigrants and assimilation as a biological process. Fairchild argues that just as foodstuff becomes an integral part of the organism which ingests it, so the assimilation of immigrants 'involves such a complete transformation and unification of the new constituents that all sense of difference between old and new disappears'.

Similarly, Park,[2] although he does not use Fairchild's biological analogy, argues that for complete assimilation to take place, it is necessary for the alien to make the language, customs, and institutions of his adopted country his own 'in some more thorough-going way than mere use implies'. In addition, Park argues that assimilation is *inevitable* in his theory[3] that whenever different races meet there occurs a 'progressive and irreversible' race relations cycle consisting of initial contact, followed by competition, then accommodation and ultimately assimilation.

All these assumptions have been challenged by later writers. Berry,[4] for example, gives a long list of products including Grimm alfalfa, Tokay grapes, spaghetti, and so on, which have been introduced into America by immigrant groups and accepted by 'native' Americans. Lieberson[5] suggests that the sharp contrasts between the relatively harmonious race relations in Brazil and Hawaii and the current racial turmoil in South Africa and Indonesia serve to illustrate the difficulty in stating—to say nothing of interpreting—an inevitable 'natural history' of race relations, as has been attempted by Park and several other writers. Useem and Useem's study of a group of Norwegian immigrants in a Prairie town and a Prairie farming community shows that it is possible for an immigrant group to be well adjusted in its relations with the host society and yet remain unassimilated. It was the very fact that the Norwegians were only superficially integrated with the out-group, the Useems conclude, that permitted them to retain as much of their cultural

[1] Fairchild, op. cit.
[2] R. E. Park, 'Assimilation, Social', *Encyclopaedia of the Social Sciences*, London, 1930.
[3] R. E. Park, 'Our Racial Frontier on the Pacific', *Survey Graphic*, Vol. 9, May 1926; reprinted in R. E. Park, *Race and Culture*, Glencoe, Illinois.
[4] B. Berry, *Race Relations*, Boston, 1951.
[5] S. Lieberson, 'A Societal Theory of Race and Ethnic Relations', *American Sociological Review*, Vol. 26, 1961.

heritage as they did without coming into conflict either with others or amongst themselves.[1]

In Eisenstadt's view,[2] the existence of such 'unassimilated' groups is an almost inevitable part of the migration process. Complete absorption,[3] he argues, is a lengthy process in that it involves wide changes in the social structure of the immigrant group and the institutional structure of the host society. In the short run, therefore, the receiving society cannot completely obliterate the distinct cultures of immigrant groups; at the most, it merely transforms them and incorporates them within itself. Thus there usually develops a 'pluralistic' structure; that is a society composed of different groups maintaining some degree of separate identity.

Moreover, whilst the host society may expect conformity from the immigrant groups in certain respects (for instance, the observance of its laws), in others (for instance, social life) they may not only be permitted but encouraged to remain distinct from the older inhabitants. Viewed in this light, Eisenstadt suggests, the mere existence of an immigrant group with different patterns of behaviour, values and so on, is not necessarily a negative index of absorption. What is more important is the extent to which the structure of such a group is *balanced* with respect to the total social structure. He concludes, therefore, that instead of looking for universal indices of total absorption, it would be more profitable to focus upon the following questions:

1. What are the types of pluralistic structure that arise from different types of immigration?

2. What, in various societies, are the limits to which pluralistic structures may develop without undermining the basic social structure? As we shall see later, both these questions are highly relevant to the differing orientations of West Indian and Asian immigrants to Britain.

One reaction to the limitations of the early theories of assimilation has been to retain the concept, but in a considerably

---

[1] O. C. Useem and Ruth H. Useem, 'Minority Group Pattern in Prairie Society', *American Journal of Sociology*, Vol. 50, 1945.

[2] S. N. Eisenstadt, *The Absorption of Immigrants*, London, 1954.

[3] Eisenstadt uses the concept of 'absorption' rather than 'assimilation'. but for present purposes we shall use the terms interchangeably.

modified form. Berry,[1] for example, defines assimilation as 'the process whereby groups with different cultures come to have a common culture.' In contradistinction to earlier theorists, he maintains that this cultural fusion is not inevitable and is a reciprocal process if it does occur. Not all assimilation theorists, however, have accepted such modifications. Brunle,[2] for example, argues that assimilation is by definition a one-way process and one which results in identity between immigrant and host.

Because the term assimilation has tended to retain some of its earlier connotations and in some cases is used in its earlier sense, some writers have rejected it altogether and attempted to find alternative concepts. One such concept, 'absorption', has been introduced in relation to Eisenstadt's theory of immigration. Another is that of 'integration'.

In his report on a U.N.E.S.C.O. conference on the cultural integration of immigrants, Borrie[3] states that in recent years:

> . . . there has been a growing awareness of the persistence of the cultural traits which immigrants bring with them, of the significance of the retention by the immigrants of many of these traits as a stabilising link between their old life and their new, and of the sheer unwisdom of trying to force the immigrants into a world which they do not understand and which oversimplifies the complexities of the social and cultural structures of the nations which have received them.

The reaction against assimilation as a concept of cultural uniformity has not, on the other hand, led to a doctrine of *laissez-faire*. Rather, Borrie states, has it been towards a policy which aims at achieving uniformity where this is felt to be necessary in the interests of the receiving society and cultural pluralism where this is essential to the welfare of the immigrant. To differentiate this newer concept of conformity within a framework of cultural pluralism from the older definition of assimilation, Borrie suggests the term integration.

Although some speakers at the conference still preferred to use the term assimilation, there was, according to Borrie, general agreement on the concept of *plurality* plus adjustment, of a pro-

---

[1] B. Berry, op. cit.

[2] H. Brunle, 'The Cultural Assimilation of Immigrants' in *Cultural Assimilation of Immigrants, Population Studies Supplement*, March 1950.

[3] W. D. Borrie, op. cit.

cess towards uniformity at some levels but preserving differences at others. It was recognized, he states, that the concept of *accommodation* was essential to the process:

The process of adjustment was seen as one which is generally accompanied by subgroups being *accommodated* within the total framework, while wholly or partially absorbed in various sectors or isolates of that framework. Hence there may be economic absorption but cultural pluralism; cultural absorption at some levels (e.g. clubs, societies), yet cultural differentiation and isolation at others (e.g. family customs, diet, etc.) . . . and so on through many permutations which arise because of variations in the social systems brought into contact through immigration.

Borrie concludes that although the ultimate aim of the immigrant receiving countries may be the merging of immigrant and native cultures, this is now recognized to be a very long process taking generations rather than years, the important and more immediate problem being the degree of adaptation which can reasonably be expected from the first generation and at what levels it should occur.

It will be apparent that for all practical purposes the concepts of absorption (as used by Eisenstadt) and integration (as put forward by Borrie) are identical. Both admit the likelihood of the culture of the immigrant group affecting that of the host society, both recognize the inevitability and value of some degree of cultural pluralism and both stress that the process, by whatever name it is called, is a long term one.

Nevertheless, the concept of integration is preferable for present purposes. This term has gained considerable currency in the United States, and more recently in Britain, in the field of race relations. This gives us the not inconsiderable advantage of being able to use the same terminology in both the main spheres with which we are here concerned: race relations and immigration theory.

We shall therefore employ the term integration in the present study. At the same time, it is recognized that, in view of the similarities between the approaches of modern theories of assimilation and of absorption and integration, the choice of any one term is more a matter of convenience than of selecting the most viable theory. Thus, whilst using the term integration it will be possible to draw upon the theoretical concepts of such writers as Berry and Eisenstadt without modifying their basic orientations.

3. Race Relations Theory

We now turn to the field of race relations. Race relations is often described, with some justification, as one of the major 'social problems' facing the world today. By this, of course, is meant 'bad' race relations; cases in which discrimination, oppression, conflict, and the like occur, although these are by no means the inevitable result of race and culture contact. Until recently, the main theoretical concept which has been used in the analysis of such situations has been that of 'racial prejudice'. Although prejudice and discrimination have been recognized as being different orders of phenomena—loosely speaking, prejudice is a mental attitude and discrimination a form of behaviour—the emphasis on racial prejudice has been justified on the grounds that it is the *cause* of the socially undesirable aspects of race relations.

This argument is advanced by Rose,[1] who in the same article gives personal advantage as one of the causes of prejudice. That is, he suggests that prejudice may arise as a means of rationalizing, justifying, and maintaining economic, social, or political inequality. But this is tantamount to admitting that discrimination may cause prejudice rather than the other way round. In fact, we need not choose between either of these causal hypotheses. As writers such as Banton[2] have pointed out, there is no simple one-to-one relationship between prejudice and discrimination; prejudice can exist without discrimination and discrimination without prejudice.

Moreover, several studies have been carried out in recent years which have suggested that racial prejudice is not even one of the main factors causing discrimination. For example, in the Pocahontas coal field in West Virginia, Minard[3] found almost complete integration in the mines and almost complete segregation above ground. Twenty per cent of miners were prejudiced in both situations and 20 per cent in neither, the remaining 60 per cent tending to switch their role and status on passing

[1] A. M. Rose, 'The Roots of Prejudice', *The Race Question in Modern Science*, Paris: U.N.E.S.C.O., 1956.

[2] M. P. Banton, *White and Coloured*, London, 1959.

[3] R. D. Minard, 'Race Relations in the Pocahontas Coal Field', *Journal of Social Issues*, Vol. 8, 1952.

through the mine's mouth to and from the outside world. Similarly, Reitzes[1] reports a case in which a group of white workers were unwilling, as members of an all white Civic Club, to admit Negroes into the neighbourhood in which they lived, but as members of a union opposed to discrimination, supported non-segregation in the work place.

These, and similar findings by Stouffer et al,[2] Biesanz and Smith,[3] Harding and Hogrefe,[4] and Irish,[5] apparently indicate that the degree of prejudice expressed by the same people in different situations may vary considerably. However, the examples given above are concerned with overt behaviour, i.e., with levels of *discrimination*, and do not in fact tell us whether prejudice in the psychological sense varied concomitantly with the variations in behaviour. Indeed, if one accepts that prejudice is 'an emotional and *rigidly* hostile disposition towards a particular group',[6] then it is difficult to see how prejudice could vary in this manner.

Thus one is led to the conclusion that the variations in behaviour were brought about not so much by changes in individual attitudes but rather by differences in the social norms governing behaviour in the different situations. Some writers have therefore suggested that the concept of racial prejudice is of only limited explanatory value in the field of race relations. Blumer states, '. . . the idea so current during the past decade that a racial relationship is sustained by individual feelings or attitudes must be recognized as puerile'.[7] Similarly, Rose claims that 'prejudice has little to do with inter-group relations',[8] and

[1] D. C. Reitzes, 'The Role of Organizational Structures', *Journal of Social Issues*, Vol. 9, 1953.

[2] S. A. Stouffer, E. A. Suchman, L. C. Devinney, Shirley A. Star, R. M. Williams, Jnr., *Studies in Social Psychology in World War II:* Vol. 1, *The American Soldier: Adjustment During Army Life*, Princeton, 1949.

[3] J. Biesanz and L. M. Smith, 'Race Relations in Panama and the Canal Zone', *American Journal of Sociology*, Vol. 57, 1951.

[4] J. Harding and R. Hogrefe, 'Attitudes of Department Store Employees towards Negro Co-workers', *Journal of Social Issues*, Vol. 8, 1952.

[5] D. P. Irish, 'Reactions of Caucasian Residents to Japanese-American Neighbours', *Journal of Social Issues*, Vol. 8, 1952

[6] *White and Coloured*, op. cit. (italics mine).

[7] H. Blumer, 'Recent Research into Race Relations: United States of America', *International Social Science Bulletin*, Vol. 10, 1958.

[8] A. M. Rose, 'Intergroup Relations vs. Prejudice: Pertinent Theory for the Study of Social Change', *Social Problem*, Vol. 4, 1956.

Raab and Lipset state that 'prejudiced attitudes do not predetermine prejudiced behaviour.'[1]

In many respects, perhaps, the swing against psychological explanations in race relations has gone too far. As Pettigrew[2] and Allport[3] point out, psychological factors are important intervening variables between societal forces and actual behaviour because societal forces do not always affect people in the same way (see, for example, Minard's study above[4]). Nevertheless, the evidence does suggest that the explanatory value of the concept of prejudice itself (as opposed to other psychological variables such as 'conformity needs') is limited to the minority of cases where an emotional and rigidly hostile attitude towards an outgroup is involved. The writer would therefore agree with Reitzes[5] that too much emphasis has been placed upon prejudice and that the study of race relations should be integrated to a far greater extent into the general field of social science research. Thus the concept of prejudice will be little used in the present study and two other concepts, social distance and social conflict, will be employed in its stead.

Social distance refers to the degree of intimacy which people are prepared to accept in social relations with members of another group. For example, Bogardus,[6] who carried out the first quantitative analysis of social distance, asked his respondents to indicate on a scale including such steps as kinship by marriage, personal friend, neighbour, fellow worker and so on, how close a relationship they would be prepared to accept with members of various ethnic groups. According to Allport:

. . . the most striking finding from this procedure is that a similar pattern of preference is found across the country (i.e. the United States), varying little with income, region, education, or even with ethnic group. Most people, whoever they are, find the English and

[1] E. Raab and S. M. Lipset, *Prejudice and Society*, New York: Anti-Defamation League, 1959.

[2] T. F. Pettigrew, 'Social Psychology and Desegregation Research', *American Psychologist*, Vol. 16, 1961.

[3] G. W. Allport, 'Prejudice: Is it Societal or Personal?', *Journal of Social Issues*, Vol. 18, 1961.

[4] R. D. Minard, op. cit.

[5] D. C. Reitzes, 'Institutional Structure and Race Relations', *Phylon*, 1st quarter, 1959.

[6] E. S. Bogardus, *Immigration and Race Attitudes*, Boston, 1928. (Referred to by G. W. Allport, see below.)

Canadians acceptable as citizens, as neighbours, as social equals, and as kinsmen. These ethnic stocks have least social distance. At the other extreme come the Hindus, Turks and Negroes. The ordering —with a few minor shifts—stays substantially constant.[1]

Owing to the problems of access outlined in the Introduction, it proved impossible to carry out a rigorous analysis of social distance of the type outlined above during the present research. The concept is therefore used rather as a mental construct or 'heuristic device' in terms of which the more qualitative interview data are interpreted.[2] Nevertheless, even for this purpose, the concept of social distance has several advantages over that of racial prejudice.

Firstly, it is affectively neutral. To say that person A is prejudiced has overtones of censure and it is desirable that this should be avoided in the interests of objectivity.

Secondly, it has wider applications in the study of inter-group relations and therefore permits greater integration of findings in the field of race relations into social science research in general. For example, there may be similarities in the relations between different ethnic groups and those between, say, members of different professions or of different departments in the same organization, and whilst it would be possible to use the concept of social distance in both cases, the term prejudice tends to be restricted to the former. Moreover, due to overlapping group membership, the same two people may be both members of different ethnic groups and members of different professions or departments, and the use of the concept of racial prejudice would lead us to concentrate upon one explanation of the social distance (or conflict) involved and ignore the other.

Finally, the term prejudice tends to be restricted to cases where hostility, or at least antipathy, is involved. As Banton points out,[3] however, social distance may arise from other sources than negative attitudes towards a particular group. It may, for example, merely reflect a lack of common interests or

[1] G. W. Allport, *The Nature of Prejudice*, New York, 1958.
[2] This, in fact, is the use of the concept of social distance advocated by Hill, although the writer does not share his mistrust of quantitative social distance scales. (M. Hill, 'Some Problems of Social Distance in Intergroup Relations', in M. Sherif and M. O. Wilson (eds.) *Group Relations at the Crossroads*, New York, 1953.)
[3] M. P. Banton, 'Social Distance: A New Appreciation', *The Sociological Review*, Vol. 8, 1960.

experiences. But such a lack of common interests or experiences is quite likely to arise between members of different ethnic groups, particularly in an immigrant situation. Thus, unless one is to posit two forms of prejudice, one hostile and the other non-hostile (which could easily lead to confusion as the term has mainly been used in the former sense), the concept of prejudice is inadequate for the analysis of a large part of inter-group relations.

On the other hand, it is quite in order to use the concept of social distance in relation to either the stiff, formal relationship between strangers or cases where hostility is involved. In either case, social distance is high, but for different reasons. It would, of course, be possible to use the concept of prejudice in relation to the hostile forms of relationship, but here again its value is limited because there are other causes of hostility than prejudice. For this reason, the concept of social conflict will be employed.

Like social distance, social conflict may result from a number of causes. Coser makes an important distinction between 'realistic' and 'unrealistic' conflict. According to Coser,[1] each social system contains sources of realistic conflict in so far as people raise conflicting claims to status, power, and resources, and adhere to conflicting values. Realistic conflicts arise when men clash in the pursuit of claims to these scarce commodities. Non-realistic conflict, on the other hand, arises from deprivations and frustrations in the socialization process or later adult role obligations, or from the conversion of originally realistic conflict which was disallowed expression. Whereas the first type of conflict takes place with the frustrating objects themselves, the second consists in a release of aggression against shifting objects. The first type of conflict is viewed by the participant as a means of gaining realistic ends, a means which may be abandoned if others appear to present a more effective way of reaching the same goal. The second leaves no such choice, however, since satisfaction is derived from the aggressive act itself.

It is interesting to note that there are marked similarities between the sources of unrealistic conflict outlined by Coser above and the nature of prejudice as described by a number of writers. Banton,[2] for example, states that the cause of prejudice

[1] L. A. Coser, *The Function of Social Conflict*, London, 1956.
[2] *White and Coloured*, op. cit.

'is in the subject not in the object of prejudice. It is an irrational, pathological phenomenon, arising from the individual's own inadequacies and resulting in displaced aggression.' Thus Coser's approach allows us to retain the concept of prejudice (as a mental attitude associated with or leading to unrealistic conflict), but at the same time his recognition of the importance of realistic sources of conflict provides a useful counterbalance to the undue stress placed on irrational factors in many theories of race relations such as the frustration-aggression hypothesis.

In conclusion, therefore, we would suggest that the concept of prejudice has, until recently, been over-emphasized as an explanatory concept in the study of race relations. This is not to say that prejudice does not exist: in face of the evidence to the contrary, this would be foolhardy. However, it does appear that the concept of prejudice cannot be applied to all aspects of race relations whereas a combination of the concepts of social distance and social conflict can. The main advantage of these two concepts is that, unlike prejudice, they do not constitute an explanation of any race relations situation. They are part of the nature of inter-group relations, but do not commit us to any reason for their existence. Once having discovered whether social distance or conflict exist in a particular situation, we can then search for the reasons. It may well be, of course, that prejudice is one of the causal factors, but there may also be others, and the present approach leaves us free to search for them.

4. *Industrial Integration*

Thus far we have been concerned with the general fields of immigration and race relations. However, as the main concern of the present study is the coloured immigrant in industry, it is now necessary to restrict our sphere of interest to this aspect of the general situation.

For this purpose we shall distinguish between three main spheres of integration:

i. *Social Integration:* measured by the extent to which race or ethnic group membership *per se* is a factor determining social distance between members of an immigrant or minority group and members of the host society.

ii. *Cultural Integration:* measured by the extent to which members of an immigrant or minority group and members of the host society come to have a common cultural heritage, or the culture of the immigrant group comes to be accepted as a legitimate (alternative) feature of the culture of the host society.

iii. *Economic Integration:* measured by the extent to which the immigrant or minority group is absorbed into, and accepted as part of, the economic system of the host society.

It is, of course, with this latter sphere that we are mainly concerned, but in a restricted form in that we are interested in integration into industry rather than the economic system as a whole.

For complete integration to have taken place, there would be no social distance between immigrant and host, complete cultural uniformity or acceptance of the immigrant culture as a legitimate alternative, and complete absorption into industry at a level of equality. As Eisenstadt points out, this is unlikely to occur in the first stages of any immigration movement. The concept of integration as embodying complete equality will therefore be retained only as a limiting case against which it is possible to measure the degree of integration which the immigrants do in fact attain. Where an immigrant group has become a functioning part of the economic, cultural, or social system, this group will be described as *accommodated;* that is, partially, but not fully integrated. These spheres therefore refer to areas of accommodation as well as areas of integration.

However, in order to avoid the reintroduction of errors contained in the earlier theories of assimilation, two points need to be made. Firstly, although the stage of accommodation is a prerequisite of integration, it does not follow that an accommodated immigrant group will necessarily proceed immediately, if at all, to the later stage of integration. Like the Norwegians in the Useems' example, an immigrant group may become integrated in one sphere, but remain accommodated in others, perhaps for an indefinite period. Secondly, it must not be thought that integration constitutes a 'better' or in some way more desirable form of adjustment. It may well be that an immigrant group would prefer to remain only accommodated in some spheres, for instance, that of social relations. In this case, lack of social integration would not imply discrimination, but would merely be indicative of a desire on the part of the immigrant group to remain within the bounds of its own social structure.

It is also necessary to point out that the three-fold distinction between the different spheres of integration or accommodation, although necessary to instil some degree of order into a complex subject matter, is somewhat arbitrary and should not be applied too rigorously. For one thing, there is considerable interaction between the different spheres. For example, a minority group's lack of social acceptance by majority group workers or customers may deter firms from employing them, thus giving rise to inequality in the field of employment. Similarly, lack of social acceptance, by making it more difficult for minority group members to become conversant with the host society's norms, customs, and values, may delay their cultural integration. More important for the present study, however, is the fact that at least two of the spheres, namely the economic and the social, appear to overlap. That is, the field of social integration extends into the works environment in that social interaction occurs within the informal organization of industrial concerns.

For this reason, in addition to differentiating between economic and other types of integration, we shall also distinguish between two types of economic integration; 'work integration' and 'social integration within the works environment'. As with social integration in general, the latter is measured by the extent to which race or ethnic group membership *per se* is a factor determining social distance between the immigrant and the British worker. Work integration, on the other hand, is concerned with the extent to which the immigrant is accorded or has achieved equality with the British worker with respect to the formal organization.[1]

The extent of work integration will be assessed in terms of three criteria: employment level, occupational level, and the treatment of coloured workers by management and supervisors. The first two are derived from Turner who defines them respectively as 'the degree of labour force participation and, for those employed, the level at which participation is attained'.[2] Thus

---

[1] It could be argued, of course, that the concept of social integration at work is superfluous, being merely a particular case of social integration in general. However, the indications are that this is not the case. In Minard's study, for example, Negro miners in West Virginia were found to be almost completely integrated at work and almost completely segregated in the community.

[2] R. H. Turner, 'The Relative Position of the Negro Male in the Labour Force of large American Cities', *American Sociological Review*, Vol. 16, 1951.

we are, in effect, concerned with the *quantity* and *quality* of jobs available to coloured workers. Applied to a particular firm, these criteria refer to the proportion of coloured workers in the labour force and the proportion of coloured workers in the various jobs at different status levels. Work integration will be said to be greater, the nearer the employment and occupational level of coloured workers approaches equality with that of the white employees.

However, whilst it is necessary for the attainment of work integration that coloured workers should obtain jobs and obtain them throughout the various levels of the status hierarchy, these two criteria do not, in the writer's opinion, fulfil all the requirements for full work integration. For even where equality of employment and occupational levels is obtained, coloured workers may receive unequal treatment in other respects. They may, for example, be given orders with less civility than white workers, be expected to work overtime without notice whereas white workers are not, be given the least wanted jobs within a particular status level, be provided with less adequate facilities than white workers, and so on. Factors such as these will be grouped under the heading of 'treatment of coloured workers by management and supervisors'. As with employment and occupation level, work integration will be said to be greater, the nearer the treatment received by coloured workers approaches equality with that received by white workers.

It must be pointed out, however, that progress towards integration with respect to employment and occupational levels may, under certain circumstances, be incompatible with the achievement of equality of treatment. It is conceivable that some firms may employ as many coloured workers as possible, not because they are believed to be better workers, but because they can be accorded treatment much inferior to that which the white worker would be prepared to accept. In popular parlance this is known as using 'sweated labour'. Where jobs are hard to come by, the coloured worker may well be placed in the position of having to make the first step towards industrial integration, the mere obtaining of a job, at the expense of the retrograde step of accepting unequal treatment. In other words, he may be forced to accept accommodation into the industrial system because full integration is not obtainable.

A discussion of equality and inequality inevitably brings to mind such topics as racial discrimination, the colour bar and so on. Before going further, therefore, it will be as well to examine the relationship between discrimination and equality. Hankins[1] defines discrimination as 'the unequal treatment of equals'. If we accept this definition, it follows that there is no simple relationship between discrimination and lack of industrial integration. For inequality of employment or occupational level to be a sign of discrimination, then the immigrant and the British worker must be equal. However, the indications are that the immigrant worker is less skilled than his British counterpart. In this sense, therefore, coloured and British workers are unequal with respect to competitive capacity. Thus, a lower employment or occupational level on the part of a particular immigrant group may merely be a sign that employers are 'discriminating' against the less skilled worker, the fact that he is also coloured being 'accidental'.

On the other hand, some employers may use the fact that the coloured workers tend to be less skilled as an *excuse* for not employing them, or for employing them only on lower status jobs. Hankins states that discrimination may also exist where competitors are unequal, but the burdens or advantages are disproportionate to the inequalities.[2] Thus, where coloured workers have a lower employment or occupational level than would be expected in relation to the difference in skill level between white and coloured workers *and this results from action on the part of management*, then discrimination will be said to exist.

However, it should be pointed out that disproportionately low employment or occupational levels may occur through reasons other than managerial discrimination. Firstly, the mere fact that the coloured immigrant is a stranger, not conversant with the full range of jobs available to him, may lead him to accept a job of a lower standard than his capabilities would merit. Secondly, discrimination in spheres other than employment may limit the range of jobs open to coloured workers. Any restriction of coloured people to particular residential areas as the result of discrimination in housing, for example, will at the same time

---

[1] F. M. Hankins, 'Social Discrimination', *Encyclopaedia of the Social Sciences*, London, 1934.
[2] Ibid.

have the effect of limiting the coloured worker to those jobs which are within reasonable travelling distance of these areas.

Thus, where there is inequality of employment or occupational level, we need to know three things before we can assert that discrimination in employment has taken place: firstly, the relative skill level of the white and coloured workers; secondly, whether the inequality is out of proportion to the difference (if any) in skill level; and thirdly, whether the inequality resulted from action on the part of management.

In the case of inequality of treatment by management and supervisors, however, none of these considerations apply. Firstly, this type of inequality by definition results from action on the part of management, and secondly, the question of skill level is only relevant to whether a man is employable or not, or whether he is capable of being promoted. Once employed or promoted, management has in effect admitted that the man is of an adequate skill level and there is, therefore, no further justification for according him treatment different from that which a white worker would receive.

Thus far, we have been concerned with levels of integration in different industrial spheres and the criteria against which these may be assessed. Little has yet been said of integration as a dynamic process, and it is to this question which we finally turn.

In the integration of any immigrant group, we would suggest, two factors or sets of factors are of vital importance before the first immigrant sets foot in his country of destination. These are, firstly, the characteristics of the migrant population and secondly, the characteristics of the receiving situation. These may be termed the 'given' or predisposing factors in a migratory movement and in large measure determine the subsequent course of the immigration process.[1]

By the characteristics of the migrant population are meant not only such attributes as age and sex ratios, skills, both social and economic, ethnic membership, and so on, but also the hopes and aspirations with which immigrants regard their new country. Similarly, the characteristics of the receiving situation include not only what might be termed the 'vacancies' which exist for

[1] This approach is largely based on Eisenstadt's theory of immigration. (S. N. Eisenstadt, op. cit.)

new members of the community, but also the expectations of the host society towards the immigrant group. The form of adjustment which ensues between immigrant and host may be seen as the result of an interaction between these two sets of factors. The adjustment will be mutually beneficial to the extent to which the two sets of factors coincide and detrimental to the extent that they do not.

With this, our discussion of the theoretical background to the present research is now complete. In the next chapter, we shall consider the economic and social background to the industrial integration of coloured immigrants in Britain.

CHAPTER TWO

Industrial Integration: The Economic and Social Background

1. *Introduction*

In Chapter One, a distinction was made between two main aspects of industrial integration—work integration and social integration at work. It was further suggested that the process of integration could be regarded as the outcome of an interaction between two sets of given or predisposing factors—the characteristics of the migrant group and the characteristics of the receiving situation. In the present chapter, we shall examine those given or predisposing factors affecting the level of both work integration and social integration at work of coloured immigrants to Britain. This we have called, for want of a better phrase, the economic and social background to industrial integration. It should be noted, however, that the term 'social' is here being used in a restricted sense, in that it refers to social relationships rather than 'social conditions' in general.

In the social sphere, we shall be concerned with the extent to which British people are prepared to accept coloured immigrants in social relationships and with the level of social acceptance which coloured immigrants expect to achieve. In the sphere of industrial integration, on the other hand, we shall be concerned with the level of industrial skill of the various migrant groups and the economic position in Britain during the fifties. Other factors, including the immigrants' expectations concerning the type of job they were going to obtain and the attitudes of British employers concerning the type of work of which they are capable, also have an important effect upon the level of work integration, but, for the most part, discussion of these questions will be delayed until later.

2. Inter-Group Relations: British Attitudes and the Immigrants' Expectations

That coloured immigrants do not receive full social acceptance in Great Britain is common knowledge. This view is amply supported by research studies such as those of Little,[1] Richmond,[2] Banton,[3] Collins,[4] Patterson,[5] Hill,[6] and so on. However, it is worth noting that this lack of social acceptance is by no means complete nor is it uniform and predictable. Ruth Landes sees the British attitude towards the coloured immigrant as being one of 'limited acceptance'.[7] This attitude is well illustrated by a respondent in Sheila Patterson's study of Brixton who stated: 'There are so many darkies about now that Brixtonians take them for granted. While the majority cannot be said to accept them fully, they are resigned to their presence.'[8]

Mrs. Patterson's study also provides evidence of situational variations in the level of social acceptance. Within the working environment, she states, there were indications that an initial hostility and rejection had been to some extent modified and a certain degree of accommodation achieved on both sides. However, such accommodation was limited to the work situation with very little carry-over of work relationships to the neighbourhood or to informal social life. A similar conclusion was reached by Senior on the basis of a survey carried out by the British Institute of Public Opinion. He states:

The experience of West Indians . . . indicates that relations at work are much better than off-the-job personal contacts. Whereas 50% of the outside relationships were felt to be 'all right' or better, 78% of the workshop contacts were so characterised. There is a four-to-one differential in the 'very well as a friend' category; 10% outside work to 40% at work.[9]

[1] K. L. Little, op. cit.

[2] A. H. Richmond, op. cit.

[3] *Coloured Quarter*, op. cit.

[4] S. Collins, op. cit.

[5] Sheila Patterson, *Dark Strangers*, London, 1963.

[6] C. S. Hill, *West Indian Migrants and the London Churches*, London, 1963.

[7] Ruth Landes, 'A Preliminary Statement of a Survey of Negro-White Relationships in Great Britain', unpublished communication, Royal Anthropological Institute, 6 May 1952.

[8] Sheila Patterson, op. cit.

[9] C. Senior, 'Race Relations and Labour Supply in Great Britain', Paper for the American Sociological Society, Race Relations Section, Detroit, 1956. Published with minor alterations in *Social Problems*, Vol. 4, 1957.

On the other hand, it must be admitted that differences in the degree of social acceptance cannot always be related to simple and clear-cut situational variations such as that between the works and the community environment. As Richmond points out,[1] the extent to which full acceptance can be achieved is often vague and unpredictable in Britain, and the resulting ambiguity can be a considerable source of anxiety, particularly for the West Indian immigrant. Thus, in any attempt to explain British attitudes and behaviour towards coloured immigrants, a number of problems arise. It is not sufficient to explain why coloured immigrants do not receive full social acceptance; one must also explain why the level of social acceptance, although relatively low, is not so low as to involve complete rejection, why it varies between different situations, and why it also varies in such apparently unpredictable ways.

However, whilst it is generally agreed that coloured immigrants are not fully accepted in Britain, there is much less agreement concerning the causes of this lack of acceptance. Little[2,3] argues that colour prejudice in Britain is linked with class prejudice, coloured people being less socially acceptable not merely because they are racially different, but because of the social stigma which may arise from associating with them. This results, he suggests, in the frequent exclusion of even well educated persons of colour from British middle-class homes. Though many of the individuals concerned may lack personal prejudice, Little states, they feel that their social reputation might be jeopardized if they were known to have coloured friends or acquaintances.[4]

Richmond, on the other hand, completely rejects Little's colour-class-consciousness approach. He states: 'It is not a question of the coloured man having low social status in our system of social stratification, but of him not fitting in at all.' The social status of the Negro is ambiguous in Britain, Richmond maintains, and this gives rise to insecurity among whites who are not sure how they should behave towards them. This insecurity is aggravated by the belief that coloured people have

[1] *Colour Prejudice in Britain.*

[2] *Negroes in Britain.*

[3] K. L. Little, 'Race and Society', *The Race Question in Modern Science*, London 1956.

[4] Ibid.

different values, especially with regard to sex. The essential point about any in-group/out-group delineation, Richmond concludes, is that differences of skin colour (or whatever it is that visibly distinguishes the group concerned) are *symbols* of real or assumed differences in values.[1]

Richmond's point is to some extent justified. One limitation of Little's theory is that it does not take into account the effect of cultural differences. These are of particular importance in the case of Asian immigrants. Little suggests that a darker skin colour makes a person less socially acceptable. Yet the Asian immigrant provides an example of a coloured man whose skin colour is, more often than not, lighter than that of the Negro, but who is equally likely not to gain social acceptance. Of course, one could argue that like a dark skin, Asian features are symbolic of low social status; but even if we ignore this possibility, lack of a common language and differences in norms and values would be sufficient to inhibit social integration to a considerable degree. Even in the case of Negro immigrants, there are some differences in norms and values, especially in the case of recent arrivals. Thus the possibility that cultural factors are involved here also cannot be excluded.

Nevertheless, Richmond's complete rejection of Little's approach cannot be accepted, as supporting evidence for his theory is to be found in other studies. Carey,[2] for example, found that landladies often objected to taking coloured students because they saw this as a confession of 'having come down in the world'. Fear of prestige loss was also found in an industrial setting in Sheila Patterson's[3] study of the coloured community in Brixton. Mrs. Patterson states that apprehension over status was shown by South London workers in their objection to an excessive proportion of coloured labour in any one department or shop, lest it should be regarded as a 'black shop'; in a certain tendency to regard some rough, unpleasant and low-paid jobs as 'darkie jobs' and to shun them even more than before; and in the very widespread unwillingness to contemplate taking orders from a coloured man. It would appear, therefore, that both questions of social status and differences in values are involved

[1] A. H. Richmond, 'The Study of Race Relations', *Man*, Vol. 57, 1957.
[2] A. T. Carey, *Colonial Students*, London, 1956.
[3] Sheila Patterson, op. cit.

in the lack of social acceptance of coloured immigrants by British people.

A theory which attempts to take into account both these factors is that of Banton.[1] From the closing years of the eighteenth century, Banton suggests, a variety of factors, such as the arguments put forward to justify the slave trade, the growth of imperialism, the activities of missionaries and so on, fostered the idea that coloured people were fundamentally different from Europeans. By the early twentieth century, Britons had become accustomed to regarding themselves as morally and socially superior to coloured people and expected the latter to conduct themselves as subordinates. In recent years, according to Banton, this pattern of relationships has largely broken down. British people have come to realize that the old norms of conduct are no longer appropriate, largely because coloured people refuse to enter into relationships on these terms.

At the same time, Banton argues, relations between British and coloured people cannot yet be assimilated to the pattern of relations between Britons. He gives two reasons why this is so. Firstly, coloured people are believed to be unfamiliar with the norms by which these relations are governed and the ways in which the parties convey to each other their expectations and interpretations. The coloured man, Banton suggests, is seen as 'the farthest removed of strangers—the archetypal stranger'. Secondly, a dark skin colour detracts from a man's social prestige, and, where the nature of the relationship is not generally recognized or approved, from the prestige of those seen associating with him.[2]

Thus although the old norms have been discarded as a general guide to conduct, no agreement has yet been reached as to the principle which is to replace it. Owing to the ambiguities as to the proper course of conduct, Banton suggests, Britons are apt to avoid entering into relations with coloured people, particularly in relationships based upon implicit norms and in which

---

[1] *White and Coloured.*

[2] Banton does not suggest, however, that all coloured colonials are thought of as socially inferior to all Britons. He states: 'A coloured doctor is not ranked below a white shop assistant, nor an African chief below a typist. But unless he is known to be better qualified or more competent, a coloured doctor will not be considered the equal of his white colleague. The coloured man always has to go one better to obtain an equal position.'

the sanctions upon deviant behaviour are weak. The Briton, he states, knows that awkward scenes may develop where people do not share the same customs and cannot take one another's hints; he feels the embarrassing scene acutely and avoids getting into a situation where it might arise. On the other hand, the coloured man is less likely to be avoided where the relationship is clearly defined and there exist adequate sanctions upon deviant behaviour. The employer, for example, is not unduly worried lest the coloured worker should prove lazy, because he can always give him the sack.

British behaviour towards coloured people, Banton concludes, cannot be explained as the outcome of prejudice. It is character-ized not by aggressiveness but by avoidance of them in relation-ships which might get out of hand or which onlookers might regard unfavourably. There is discrimination, he states, but this does not represent an attempt to confine immigrants to a sub-ordinate role in the national life. It is a form of the avoidance of strangers that can be discerned in any society.

Banton's theory is one of considerable explanatory power. It accounts for many of the different, and sometimes paradoxical, aspects of the British racial scene. For example, why British people in general should be strongly opposed to discrimination in the public treatment of coloured immigrants and yet be so hesitant about treating them equally in private relations; why British conduct towards coloured people should be so uncertain and inclined to sudden change, and so on. Of particular interest as far as the present study is concerned is Banton's analysis of a finding reported both in a British Institute of Public Opinion Poll (see Senior[1]) and in Sheila Patterson's[2] study of the coloured community in Brixton, namely that coloured immi-grants are accepted to a much greater extent in the works than in the community environment. This Banton explains as follows:

In the course of his work (the Briton) may be brought into deal-ings with the immigrants, but this gives him no cause for concern as his association is legitimised by the work relationship. If the new-comer does not understand the norms of the relationship this need not disturb the Briton, for the sanctions are such that if the coloured

[1] 'Race Relations and Labour Supply in Great Britain'
[2] *Dark Strangers.*

man fails to conform to the accepted usages, he may lose his job. This holds to a lesser extent of relations which are independent of the work process—such as with whom a man sits down in the canteen to eat his lunch, or in informal work arrangements that have not received the approval of the management. While in the district in which the British workers live the structure of relations may be quite radically different. They are not bound to mix with the newcomers, and if they do so they have little defence against either the failure of the immigrant to behave in the expected fashion or the misinterpretation of the relationship by their neighbours. The workers' psychological make-up does not change when they come home from work; their different pattern of conduct is a response to a different social situation.[1]

This explanation cannot be accepted in its entirety. It does not appear to be the case that association with coloured people in the course of his work gives the British worker no cause for concern whatsoever. Certainly he tends to become anxious over his status and job security when a high proportion of immigrants are employed on his job, in his department or in the works as a whole. However, the important point is that the British worker does seem to be *less* concerned about associating with coloured people at work, and Banton's theory provides a convincing explanation of this.

There are two further aspects of Banton's theory with which the writer would not entirely agree. Firstly, Banton's stress upon the lack of aggressiveness in British behaviour towards coloured people has not been upheld by subsequent events such as the 'riots' in Nottingham and Notting Hill. The fact that both disturbances took place in areas of relatively high coloured settlement would suggest that aggressiveness may take place where avoidance is difficult or impossible. Secondly, in the writer's view, Banton's theory does not take sufficient account of actual, as opposed to ascribed, differences in norms and values. Some degree of social distance is to be expected when actual differences in norms and values exist, and Banton's theory provides not so much an explanation of why coloured people are avoided, but of why they are avoided more than would be expected were actual differences in norms and values the only factor involved.

However, these are largely matters of emphasis rather than

[1] *White and Coloured*

fundamental objections, and on the whole, the writer would accept both Banton's general theoretical approach and the specific hypotheses concerning race relations in Britain which he puts forward.

A major advantage of Banton's theory is that, unlike those of Little and Richmond, it is not based upon the concept of prejudice. As noted in Chapter One, research in the United States has shown that the concept of prejudice has limited explanatory value in the field of inter-group relations. Studies by two American social scientists, Landes[1] and Burt,[2] suggest that the concept may be of even less value in Great Britain. Ruth Landes, who came to this country to study mixed marriages, states: 'Prejudice seemed to muddy up the approach; it didn't seem a helpful assumption in Britain.' A similar conclusion was reached by Burt:

It may even be possible to deny completely the existence of a race problem as such—a concept which would be impossible in discussing the United States—and to assert that the present situation in Britain is an 'immigrant problem' in which race is a complicating but not defining factor.

Moreover, some support for Banton's 'stranger' hypothesis is to be found in two studies by British social scientists, Sheila Patterson[3] and Judith Henderson.[4] Both writers point out that social distance between white and coloured people in areas of coloured settlement cannot be interpreted in terms of colour alone. Sheila Patterson notes that the unwillingness of Brixtonians to accept coloured people was 'reinforced by the reserve, lack of sociability and fragmentation that characterizes informal social life in large English cities'. Similarly, Judith Henderson states: 'Keeping to oneself is a characteristic of the British townsman, and even when long standing propinquity has broken down the barriers within the street, they are more than likely to be re-erected round the newcomer, particularly a coloured

[1] Ruth Landes, op. cit.

[2] R. Burt, 'Colour Prejudice in Britain', unpublished senior thesis, Princeton University, 1960.

[3] Sheila Patterson, op. cit.

[4] Judith Henderson, 'A Sociological Report', *Coloured Immigrants in Britain*, London, 1960.

man.' In other words, some degree of social distance is to be expected even between members of the host society in a community situation, and the relative social isolation of the coloured person is an exaggerated form of an already existing social process.

Nevertheless, the coloured man's reaction to this lack of social acceptance will depend not so much on the objective situation, but upon how he perceives it, and being unused to the norms of the receiving society, his colour may seem to be the only factor involved. This brings us to the question of the migrant's expectations towards the receiving country.

We have already noted that, according to Richmond,[1] lack of social acceptance is a source of anxiety to the Negro immigrant. The majority of West Indians, Richmond states, very much desire to be fully accepted as British subjects, with all the privileges that such status implies. Yet the more he attempts to gain such acceptance, the more frustration he experiences and the more anxiety about his status and security he feels. This frustration and anxiety, Richmond suggests, in their turn create a great deal of conscious and unconscious aggression which sometimes earns the Negro a reputation for undue truculence.

A similar conclusion was reached by Banton[2] in his study of the coloured community in Stepney. The behaviour and attitudes of Negro immigrants, he states, were profoundly affected by the withholding of acceptance and social equality on the part of British people. In many cases, the frustration of their hopes and the denial of what they felt was due to them as British citizens led to the rejection of British values and the development of 'anti-social' attitudes. Supported by the belief that the coloured man must throw his weight around to get his due, abuse and truculence were common.

The lack of congruence between the expectations of Negro immigrants and British attitudes towards coloured people was also noted by Ruth Landes.[3] The coloured man, she concluded, 'guides himself in terms of the logic of complete acceptance, whereas Britons act in terms of a more limited acceptance.' This point was reiterated more recently by Burt who states:

[1] *Colour Prejudice in Britain.*
[2] *Coloured Quarter.*
[3] Ruth Landes, op. cit.

It is fair to say, I believe, that the British have an unreasonable aversion to foreigners within their community, and that the West Indian arrived in Britain with unreasonable expectations of the warmth with which he would be received. The 'collision' of these attitudes can be seen in the numerous petty complaints that Britons may be heard to give about their West Indian neighbours and that the West Indians may be heard to return.[1]

According to Burt, 58 per cent of a sample of 320 West Indian workers interviewed in 1955 had received no information concerning conditions in this country before they migrated from the West Indies. Furthermore, over half of the remaining 42 per cent had received no unfavourable information. Until the summer of 1958, he goes on, the information bulletins sent to the Islands by the Commission for the West Indies did not mention the fact of colour discrimination existing in any form in Great Britain and the individual migrant was ashamed to write home of personal frustration in the land where—as everyone knew—life was perfect.

Following the publicity given to the Notting Hill and Nottingham riots, it would be possible to argue that the migrants' expectations with regard to British society are no longer so unrealistically high and that the contrast in expectations between immigrants and host is, therefore, no longer an important factor in inter-group relations. However, this would be to confuse two meanings of the word 'expect'. It is unlikely that the West Indians still expect to obtain full acceptance in the sense that they think that it will be easily achieved. On the other hand, this does not mean that they do not think that it *should* be easy to obtain, and in this sense their expectations are still high and are still a possible source of friction.

In the case of the Asian immigrants, however, such considerations do not apply. To a large extent, they do not expect social acceptance and what is more important, do not appear to desire it. According to Desai:

The relations between the Indians and the non-Indian neighbours are to a great extent negative. This is partly due to the pattern of English behaviour, of which the immigrants are totally ignorant. But it is also due to the fact that the immigrants themselves desire exclusion. . . . The male immigrants sometimes develop a friendship

[1] R. Burt, op. cit.

with neighbours at the local public house. But it does not extend outside the pub. The children of the immigrants also enter into relationships with non-Indian children in school or in the street. But this also does not extend to parents. The immigrants cannot easily communicate in English. Both sides lack common cultural interests and do not desire interaction. The Indian immigrants recognise as neighbours only those who belong to their own linguistic regional group, and find this sufficient. They ignore the rest.[1]

Similarly, Alavi states with respect to Pakistani immigrants:

Pakistanis keep to themselves and tend to look upon this as a virtue. This way, they hope to minimise the opportunities for conflicts. But they all feel very insecure and have a great deal of anxiety about the outbreak of racial trouble. This fear tends to drive them inwards into their own community rather than to induce them to consciously seek to establish relationships with locals.[2]

Nevertheless, this pattern of voluntary segregation is not entirely successful in avoiding conflict. According to Desai, the 'avoidance' relationship between Indians and non-Indians makes it difficult to pick quarrels readily, but once a quarrel starts it is likely to be more violent than if it were within the Indian group. In the latter case, there are conventions for the settlement of the conflict without violence, but these are not available in a quarrel with outsiders. Furthermore, Alavi suggests that avoidance may only intensify suspicions on both sides and thereby perhaps even cause rather than prevent conflict.

 Banton[3] found marked differences in the orientation of Asian and Negro immigrants, not only in the community but also in the industrial environment. The jobs offered West Indian and West African immigrants, Banton states, rarely came up to their level of expectation. As a result severe disappointment was experienced and they tended to change jobs frequently searching for something better. Many were unwilling to do jobs which they considered degrading and developed the view that it was necessary to make trouble to get their due. By contrast, Pakistani workers avoided conflict, made few demands and were willing to put up with conditions which the African would reject.

[1] R. Desai, *Indian Immigrants in Britain*, London, 1963.
[2] H. A. Alavi, 'Pakistanis in Britain', London Council of Social Service; extract from a report prepared for the Overseas Socialist Fellowship, 1963.
[3] *Coloured Quarter.*

The general mode of adjustment of Asian immigrants in Britain, Banton suggests, is that of a non-assimilating or *accommodating* group. They wish to preserve their own culture and adopt as little of the customs of the receiving country as possible. The Afro-West Indian group, on the other hand, he describes as an *adapting* group. They largely accept the norms and values of the host society and wish to become assimilated, but are prevented from doing so as noted previously, by lack of acceptance on the part of British people.

Collins[1] comes to a somewhat different conclusion on the basis of his study of two coloured communities on Tyneside. Like Banton, Collins found a tendency towards self-segregation on the part of Asian immigrants and towards integration on the part of Negroes. He suggests, however, that *both* tendencies were present in each case. During the process of migrant settlement, Collins argues, two opposing social forces are to be observed. At first, on arrival, there is a tendency for the migrants to remain within their own community, since, unused to the ways of the host society they find amongst people of their own culture common ground for close social relationships. Later, however, as the immigrants begin to learn the mores and values of the host society, there is a counter-tendency for them to become less dependent on their own groups, to make contact with British people and to share in greater or lesser degree the life and privileges of British society.

The differing patterns of adjustment of Asian and Negro immigrants, Collins suggests, results from the fact that these opposing social forces do not operate with the same strength on different immigrant groups. The Asian immigrants wish to preserve their traditional institutions and are orientated towards the countries of origin. They therefore tend to maintain their social cohesion and to be more resistant to assimilation. On the other hand, the West Indians, because of their early acquaintanceship with British ways of life, associate more freely and more quickly with members of British society.[2] Nevertheless, it is apparent from Collins' description of the communities he

---

[1] S. Collins, op. cit.

[2] The Africans, Collins suggests, fell between these two extremes: they tended to maintain their tribal groupings, but in their new social environment these tended to loose their intrinsic traditional functions and to become orientated towards British society.

studied that both forces were operating, at least to some degree, with respect to both groups: many West Indians remained within the bounds of the immigrant community and some Asian immigrants moved outside their own social grouping. Support for Collins' thesis is also to be found in Banton's[1] study of Stepney, for Banton states that although the more ambitious West Indian and African migrants tended to move out of Stepney once they had become acclimatized to life in Britain, they tended to return in the evenings and at weekends to meet their friends.

Thus, in spite of their differing orientations, the West Indian and Asian groups have, for the moment, made a remarkably similar adjustment to their life in Britain. Both tend to be concentrated in certain areas; both, although for different reasons, are reliant upon their fellows for the fulfilment of their social needs; and both, again for different reasons, may find themselves in conflict with members of the host society.

In the future, however, assuming that both groups remain in Britain, these patterns of adjustment may develop along divergent lines. At the moment, the West Indians—speaking English as their native language and largely conversant with and accepting British norms and values—are capable of achieving a high degree of social integration. They are prevented from doing so mainly by the lack of acceptance on the part of the host society. Any future increase in acceptance is therefore likely to lead to greater integration. In the case of the Asians, however, their voluntary segregation from the host community has aided their accommodation in the short run but at the same time decreased their opportunities to acquire British norms and values and to learn the English language. Thus an increase in social acceptance is less likely to occur, and even if it did they would be less likely to take advantage of it. For this reason, the social integration of Asian immigrants, if it occurs at all, will be an extremely long-term process.

3. The Economic Background to Migration

Data collected in the course of the present research do not provide an adequate basis for the assessment of the general level of skill of coloured immigrants to Britain. In the interviews with

[1] *Coloured Quarter.*

coloured workers, information concerning their previous occupations was obtained. However, the number of respondents was too small, and their manner of selection too arbitrary, to accept this sample as a representative cross-section of coloured immigrants in general. It is necessary, therefore, to rely mainly upon the literature for this information.

Unfortunately, the literature does not provide us with any clear cut answers. With regard to the skill level of West Indian immigrants widely differing views have been expressed. On the one hand, there is the Earl of Swinton's statement in the House of Lords that 'the great majority of people who come to this country, certainly from the West Indies, are unskilled men'.[1] On the other hand, there is the conclusion reached by Ruth Glass,[2] on the basis of data concerning the previous occupation of a sample of West Indian immigrants in London, that the 'great majority' of West Indians are in fact 'black coated and skilled workers'. Between these two extremes fall the assessments of various other writers.

In the *Civil Service Argus*[3] for February 1955, it was suggested that 13 per cent of West Indian immigrants were skilled, 22 per cent semi-skilled and 65 per cent unskilled. A much higher level of skill amongst West Indian immigrants was found in a survey carried out by the Economist Intelligence Unit in 1961 (see Table 1). Even if we recalculate the data to provide details of manual workers only, the occupational distribution is as follows: 42 per cent skilled, 13 per cent semi-skilled and 45 per cent unskilled (including agriculture and fishery).

Several studies of the skill level of West Indian migrants have been carried out in the West Indies. Taken at their face value, the results of these studies tend to support Ruth Glass's viewpoint. During October 1954, Maunder[4] interviewed 773 Jamaican migrants, 479 men and 294 women, as they left Kingston for Britain. Amongst the 428 men who had been in work during 1954, 36 per cent had been skilled tradesmen, 8 per cent semi-skilled workers and 5 per cent unskilled labourers.

---

[1] Parliamentary Debates, H.o.L., 19 November 1958, col. 646.
[2] Ruth Glass, *Newcomers*, London, 1960.
[3] The official journal of the Ministry of Labour Staff Association.
[4] W. F. Maunder, 'The New Jamaican Migration', *Social and Economic Studies*, Vol. 4, No. 1, 1955.

4

The remainder were made up of 22 per cent farmers, fishermen and farm workers, 13 per cent handicraft workers, 8 per cent shop and clerical workers, 5 per cent personal service occupations and 2 per cent miscellaneous. Comparison with the available data concerning the distribution of these occupations in the general population[1] reveals that skilled workers were considerably over represented and unskilled labourers, farmers, fisherman and farm labourers considerably under represented amongst the migrants. Maunder concludes: 'The evidence . . . is that the emigrants are educationally a superior group. . . . Particularly striking are the relatively high percentages of those with practical training or secondary education.'

In a more detailed study, Roberts and Mills[2] provide data concerning the previous occupations of 17,373 Jamaicans who emigrated to Britain during the years 1953 to 1955. Taking the three years together, the occupational distribution was as follows: skilled workers (carpenters, mechanics, etc.) 55 per cent; unskilled 6 per cent; planters, senior persons in trade, managers and executives 2 per cent; domestic and personal service employees 2 per cent; nurses, teachers, professionals, civil servants, clerks, tailors 11 per cent; farm workers 20 per cent; others 3 per cent.[3] Thus, as in the case of Maunder's survey, Roberts and Mills' data show a higher proportion of skilled tradesmen than amongst the population as a whole.

On the other hand, the data also reveals a considerable change in the occupational distribution of Jamaican migrants between 1953 and 1955. Whilst the total unskilled males emigrating to Britain experienced a fourteenfold rise during the period in question, there was only a sevenfold increase in the number of skilled emigrants. At first the emigrants had been mainly skilled and semi-skilled with a few unskilled, but by 1955 the position had largely been reversed. Roberts and Mills conclude:

[1] On the basis of an 'approximate reclassification' of census data, Maunder gives the following occupational distribution for the general population in 1943: 8% skilled tradesmen, 5% semi-skilled workers, 14% unskilled labourers, 55% farmers, fishermen and farm workers; 5% handicraft workers, 7% shop and clerical workers, 5% personal service occupations and 1% miscellaneous.
[2] G. W. Roberts and D. O. Mills, 'Study of External Migration Affecting Jamaica: 1953–1955', *Social and Economic Studies*, Vol. 7, 1958.
[3] Percentages obtained by a re-analysis of Roberts and Mills' original data.

The departures of unskilled workers from the island over the three year period strongly suggest that this phase of emigration may continue its increase into 1956 and that the unskilled, the rural dwellers and the illiterates will appear in mounting proportions in the emigration stream to the United Kingdom after 1955.

During October 1955, a survey similar to that previously carried out in Jamaica by Maunder was undertaken in Barbados by Cumper.[1] A total of 384 emigrants (272 men and 112 women) from three boats embarking for Britain were interviewed. The previous occupations of the men were as follows, the figures in parentheses being the distribution of these occupations in the general population in 1955: skilled and factory workers 70 per cent (29 per cent); professional, clerical and salespeople 12 per cent (16 per cent); agricultural labourers 5 per cent (26 per cent); others (mainly general labourers) 12 per cent (29 per cent). Cumper concludes that in general the men were of a higher educational standard than the population as a whole—comparable with the upper range of skilled persons. He states:

> Skilled workers were greatly over represented amongst the emigrants to an extent which does not appear explicable on the grounds of misreporting of occupation. . . . Agricultural labourers were less common than in the whole population and so were . . . general labourers.

Finally, Davison[2] carried out a survey of the previous occupations of Dominican emigrants to Britain. Amongst those working for wages (as opposed to on their own account) the following occupational distribution was obtained: 34 per cent skilled; 42 per cent unskilled; 15 per cent domestic servants; 6 per cent clerical; and 3 per cent professional. A similar survey of the occupational level of Jamaican migrants was also planned, but had to be abandoned for reasons to be given later.

We now turn to Mrs. Glass's data,[3] which she obtained from a random sample of the case histories of those West Indians who had been interviewed by the Migrant Services Division of the

---

[1] G. E. Cumper, 'Working Class Migrants to the U.K., October 1955', *Social and Economic Studies*, Vol. 6, 1957.

[2] R. B. Davison, *West Indian Migrants*, London, 1962.

[3] Ruth Glass, op. cit.

West Indies Commission in London. The total number of men in this sample was 782, but in 174 cases (22 per cent) employment details were vague, employment status was unknown, or the person had definitely never worked before. The previous occupations of the remaining 608 men were as follows: professional workers 1 per cent; quasi-professional workers 6 per cent; shopkeepers, shop assistants, salesmen 5 per cent; clerks and typists 12 per cent; skilled manual workers 46 per cent; semi-skilled manual workers 5 per cent; unskilled manual workers 13 per cent; farmers 9 per cent; farm labourers and fishermen 3 per cent. These data, Mrs. Glass claims, will provide no support for those people who write to newspapers complaining that England has become the 'dumping ground of the world's riff-raff'.[1]

Indeed they do not! But whilst the writer has no desire to support such claims (which the findings, not only of Mrs. Glass, but also of Maunder, Roberts and Mills, Cumper and Davison demonstrate to be completely without foundation), it must be pointed out that the contrary conclusion that the great majority of West Indian migrants are black-coated and skilled workers, is itself questionable on several grounds.

Firstly, the proportion of unskilled immigrants in the sample is probably higher than it appears at first sight. Farmers, farm labourers and fishermen are not classified with respect to skills but are placed in a different category from manual workers. However, once in Britain, they tend to *become* manual workers. Wood,[2] for example, states that although coloured immigrants work in a variety of industrial jobs, there are hardly any in agriculture. This being the case, then as far as industrial work is concerned, the farmers, farm labourers and fishermen are unskilled. Not only this, they are amongst the most unskilled of the West Indian immigrants, for not only do they lack specific industrial skills, they also lack the general experience of working in industry which even the most unskilled manual worker has. If this is taken into account, then the proportion of unskilled workers becomes 25 per cent not 13 per cent.

Secondly, Mrs. Glass's data depend for their validity upon reports by the immigrants themselves. This is also true of the

---

[1] Quoted from a letter to the *North London Press*, 8 May 1959.
[2] D. Wood, 'A General Survey', *Coloured Immigrants in Britain*, London, 1960.

other studies we have examined, with the exception of that of the Ministry of Labour Staff Association. Thus it is possible that the respondents exaggerated the amount of training they had received and the skills they possessed, a point which is made both by Roberts and Mills, and by Davison. The former state:

> . . . the dubious nature of the claims to skill made by many of the emigrants should be emphasised, especially as some of them may deem it in their interest to profess such skills in the hope that they might thereby command a much better position in the United Kingdom.[1]

Roberts and Mills found very few illiterates amongst the emigrants. However, an appreciable proportion of these illiterates —44 per cent in 1954 and 25 per cent in 1955—declared themselves as possessing some skill, a fact which Roberts and Mills suggest is in keeping with the tenuous nature of some of the occupational classes delineated in their study.

Similarly, Davison states that, because it relies on personal reports and exaggeration might have occurred, his Dominican data 'is of very doubtful value as an accurate assessment of the real skill of the immigrants'. Furthermore, he abandoned his attempt to obtain data concerning the previous occupations of a sample of Jamaican emigrants because reliable information could not be obtained:

> A man would claim to be a 'painter' or a 'mechanic' simply because, in some remote past, he had held a brush or a spanner in his hand or even watched someone handling these implements. Without some simple trade testing scheme, the attempt to register occupation simply on the word of the respondent seems a somewhat futile exercise when it is borne in mind that for the sake of prestige, to say nothing of future employment prospects, it is a human reaction to exaggerate attained skill.[2]

Even when a more stringent check on accuracy is kept, however, errors may still occur. During World War II, skilled technicians were recruited in Jamaica to help with the war effort. Richmond[3] reports that when the first three contingents

---

[1] G. W. Roberts and D. O. Mills, op. cit.
[2] *West Indian Migrants.*
[3] *Colour Prejudice in Britain.*

arrived, 'it came to light that a considerable number of men had succeeded in convincing the authorities of their qualifications when in fact they had little or no skill'.

Finally, there is the question of the standards by which the accuracy of the data is to be assessed. A man who thinks of himself as skilled and may, in fact, be skilled according to West Indian standards, need not necessarily be skilled in relation to British criteria. Senior and Manley, in an enquiry carried out for the Jamaican government, state that: 'It is extremely difficult to transfer at the same level from one economic system to another the product of specific vocational training, apprenticeship, or industrial experience.'[1] Now this is often true even when the two countries concerned are at roughly the same level of economic development, but when the immigrant comes from an under-developed area such as the West Indies to one which is economically more advanced, then his skill level may well fall considerably below the required standards of his new country.

In relation to British requirements, the training received by West Indian immigrants may be inadequate in two respects. For one thing, it is likely to have been less rigorous and systematic than that received in Britain. Writing in 1953, Ella Campbell claimed that: 'For all practical purposes there is no apprenticeship system in Jamaica.' She further states that the report of the Apprenticeship Committee of 1943 gave the following reasons for the unsatisfactory state of affairs with respect to apprenticeships, especially in the smaller industries and enterprises:

... the lack (in most cases) of any system of training or well defined conditions of employment: the lack of co-ordination with the training offered by technical and vocational schools, little or no regard being paid to basic educational qualifications of apprentices or learners; the exploitation of juveniles by some employers who utilize nominal apprenticeships as a means of securing cheap labour; the attitude of some parents and guardians, who are more interested in immediate increases of family income than in a career for the boys and girls they seek to place under apprenticeship; the tendency of apprentices and learners, under such conditions, to shift from one employment to another, or to open up in business on their own account before completing training; and the frequent abuse of the

[1] C. Senior and D. Manley, op. cit.

system by partially trained apprentices, who in the absence of regulations requiring certification of apprentice and master, are able, when they set up for themselves, to employ apprentices of their own.[1]

Secondly, even when the training is of the highest standard, the equipment on which the apprentice is trained, and therefore, the techniques which he can be taught, are likely to be less advanced than those used in Britain. Senior and Manley[2] state, for example, that several immigrants who had correctly looked upon themselves as skilled lathe turners in West Indian plants told the same story of being sent by British Employment Exchanges to work as turners, only to find that the measurement was done with micrometers instead of calipers and that they were expected to achieve the much finer tolerances indicated by the former.

Considerations such as these were taken into account by Cumper[3] in his analysis of his data. He suggests that skilled workers were over-represented to an extent which does not seem explicable on the grounds of misreporting of occupation, but emphasizes that he uses the term 'skilled worker' to denote those who would reasonably so classify themselves in Barbados. In an economy with more advanced technical standards, he states, many would be regarded as semi-skilled or unskilled. Similarly, Roberts and Mills state that throughout their study, 'the occupational classes designated skilled in terms of conventional West Indian standards bear little relation to the classes of skilled workers as understood in Great Britain.'[4]

We may conclude, therefore, that by British standards Mrs. Glass's assessment represents an overstatement of the skill level of West Indian immigrants. It is, of course, impossible to specify the exact degree of error involved, but my own opinion is that it is probably quite large and that the estimate of the Ministry of Labour Staff Association is much more realistic, at least as far as manual workers are concerned. The fact remains, however, that whilst the majority of West Indian immigrants may be unskilled by British standards, they are amongst the

[1] Ella Campbell, 'Industrial Training Methods and Techniques', *Social and Economic Studies*, Vol. 2, No. 1, 1953.

[2] C. Senior and D. Manley, op. cit.

[3] G. E. Cumper, op. cit.

[4] G. W. Roberts and D. O. Mills, op. cit.

most skilled workers in the West Indian economy. This state of affairs is one which, as Wood points out, is very likely to give rise to misunderstandings and difficulties. He states:

> Some (West Indians) were well taught at home, but there are fairly widespread complaints that some of those who think they are skilled fall short of the standards demanded by craft unions and employers in this country. This is often felt by West Indians to be an unfair discrimination made because of their skin colour whereas in fact *it is usually an objective decision based on professional standards of skill*.[1]

Much less research has been carried out with respect to the skill level of other groups of coloured immigrants. According to Wood: 'Amongst the West Indians there are more skilled workers than amongst other nationalities.'[2] This conclusion is largely supported by data from other sources. In the Economist Intelligence Unit survey mentioned earlier, details were obtained of the previous occupations of seven immigrant groups including West Indians, Indians and Pakistanis. These data are presented in Table 1. It will be seen that although more Indians and Pakistanis fall into the 'Professional', 'Business and Managerial' and 'Office and Clerical' categories, there are more skilled manual workers in the West Indian group.

Nevertheless, the proportion of skilled workers amongst the Indian immigrants is still relatively high, being only slightly smaller than combined percentages of those whose previous occupations had been in unskilled work, agriculture and fishing. This finding is contrary to Desai's conclusion that: 'Most (Indian immigrants)[3] have an agricultural background, the great majority of them belonging to the agricultural castes. The rest are usually craftsmen who depend for their livelihood on the agricultural castes.'[4] In view of the smallness of the sample, therefore, it seems likely that the Economist Intelligence Unit's survey over-estimates the number of skilled workers amongst the Indian group.

[1] D. Wood, op. cit. (Italics mine.)
[2] Ibid.
[3] It should be noted that Desai defines as immigrants 'Those who came (to Britain) to work, usually as unskilled or semi-skilled labourers, in order to pay for their stay and earn money.' The remainder—students, qualified medical practitioners, technical trainees, business men, High Commission officials and so on—are not defined as immigrants and do not come within the scope of his study.
[4] R. Desai, op. cit.

TABLE 1   *Percentage Distribution of Previous Occupations of Coloured Immigrants in Britain, Summer 1961*

	West Indians	Indians	Pakistanis
Professional	2	8	4
Business and Managerial	1	10	6
Office and Clerical	2	2	4
Skilled Manual Work	28	14	8
Semi-skilled Manual Work	9	5	4
Unskilled Manual Work	18	2	9
Nursing and Welfare Work	2	—	—
Agriculture, Fishing	12	14	31
Students too young to work	3	18	6
Unemployed	12	13	19
Other answers	11	14	9
Number in sample	603	83	165

The occupational distribution of the Pakistani immigrants, on the other hand, largely corresponds with other assessments which have been made. According to Kathleen Hunter, most of the Pakistani manual workers, who form the largest section of their co-nationals in Britain, have come from villages where factories and their purposes are largely unknown. Similarly, Alavi states that the Pakistanis who came to Britain in the post-war years:

. . . were often men who had seen little outside their village. Those who were literate amongst them knew Bengali, but very few knew English. They were quite unsophisticated in their ways and bound very much by custom and traditional modes of behaviour.[1]

If it is accepted that a high proportion of Indian and Pakistani manual workers came from such rural backgrounds, then there is little doubt that, on the whole, their opportunities for developing industrial skills were much more limited than in the case of the West Indians. However, to describe these rural

[1] H. A. Alavi, op. cit. The immigrants who arrived prior to and immediately following the Second World War, Alavi states, had been more sophisticated. Small in numbers, they were mainly ex-sailors and ex-soldiers who had 'seen the world'. They were detribalized, individualistic, and tended to adopt British ways much more readily than those who were to follow.

immigrants simply as 'unskilled' could be misleading. The mere fact of growing up in an industrialized community provides even the most unskilled worker with a background knowledge and experience of industry and industrial methods. He can also speak the language of that community, and can therefore be told how to do relatively simple tasks in a short time. This applies in the case of the West Indian worker to almost the same degree as the native British worker. But it is much less true of Indian and Pakistani immigrants, in that, firstly, they tend to lack industrial sophistication, and secondly, the majority cannot speak English. This means that not only do they have to be trained for specific skilled or semi-skilled jobs, but in many cases they may also have to be taught how to be unskilled labourers.

To summarize: the writer is of the opinion that West Indian immigrants are in general less skilled than native British workers. Although the data are conflicting, it seems likely that the estimate of the Ministry of Labour Staff Association of 13 per cent skilled, 22 per cent semi-skilled and 65 per cent unskilled, is the most realistic assessment of the skill level of manual workers in this group of immigrants. Such evidence as there is indicates that Indian and Pakistani immigrants are, on the whole, less skilled than the West Indian immigrants, both with respect to specific industrial skills and industrial sophistication. Their lack of facility with the English language is an additional handicap and, in effect, lowers their skill level even further.

We now turn to the employment position in Britain during the 1950s. Until the late 1940s the coloured worker was a comparative rarity in British industry. Admittedly, coloured workers were employed in industries essential to the war effort during both World Wars, but except in times of national emergency, British firms seem to have been reluctant to employ coloured labour. In fact, during the inter-war years, Little[1] tells us, sea-faring was the only occupation in which the coloured worker had any chance of obtaining employment, and even here, opportunities were to a considerable extent limited.

Between 1948 and 1960, however, work in industry became increasingly available to coloured immigrants. The large concentrations of the coloured population shifted from the ports

[1] *Negroes in Britain.*

to the large inland industrial centres. Whereas the 'old' immigrants consisted mainly of sailors who had settled in the ports, the 'new' immigrants came specifically to obtain jobs in industry. Firms which had never done so before, began to employ coloured workers. Of the firms from which data were obtained in the present study, only two had employed coloured workers for more than thirty years and only three as far back as World War II. In the remaining fifty-four cases, coloured workers were first employed between 1947 and 1960. What brought about this dramatic change in policy on the part of these firms?

Writing in 1956, Senior[1] related the increase in Britain's coloured population directly to changes in the supply of labour. He states that the unfavourable effects of emigration on the expanding war and post-war economy, together with a long term decline in the British rate of natural increase had combined to produce a declining rate of growth in the labour force. One result had been that in only two of the previous ten years, 1947 and 1952, had the number of unfilled vacancies registered at Labour Exchanges at mid-year failed to exceed the number of unemployed. In June 1956, for example, there had been a total of 223,000 unemployed and 397,000 vacancies, or a total deficit of 174,000 persons.[2]

It was this desperate shortage of labour which was filled in part by the large-scale immigration of coloured people. However, the vacancies open to coloured people, Senior claims, were not spread evenly throughout industry. There had been a tendency for British workers to move from industries in which the value of output was low to those where it was higher, thus leaving the lower paid and the 'dead-end' jobs to be filled by the newcomers. Such jobs, though unwanted by the British workers, represented greater economic opportunities than were afforded by the colonial areas.

Senior's account of the economic background to coloured immigration in the post-war years is largely supported by data from the present study. The employment of coloured workers

[1] C. Senior, op. cit.

[2] Quoted from 'Britain's Manpower Situation', *Labour and Industry in Britain*, March 1956, pp. 7–10. It should be noted that the demand for labour decreased sharply during the following two years, 1957 and 1958, due to a trade recession. Coloured immigration to Great Britain slackened during this period, but increased again after the state of trade improved.

as a means of overcoming a shortage of labour was a recurrent theme in most of the firms visited in the course of the interview surveys. When asked why their firms had begun to employ coloured workers, four managers said succinctly:

We couldn't get enough non-coloured labour. (Works Director, Torrington Cutlers)
Shortage of labour—we had no alternative really. (Personnel Officer, Leigham Cannery)
Labour was tight in that day. (Personnel Manager, Sterling Metal Co.)
Shortage of white labour. (Works Manager, Annerley Iron Foundry)

Others, however, went into greater detail and it might be worth examining these examples further as several interesting points arise. Some of the firms, for example, first turned to foreign white workers, such as Poles, Italians, Irish and so on, in an attempt to solve their labour shortage. These firms later employed coloured workers, either because they still could not obtain enough workers or because foreign white workers had proved unsatisfactory.

The big influx of immigrant labour began in 1954. At this time you couldn't get an armless, legless man, never mind an able bodied one. Any worker could leave the works and get a job literally within three or four minutes simply by going to the factory next door. We tried recruiting Irish labour but this didn't come off. The Manager went over to Ireland himself and recruited 36 men. Of these, only 8 actually turned up at the works, and only one stayed for any length of time. (Works Superintendent, Bradfield Foundry)

The first foreign labour we employed were German and Italian prisoners of war. When these men were repatriated, the firm found itself short of labour. Poles were employed and a number still work here. They were very good workers, but we couldn't get enough to make up for the labour shortage. The Ministry of Labour had coloured people. We wouldn't look at them at first, but eventually we succumbed. It was a case of necessity: there was no one else. Well, there was the Irish, but they were dreadful. Only about one in twenty was any good. (Labour Manager, Edge Tools Ltd.)

After the war there was firstly a shortage of workers, and secondly, a sense of freedom amongst the workers generated by the attitude of the people coming home from the forces. They felt that because they had fought for freedom, they deserved a job, and could pick and choose, so they didn't like settling down. We tried employing continentals and refugees, etc., but it didn't work out in our industry. The Chairman after the war wouldn't have foreigners (this meant coloured workers). He died in 1949, and in 1950 the succeeding Chairman employed Indian workers. (Labour Officer, Westwood Foundry)

We began employing coloured workers in 1958. At that time we were having labour trouble, especially with the Irish. You didn't know on a Monday morning whether you would have 40 men at work or 20, and by Wednesday, you might have 50. So we got in touch with the local employment exchange and asked them if they could send some reliable men along. They recommended a Pakistani. We were a bit dubious at first, but we took him on. (Works Manager, Omega Metals Ltd.)

Often managers made it quite plain that it had not been a general shortage of labour which had led them to employ coloured workers, but a shortage of labourers to do the kind of job which was least attractive to the British worker.

We began employing coloured workers in 1956. You couldn't get a good white worker unless you were prepared to pay over the odds, and good coloured people are better than bad white people. You can't get white people to do the menial tasks that have to be done in any foundry, not even the floating workers like the Irish. (General Manager, Stainless Steel Ltd.)

There was a shortage of labour and coloured workers were available. There were certain jobs the white workers steered away from and the coloured workers filled the bill. Up to three years ago you couldn't get a white labourer. Things are different now, of course. (Personnel Manager, Sovereign Steel Works)

We first employed coloured workers in 1951. The primary reason was the great difficulty in recruiting foundry labourers. We were particularly hard hit in the foundry. (Personnel Manager, Major Castings Ltd.)

It wasn't easy to obtain unskilled labour. Non-coloured labour won't have it. It's hard work under rather bad conditions. (Production Services Manager, Blackford Rolling Mills)

In another case, the manager indicated that it was possible to obtain some white workers but these were of a prohibitively low standard.

In the early fifties, white labour was virtually impossible to get. You could only get what we call tramps: he doesn't want to work and wants his money for nothing. They stay for a couple of months, then leave. Then later on they come back for their job again. We set some of these drifters on four or five times. Then the Arabs came. We set two on—one was a brick, the other a dud. The dud couldn't speak English. We got rid of him, but replaced him with another Arab. We have a contact man, an English-speaking Arab, who brings men when we need them. (Works Director, Steel Bars Ltd.)

In all, ten[1] of the fourteen firms visited during the non-directive survey had employed coloured immigrants as a result of difficulties in obtaining white workers, either in sufficient numbers or of an adequate standard. In the remaining four firms, no mention was made of the initial reason for employing coloured labour. In the directive interview survey, managers in twelve[2] of the seventeen firms directly attributed the employment of coloured workers to the labour shortage, and it was mentioned as a possible contributing factor in two further cases.[3] In another firm, the manager stated: 'We could get the coloured worker to do a job at a smaller rate of pay, still within union agreements, but which would not interest the white workers.' (Personnel Officer, Quality Steel Co.) In effect, the reason here is again shortage of labour. The lower paid jobs were open to coloured workers because the white workers were not prepared to do the jobs at that rate of pay.

In the remaining two cases, managers said that coloured workers were employed for reasons other than shortage of labour.

We never had any trouble with labour shortage, so unlike several other firms in the area we were never placed in the position of *having* to employ coloured labour. As a result, as a firm, we turned our face against coloured workmen. This bothered me, and I suggested to the Board on several occasions, that we should employ some coloured workers as a matter of policy. Eventually it was agreed that we should. After having seen the difficulties other firms in the area had had, we decided it was essential to employ only English speaking

[1] Firms 2, 3, 5, 6, 7, 8, 11, 12, 13, 14. (For identification of the above firms see Appendix.)
[2] Firms 15, 18, 19, 20, 21, 22, 23, 24, 26, 28, 29, 30.
[3] Firms 17, 27.

coloured labour. This meant West Indians only. (Personnel Manager, Pentland Alloys Ltd.)

It happened by coincidence. We weren't really looking for coloured labour. We needed a boiler firer and this man (a Pakistani) needed a job, so we took him on. A year or eighteen months later, he asked for a job for his nephew. He was employed as an annealer. He was so good at his job that we employed other Pakistanis and they took over these jobs under a white man. And then other jobs were given to Pakistanis. It is left up to the managers of the different departments as to whether they will take coloured workers. They won't take West Indians and some won't take Irish. Some won't accept Pakistanis or any coloured people, and one won't take Irish, but will take Pakistanis. (Personnel Manager, Ridgeway Steel Ltd.)

Thus, although neither firm employed coloured workers because of a shortage of labour, a resistance to the employment of coloured workers is still evident. In the first example, this resistance was only overcome because one man (the Personnel Manager) felt that it was wrong to exclude coloured workers from employment, and managed to bring the rest of the management round to his way of thinking. Nevertheless, only West Indians were employed, and, as we shall see later, these men were employed only in restricted numbers, and on certain restricted jobs. In the other case, coloured workers were employed on their merits and without reference to any labour shortage. Even here, however, only Pakistanis are employed and then only in certain departments.

Further evidence of the relation of labour supply to the employment opportunities of coloured workers was found in two firms, visited for purposes of comparison, which did not employ coloured labour. Both were situated on the outskirts of the industrial centre and were able to obtain sufficient workers from the immediate vicinity. In both cases, this adequate supply of local labour was advanced as the reason why coloured workers had never been employed. In one firm, there had been a meeting between management and the workers to discuss the recruitment of coloured labour. According to the Personnel Manager, the workmen were of the same opinion as management: 'They weren't against employing coloured labour, but they didn't see any reason to do so while there were local people out of work.' Nevertheless, the firm had employed Poles in 1947. Thus, apparently, foreign white workers are employed at a time when there is no shortage of labour but coloured workers are not. In the other firm, the Personnel Manager stated that if it came to a choice between employing coloured labour and closing down part of the works, then undoubtedly coloured workers would be employed. But, he added, this situation had never arisen.

Finally, in the questionnaire survey, managers were asked to indicate why coloured workers had first been employed in their firms. The answers are given in Table 2.

TABLE 2   *Reasons given for Initial Employment of Coloured Workers (Questionnaire Survey)*

	No.	%
1. Lack of alternative source of labour	19	51·4
2. Humanitarian reasons	1	2·7
3. As a matter of course when they became available	10	27·0
4. (1) and (2)	2	5·4
5. (1) and (3)	2	5·4
6. (1), (2) and (3)	3	8·1
7. Any other reasons	—	—
	37	100

It will be seen that the main reason given was shortage of labour alone, or shortage of labour in combination with other factors. In one case, it should be added, it was claimed that coloured workers were employed 'as a matter of course', but the respondent wrote at the end of the questionnaire: 'We do not usually employ coloured people simply because we can get all the white labour we require.'

Taken together, the interviews and questionnaire surveys demonstrate a general reluctance to employ coloured workers, which, in the main, is overcome only when adequate alternative sources of labour are not available. Furthermore, the interview survey indicates that the shortage of labour and thus the distribution of jobs available to coloured people did not occur evenly throughout status levels. Generally speaking, the coloured worker tended to obtain the jobs which the white workers valued least—foundry labourers in Major Castings Ltd., the 'menial tasks' in the Quality Steel Co., the labouring jobs which the white workers 'steered away from' in the Sovereign Steel Works, and so on.

Thus the present data amply supports Senior's[1] thesis concerning the economic basis of the large scale immigration from the Commonwealth during the 1950s. Without the severe shortage of labour, it seems highly unlikely that more than a small minority of the coloured immigrants who actually came to Britain would have been able to find jobs and support themselves. At first sight, these data also seem to support Senior's further contention that the employment available to coloured workers was in the lower paid and 'dead-end' jobs in industries where the value of output was low. However, this is not entirely the case. No doubt British workers did tend to avoid these jobs, but the present study shows that jobs which were relatively highly paid, or provided relatively good opportunities for promotion, or were in industries in which the value of output was high (although perhaps not all three) were also in some cases avoided, thus providing employment opportunities for coloured workers.

Industries in which the value of output is low do not have a monopoly of the lower paid and 'dead-end' jobs. Even in the most successful industries there are likely to be requirements for, say, sweepers-up, general labourers, window cleaners, and so on, and one cannot assume that British workers will be any more prepared to do these jobs in an expanding than in a declining industry. To take only two examples from the present sample of firms, neither Precision Engineers Ltd., a light engineering firm of national repute, nor Westwood Foundry, which was undertaking a million-pound expansion programme in 1962, could be called firms in which the value of output was low. Yet both had difficulty in recruiting labour and both resorted to the employment of coloured workers to overcome this problem.

Money is, of course, an important consideration as far as the attractiveness of a job is concerned. In Stainless Steel Ltd. and Quality Steel Co., managers indicated that they *could* have ob-

[1] C. Senior, op. cit.

tained white workers to do the lower status jobs providing they had been prepared to pay higher wages than usual. On the other hand, the moulders employed in Bradfield Foundry were in relatively highly paid skilled jobs, and yet white workers still avoided them, presumably because they were dirty and strenuous, to such an extent that it became necessary to employ European and coloured workers.

Similarly, not all the jobs on which coloured workers were employed, could be described as 'dead-end' jobs. Brierley Metal Works and Westwood Foundry had a policy of promoting their own employees when a skilled vacancy occurred rather than employing an already skilled worker from outside. There was therefore a very good chance that promotion would occur, yet white workers were not prepared to accept a lower status job even on what was in all probability a temporary basis. Again, in the Quality Steel Co., coloured workers were employed on the lower grades of set work, the first step in the promotion ladder, so this could hardly be described as a 'dead-end' job. Of course, the fact that it would not be a 'dead-end' job to a white worker does not mean that promotion would necessarily be open to a coloured worker, but this is another matter which will be examined in the next chapter.

Thus Senior's[1] assessment of the employment opportunities for coloured workers seems to be too narrow. Coloured workers could obtain jobs which were not lower paid, or were not 'dead-end', or were not in industries where the value of output was low. Where they did, however, it was usually because these jobs were avoided by white workers for other reasons, e.g., they were dirty, strenuous, tedious and so on. One is reminded of Ruth Landes' description of the coloured man's attitude towards life in Britain:

Sure there's freedom in Britain, but a man don't stand a chance. In the States, there's Jim Crow, sure. Only certain jobs and so on. But he gets any job he goes after. Here the job disappears with a black face. With the Yanks you know where you are. Here you don't. But you learn this much: you can have what the Englishman don't want. You can have the room he won't live in, the job he won't take, and the woman he throws out.[2]

[1] C. Senior, op. cit.
[2] Ruth Landes, op. cit.

As far as employment is concerned, the present data provide considerable justification for this assessment of the situation. Indeed, it would appear that in one respect the man underestimates his case. From City Transport and Precision Engineers recruiting trips were made to Ireland and to Italy respectively. In other firms, Polish, Italian, Irish and other foreign white nationalities were employed before coloured workers were turned to, more or less as a last resort. All this suggests that, at least initially, the coloured worker does not automatically get the job the Englishman won't take: he may only get those which foreign white workers do not want either.

4. *Summary*

In this chapter, we have discussed the background factors relating to the level of industrial integration achieved by coloured immigrants to Britain. It was concluded that British people are generally reluctant to accept coloured immigrants in the realm of social relationships, although there is evidence that the level of social acceptance is higher in the works environment than in the community. It was further suggested that whereas West Indian immigrants wish to achieve full social acceptance, Asian immigrants, in general, prefer to remain within their own social groups.

With regard to work integration, it was concluded that: (a) coloured immigrants have, in general, tended to be less skilled than the British workers; (b) amongst the various coloured groups, West Indian immigrants are both more skilled and more industrially sophisticated than Asian immigrants, and have a considerable additional advantage in speaking English as their native language; and (c) during most of the 1950s, owing to an acute labour shortage, there were a large number of vacancies in British industry, especially in unskilled jobs. The extent to which the immigrants' qualifications and the vacancies available to them were compatible, it is suggested, played a major role in stimulating the large scale immigration from the Commonwealth in post-war years.

On the basis of this evidence alone, it might seem to follow that: firstly, within the works environment, there would be greater social conflict between British and West Indian workers than between British and Asian workers; secondly, coloured

immigrants would experience relatively little difficulty in achieving a satisfactory level of accommodation within the British
industrial system; and thirdly, employers would have a marked
preference for West Indian workers in view of their obvious
advantages over the other immigrant groups. To a large extent,
however, none of these 'predictions' turned out to be the case,
for reasons which we will examine in subsequent chapters.

CHAPTER THREE

Integration into the Work Organization: Employment and Occupational Levels

1. *Introduction*

In the previous chapter, we examined the conditions under which coloured immigrants were first employed in the present sample of firms. It was concluded that, owing to a reluctance on the part of managements to employ coloured workers and the uneven distribution of job vacancies, they tended to be introduced only when sufficient white workers could not be obtained, and to be given the unskilled, labouring type of jobs which the white workers valued least. It still remains to be seen, however, whether this merely represents an initial phase in the employment of coloured workers or a more rigid situation with long-term repercussions.

We now turn, therefore, to an examination of the subsequent employment pattern of coloured workers, to ascertain what progress has been made from these somewhat inauspicious beginnings towards industrial integration. In this we shall follow the scheme outlined in Chapter One (pages 13–14). For the moment, however, we shall be concerned only with employment and occupational levels. Consideration of the treatment of coloured workers by management and supervisors will be delayed until we have examined the general question of supervision in a later chapter.

2. *The Employment Level of Coloured Workers*

(a) *Employment Statistics*

On the basis of a survey carried out by the Institute of Race Relations in 1959, Wood concludes that:

> Coloured unemployment rates are . . . everywhere higher than the corresponding white figures . . . no-one knows the exact coloured

population of any one town, but it seems certain that the coloured rate is at least twice as high as the white rate and probably higher.[1]

This conclusion is supported by official statistics which have been given from time to time. For example, it was stated in the House of Lords in November 1958 that the coloured unemployment rate was about 8 per cent compared with a national average of under 3 per cent. Similarly, in early 1961, a government spokesman stated that the coloured unemployment rate was about 5 per cent compared with a national average of 1·9 per cent.[2]

In particular areas, higher unemployment rates amongst coloured workers (and also greater disparities between white and coloured unemployment rates) have been reported. According to Richmond,[3] Negro unemployment on Merseyside rose much more rapidly than white during the post-war years and by 1948 was some three times higher. Since 1950, he states, the position has remained much the same with unemployment amongst coloured workers fluctuating between 15 and 20 per cent. Banton[4] found a similar rate of unemployment (approximately 15 per cent) amongst coloured workers in East London in 1951.

Wickenden[5] states that in 1958 about 14·5 per cent of the coloured people in Nottingham were unemployed, whilst the figure for the city as a whole was less than 1 per cent. According to Argyle,[6] 'Unemployment is much higher amongst the coloured population—30 per cent v. 1·5 per cent in one area.' Unfortunately, he does not name the area nor give the source of his data.

In the period during which the present research was carried out, high rates of coloured unemployment were reported in the Midlands and North of England. In the Midlands, according to the Midland Regional Board for Industry,[7] the proportion of coloured workers amongst the unemployed had risen from 8·8 per cent in February 1961 to 21·8 per cent in February 1962. In May 1962, the East and West Riding Regional Board for In-

[1] D. Wood, op. cit.
[2] Hansard, 17 February 1961; quoted by Sheila Patterson, op. cit.
[3] A. H. Richmond, *The Colour Problem*, Harmondsworth, 1961.
[4] *Coloured Quarter.*
[5] J. Wickenden, op. cit.
[6] M. Argyle, *Psychology and Social Problems*, London, 1964.
[7] Quoted by *The Guardian*, 28 February 1962.

dustry[1] gave figures of the number of unemployed immigrants compared with the total unemployed in five Yorkshire towns. These reveal that coloured workers constituted 12 per cent of the unemployed in Leeds and Sheffield, 29 per cent in Halifax, 33 per cent in Huddersfield, and 64 per cent in Bradford. It is impossible to draw firm conclusions from either of the above sets of data because the proportion of coloured workers in the total working populations of these areas is not known. However, given that the proportion of coloured workers in the total working population of the country was 0·6 per cent in 1961,[2] then the unemployment rate amongst coloured workers was probably much higher than amongst white, even allowing for a wide margin of error due to regional variations and an increase in the coloured population in 1961.

Finally, Davison,[3] in what is perhaps the most comprehensive attempt to obtain comparative data concerning white and coloured unemployment, estimates that between August 1961 and February 1963, the average rate of unemployment amongst West Indians, Indians and Pakistanis was at least 7·5 per cent and probably in the region of 10 per cent. These figures, he suggests, should be compared with the usual national average of under 2 per cent. If Davison's estimates are correct, therefore, unemployment amongst coloured workers during this period was roughly four or five times higher than amongst white.

On the other hand, it must be admitted that the period studied by Davison was in some respects atypical. Between August 1960 and May 1962, coloured unemployment increased considerably. There can be little doubt, Davison claims, that this increase was due to the threat of the Commonwealth Immigration Act which came into operation on 1 July 1962. Whilst the Bill was passing through Parliament, he states, travel agents in the Commonwealth worked overtime packing every available ship and plane with immigrants hurrying to Britain to 'beat the ban'. Very few of them came with definite job prospects and

[1] Quoted by *The Guardian*, 16 May 1962.
[2] The Economist Intelligence Unit in *Studies on Immigration from the Commonwealth 4. The Employment of Immigrants*, London, 1962, gave the total number of Commonwealth Immigrants registered for work with the Ministry of Pensions and National Insurance as 144,400 in 1961 and the total working population for the same year as 24,590,000.
[3] R. B. Davison, *Commonwealth Immigrants*, London, 1964.

they crowded the Employment Exchanges seeking work, thus causing unusually high unemployment figures.

Another factor which may have affected coloured unemployment rates during this period was the 1962–3 recession. Wood[1] suggests that in times of economic recession, coloured workers are particularly hard hit by the shortage of jobs. In the boom conditions of 1955–6, he states, many coloured immigrants found jobs within a week of their arrival. Two years later, with the advent of the 1957–8 recession, many newcomers were unemployed for eight weeks or longer. Moreover, Wood maintains that as the unemployment rate goes down for white workers, it also goes down for coloured immigrants, *but more slowly*.

Wood's assessment of the effect of the 1957–8 recession on employment prospects for coloured workers is supported by other evidence. As noted in the Introduction, whilst Senior and Manley stated in 1955 that coloured immigrants seldom reported any difficulty in finding a job, by 1958, according to Wickenden, employment rather than housing had become the main problem facing coloured immigrants in this country. Sheila Patterson[2] states that in June 1957, reports from areas of coloured settlement indicated a considerable, if temporary, improvement in the employment situation. At the same time, however, the Ministry of Labour reported that it was taking much longer to place immigrants than in previous years. This seems to support Wood's contention that coloured unemployment rates go down more slowly than white following a period of high unemployment.

On the other hand, Davison's data[3] show that whilst unemployment generally rose by 61 per cent during the winter of 1961–2, coloured unemployment rose by only 24 per cent. Thus, in this case, the proportion of coloured unemployed *fell* during a period of general heavy unemployment. Davison suggests that this may be explained in terms of the high geographical and industrial mobility of newly arrived immigrants. Having no roots in Britain, they are willing to settle where they are most needed and to take those jobs which the unemployed Englishman refuses to touch.

[1] D. Wood, op. cit.
[2] Sheila Patterson, op. cit.
[3] *Commonwealth Immigrants.*

It could also be argued that the fall in the proportion of coloured unemployed found by Davison represents, at least in part, a recovery from the abnormally high unemployment rates due to the effect of the Immigration Act. However, it does appear to be the case that the high geographical mobility of coloured workers can, in some degree, offset the adverse effect of a recession on their rate of unemployment, particularly if the recession is localized. Banton[1] reports that there was considerable apprehension in Birmingham in January 1956 when the coloured unemployment count was 600 at a time when workers in the Midlands car factories were being laid off and a general recession threatened. By August 1956, however, there were no more than 700 unemployed coloured workers in Birmingham, many of them new arrivals. Discharged coloured workers had moved fairly readily to the North West where there was a surplus of vacancies. Enquiries by the National Assistance Board carried out at about this time showed that there was no 'hard core' of coloured unemployed. In other words, the higher rate of unemployment amongst coloured workers was due to the fact that they suffered somewhat longer periods of unemployment *between* jobs, rather than from permanent or long term unemployment.

Thus it is impossible, on the basis of the present evidence, to come to any firm conclusions concerning the 'usual' or 'normal' rate of unemployment amongst coloured workers. The particular areas quoted may be atypical, and the various national figures given may have been inflated to an unknown degree by periods of recession or the effect of the Immigration Act. Nevertheless, the general picture which emerges is that coloured unemployment rates *are* higher than white, and in all probability, as Wood suggests,[2] at least twice as high if not higher. Undoubtedly, employment opportunities are more limited for coloured immigrants than for British workers. The remainder of this section will be devoted to an examination of what these limitations are.

(b) *Factors Limiting Employment Opportunities for Coloured Workers*

With respect to individual firms, these limitations can be reduced to two types: firms which employ no coloured workers

---

[1] *White and Coloured.*
[2] D. Wood, op. cit.

and firms which *do* employ coloured workers but limit their number in one way or another. In its official journal, the *Civil Service Argus*,[1] the Ministry of Labour Staff Association reported on an analysis of job vacancies throughout the country for men of 18 and over. It was stated that 'only about half of them (were) likely to be open to coloured workers, because the following points (had) to be taken into account:—skill, location, colour prejudice, work which is done by both sexes, the attitude of trade unions, and the type of work.' We shall begin by examining these factors in relation to firms which employ no coloured workers.

The effect of location upon the range of jobs available to coloured workers was mentioned in Chapter One. However, the question is quite complex and requires more detailed examination. According to Wood:

> In towns where coloured people have gone for the first time during the past ten years there are no ghetto-like 'coloured quarters' like in some American cities. But there are concentrations of coloured people in certain districts. New arrivals go to these areas where friends and compatriots live and a 'snowballing' process begins.[2]

There are probably many factors which contribute to the formation of these 'concentrations'. Discrimination in housing and accommodation is undoubtedly one, as is lack of seniority on Council house waiting lists. In addition, lack of funds to buy the better type of house in these towns and lack of social integration into the host community (leading coloured people to prefer the security and companionship of living amongst their compatriots in the 'coloured quarters' to the uncertainties of the white world outside) may also be relevant. Thus, in as much as such factors as the above limit the range of jobs available to coloured workers to those within reasonable travelling distance of the 'coloured quarters', then these limitations may be said to result from extra-industrial factors.

However, this differentiation between industrial factors (for instance, skill or managerial discrimination) and extra-industrial factors such as housing, is an arbitrary theoretical distinction. In practice, both may be relevant even in areas where there are

---

[1] February 1955.
[2] D. Wood, op. cit.

very few coloured people or none at all. Some coloured workers are prepared to travel comparatively long distances to work if employment nearer home cannot be obtained. Thus to advance the argument, as did one manager interviewed during the present research,[1] that coloured workers are not employed because there are none in the district may be somewhat specious. Whilst it is true that the firm in question was situated some five or six miles from the nearest concentration of coloured people, so was Hamilton Engineering Co. and this did not deter coloured workers from working there. Furthermore, coloured workers had approached the firm for jobs, so obviously they were prepared to undertake the long journey to and from the firm, or to find nearer accommodation had they been offered jobs.

In fact, it is probably the case that it is the availability of employment which gives rise to coloured settlements in certain areas rather than availability of housing. Housing discrimination and so on may determine the district in which they settle within the area, but coloured people would not move into the area as a whole, no matter how easy it was to obtain accommodation, unless they could obtain work there. In most of the large industrial areas in England—London, the Birmingham conurbation, Manchester, Liverpool, Leeds, Sheffield, Bradford, Newcastle, and so on—there are now areas of coloured settlement, and often more than one. It is doubtful whether any job within these areas and also the outlying districts would be so far away from the centres of coloured population as to be unavailable to coloured workers on the grounds of location. Where the question of location may be relevant is in the smaller industrial towns which have not yet attracted coloured settlement, but it is also likely that there are only a limited number of vacancies in these areas in any case.

We turn now to the firms within areas of coloured settlement which employ no coloured workers. It is evident that although coloured workers are available to these firms, there is nevertheless considerable resistance to their employment. In Chapter Two it was suggested that, in general, firms did not employ

[1] The firm in question was the first of the two firms already mentioned on page 45, which employed no coloured workers and were visited by the writer for purposes of comparison. The above reason for the lack of coloured workers in the labour force was advanced in addition to the fact that there was no shortage of white workers.

coloured workers unless a shortage of labour left them no alternative. Unfortunately, no clear conception of the proportion of
firms not employing coloured labour can be gained from the
present data. The postal questionnaire was designed primarily
to provide some test of the generality of the interview data, and
was, therefore, sent mainly to firms where it was known that
coloured workers were employed or where it was thought likely
that they would be. Nevertheless, 29 per cent of the firms from
which data were obtained reported that they did not employ
coloured workers. No doubt the figures would have been much
higher had random sampling been used.

The question of firms refusing to employ coloured workers
gave rise in 1964 to a controversy in the letter columns of a
national newspaper.[1] The point at issue was whether it was
better for Employment Exchanges not to send coloured workers
to employers who had let it be known that they would not
accept them, thus protecting the coloured worker from the possible humiliation and discouragement of rejection, or to send
them to these firms and thus at least give them the opportunity
of speaking for themselves.[2]

According to the initial letter and also Frank F. Lee,[3] Employment Exchanges employ the former method. Lee refers to
this as a form of 'structured shielding', that is, the protection of
coloured people from experiencing discrimination. With reference to Port City, the pseudonym for an industrial town of
nearly half a million population in the South West of England,
Lee states that 'there are many firms . . . that will hire no
coloured workers regardless of the labour shortage or their
qualifications'. Similarly, one of the correspondents noted above,
a youth employment officer, stated that she would like to say
that if any employer discriminated against coloured people,
they would refuse to send him anyone else, but *they were so
numerous that this would be impossible to carry out.*[4]

[1] See Letters to the Editor, *The Guardian*, 27, 30 May, and 1, 5, 9, 11, 15 June
1964.
[2] Another point made by some of the writers was that by not sending coloured
workers to prejudiced employers, they were, in effect, condoning discrimination,
and the practice was reprehensible for this reason.
[3] F. F. Lee, 'Racial Patterns in a British City: An Institutional Approach',
Phylon, 1st Quarter, 1960.
[4] *The Guardian*, 1 June 1964.

Several reasons can be advanced for this resistance to the employment of coloured workers: an adverse assessment of the standard of coloured workers, managerial prejudice, fear of racial friction, objections from the white workers, and so on. Very few of the twenty-five firms in the postal questionnaire survey employing no coloured workers gave any reason for not doing so. Of the few that did, the most common explanation was that there was no shortage of white workers. But this is only a partial explanation. It takes for granted a preference for white rather than coloured workers when both are available, but does not give any reason for this preference. In these cases, the hidden reason may be one of those mentioned above (adverse assessment of the standard of coloured workers and so on). On the other hand, it may be a question of sheer inertia. Never having been forced seriously to consider the employment of coloured workers, some managers may feel it is best to 'leave well alone' rather than to take a chance on an unknown quantity.[1]

The question of skill has already been discussed in Chapter Two, and will be examined further in Chapter Four when we will analyse managerial beliefs and attitudes towards the employment of coloured workers. A discussion of the part played by managerial prejudice in limiting the number of jobs open to coloured workers is no easy matter. It is highly unlikely that any manager, when asked why he does not employ coloured labour, will say, 'Because I'm prejudiced' or 'Because I just don't like them'. Instead, he will give reasons such as 'Because they are not skilled enough'. Now this may be a rationalization, in which case we can say that prejudice, though perhaps of an unconscious nature, is involved. On the other hand, he may be quite justified, especially if the job is of a highly skilled nature, and no prejudice may be involved. Thus when faced with such a

---

[1] With regard to American industry in the Northern states, Myrdal (G. Myrdal, *An American Dilemma*, New York, 1944) states: 'There are tremendous elements of inertia which resist the introduction of Negro labour where there has previously been none.' (pp. 392–3.) He claims that Negro labour can be introduced successfully, provided employers are prepared to go to some lengths to obtain the white workers' acquiescence, but adds: 'Under ordinary circumstances, however, there are few employers who would take so much trouble voluntarily, just for the purpose of contributing to the solution of the race problem. After all, the employer's main interest is to run a business. To continue to employ white labour only is always the easier way out.' (p. 389.)

response, each individual case must be examined on its merits.[1] This question is also examined in Chapter Four.

Another reason for the reluctance to employ coloured workers is the fear, not always justified, that racial friction might ensue. According to the Works Superintendent of Bradfield Foundry: 'When we first began employing coloured workers, I envisaged race riots and all kinds of trouble, but by and large they have settled down and been accepted.' It has been suggested that, due to jealousy on the part of white workers, friction is particularly likely to arise when coloured men are employed in the same department as white women. Work which is done by both sexes was noted in the *Civil Service Argus*[2] as one of the factors decreasing the number of jobs available to coloured workers. It would appear, then, that there is a tendency for firms to avoid such friction simply by not employing coloured men under conditions where they are likely to come into contact with white women.

Owing to the limited data obtained from firms not employing coloured workers, it is impossible to come to any firm conclusion concerning the prevalence of this state of affairs on the basis of the present evidence. Only two firms mentioned this question. One stated:

We do not employ coloured workers—the whole of our production staff is female and we feel that we would have some difficulties if we introduced coloured labour into the factory. The supply of labour in this district is sufficient for our requirements both on actual production and for ancillaries such as labourers, etc.

In the other case, it was apparently the white women who

---

[1] If the response is 'Because racial friction might arise', the situation is even more complex for, objectively speaking, the manager is right. The fact that many other firms have employed coloured workers without friction arising does not prove that there is not a chance, however remote, that it will on this occasion. The question is then a moral one: how far the manager concerned is justified in putting the firm's interests before those of society as a whole. Whether the man is prejudiced or not will depend upon whether he is genuinely acting in the firm's interests or is merely using his loyalty to the firm as a means of hiding his own personal bias. As the man quite probably does not know himself, some sort of depth interview would be needed to discover the answer. It is this kind of consideration which makes the writer dubious about the value of the concept of prejudice in studies such as the present one. On the other hand, there is no doubt that the man is discriminating, whatever his reasons, latent or manifest, for doing so.

[2] Op. cit.

objected to the employment of coloured men,[1] although the firm had employed West Indian women as machine operators since June 1960. The respondent stated: 'Only on one occasion did we employ coloured men. This seemed to upset our female employees and we were obliged to cease employing coloured men.' On the other hand, it should be pointed out that in at least three of the interview survey firms (Bradfield Foundry, Edge Tools and Sovereign Steel Works) white women and coloured men worked in close proximity and no friction arising from this situation was reported by any of the managers concerned.

The situation sometimes arises (as in the case reported above) where management is prepared to accept coloured workers, but the white employees object. One of the firms in the postal survey replied: 'We have never been short of "white labour" (unskilled) and on one occasion only were we, as a company, prepared to accept coloured labour, but the men on the shop floor were not agreeable which attitude we accepted.' Another firm employing no coloured workers returned most of the questionnaire blank but gave the following answers to two of the questions:

(a) Was there any initial resistance to the employment of coloured workers? .... There is!!

(b) Are the white employees willing to accept coloured workers as work-mates? .... No!!

The respondent stated that one of the major objections was over the coloured workers' use of toilets. Other complaints included slovenliness and idleness. In this case, however, the respondent did not state whether management would have been prepared to accept coloured workers even if there had been no objections from white workers.

Resistance to the employment of coloured workers on the part of white employees has perhaps received most publicity with respect to public transport. According to press reports, bus company employees in several towns (e.g., Bristol, Coventry, West Bromwich, Birmingham, Wolverhampton, Nottingham, and Newcastle-upon-Tyne) and also railway workers in Birmingham and London have at various times objected to the

[1] N.B. It may be that the previous respondent had also been concerned about the possible objections from white women rather than men, as he did not stipulate the nature of the 'difficulties' which he thought might arise if coloured men were employed.

employment of coloured workers.[1] In these cases, pressure was brought to bear on management, often by threats of strike action or work to rule, not to employ coloured workers. Where there is a closed shop, the same effect is sometimes attained by slightly different means: coloured workers are excluded simply by refusing them union membership (usually on grounds of inadequate training). In the writer's experience, this tends to limit the range of jobs available to coloured workers within a firm rather than to exclude them altogether, but here again this may be an artefact due to the fact that most of the firms studied in the present research employed at least some coloured workers.

We now turn to the further limitations of the employment level of coloured workers which occur even within those firms which employ them. The first is a logical extension of the reluctance to employ coloured workers noted in Chapter Two. Having been constrained to employ coloured immigrants owing to the shortage of labour, some firms subsequently employ further coloured workers only when white workers cannot be obtained. For example, the Personnel Officer of Components Ltd. said: 'The coloured workers came in gradually, possibly where local people could not be obtained. . . . They were employed gradually and then only as necessary. It has always been a matter of keeping the labour force up to the amount required.'

Another manager said unequivocally:

> Coloured workers are not employed unless they are urgently needed for specific jobs. We do not hire them unless absolutely necessary. . . . We get a lot of coloured people coming for jobs and we have to turn them away. If a coloured man comes for a job, they (the Personnel Department staff) tell him that there is no vacancy, but if a white man came along within a few minutes they would take him on. Experience is needed and Jamaicans haven't got the experience. (Personnel Manager, Ensign Spring Co.)

Had all the work carried out by the firm been of a highly skilled nature there would, perhaps, have been some justification for refusing coloured workers on the grounds that they did not possess the experience required. However, this was not the case in the Ensign Spring Co. Many of the jobs apparently

[1] For reviews of these reports see Sheila Patterson, op. cit., Appendix IV, and D. Wood, op. cit., Appendix.

required no skill whatsoever. Whilst walking round the factory, the writer noticed one job in particular, on which both white and coloured workers were employed, which consisted merely of feeding long strips of metal into a machine and then making sure that the small, shaped pieces which emerged at the other side fell clear of the machine and did not jam the mechanism. Other jobs on which coloured workers were employed included pushing a trolley load of raw materials round the machine operators to ensure that they always had enough metal to work with, or collecting the finished product in similar trolleys and wheeling them to the store. It is difficult to see how lack of experience could be a very great handicap in such jobs.

The Personnel Manager of the above firm added that, although the British workers accepted coloured labour, they (management) had to be careful not have a preponderance of coloured workers in any one shop as this might lead to trouble. As the firm employed only twenty to twenty-five West Indians out of a total of 800 to 900 employees (that is, about 2·5 per cent), the danger of having a 'preponderance' of coloured workers in any one shop was not very great. Similarly, in the Quality Steel Co., where the proportion of coloured workers was less than 1 per cent, the Personnel Officer stated that some of the white workers would resent the intrusion of the coloured immigrants if their numbers rose to 50 per cent of the labour force. However, concern over the ratio of white to coloured workers is quite common and in some cases perhaps a little more realistic. This concern has sometimes led to what is generally known as a 'quota system'.

The quota system may be defined as a method whereby the number of coloured workers employed by a firm is kept at or below a given percentage of the total labour force. The intention in these cases is not to keep the number of coloured workers as low as possible, but to limit their number to below a certain maximum. The motivation is a belief that the employment of a greater number of coloured workers would lead to unrest amongst the white employees and ultimately their refusing to work for the firm. At Drop Forgings Ltd., where about 12 per cent of the workers were coloured, the Personnel Manager said:

The firm is at saturation point now with coloured labour. There is a danger that if any more were employed the white workers would

6

possibly object. . . . If over half the employees were coloured, the firm would get a name for being a coloured works and we wouldn't get white workers. This would not be a good thing because in general Jamaicans are not skilled enough for the highly skilled jobs, especially the highly skilled jobs requiring apprenticeship.

We are turning coloured workers away at the rate of 15 to 20 per day. We could employ another 300 coloured workers without difficulty if we wanted to. We get no end of enquiries from coloured employees to bring relations in, but we can't possibly satisfy all demands. We haven't enough jobs.

Similarly, in the Grange Graphite Co., where the proportion of coloured workers was again 12 per cent, the Personnel Officer stated:

We must be careful not to overload a department with coloureds. You might have a department full of men who can do any labouring job, but no skilled man to operate the press. We need adaptability according to the state of the market and these people are not so adaptable.

In these firms, management was apparently limiting the number of coloured workers of their own accord. In one of the postal questionnaire firms this also appeared to be the case. The Personnel Officer stated:

In the working groups relations are quite satisfactory, but in some workshops white workers start to express concern if the proportion of coloured people rises above 15%. Apart from this minor factor, we have had no difficulty in employing coloured labour and we are continuing to recruit them.

At Central Glass Works, however, the white workers in one department operated their own quota system and in another firm the percentage of coloured workers to be employed had been settled in an unofficial (gentlemen's) agreement between management and union. No further data was obtained on quota systems, but whether this was because they did not exist or because the firms concerned preferred not to let it be known, it is impossible to say.

With respect to quota systems, Wood states:

Employers say that the quota system ensures a fair balance between white and coloured labour. It helps to scatter coloured workers throughout the industries of a town and prevents a firm getting the reputation of being a 'coloured firm' amongst its competitors. The system does cause a feeling of injustice amongst coloured workers who apply in vain for an advertised vacancy in a firm which has its full quota. And it is in a mild sense a colour bar.[1]

Whilst one must sympathize with the coloured workers who fail to obtain jobs because of a quota system, it should be pointed out that firms with a quota level of 10 per cent are employing a very much higher proportion of coloured workers than there are coloured people in the country. The major limitation on the employment level of coloured workers is not the firms which impose a quota system, but those which do not employ coloured workers at all. Were coloured workers evenly distributed throughout British industry, then the need for quota systems would disappear. Thus the fact that a firm imposes a quota level of, say, 10 per cent is a sign that it is discriminating much less than the average firm rather than more. This is not to say that the writer wishes to recommend a 10 per cent maximum for all firms: several firms in the present sample employed a much

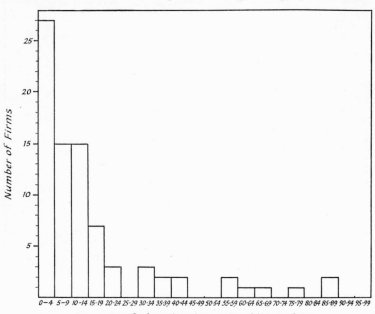

Fig 1

[1] D. Wood, op. cit.

higher proportion and seemed quite satisfied with this situation. Nevertheless, it does seem unjust to unduly criticize firms which operate a quota system when other firms avoid the whole question simply by 'finding' that all coloured workers are insufficiently skilled to be employed.

Some idea of the proportion of coloured workers employed by firms in the present sample can be gained from Figure 1. It will be seen that although most firms employed relatively few coloured workers, some firms did employ well over the 12 per cent which the Personnel Manager of Drop Forgings Ltd. regarded as saturation point. One interesting point emerges, however. As can be seen in Figure 2, in most of the cases where a high proportion of coloured workers were employed, they were Asian (Indian, Pakistani and Arab) workers rather than West Indian.

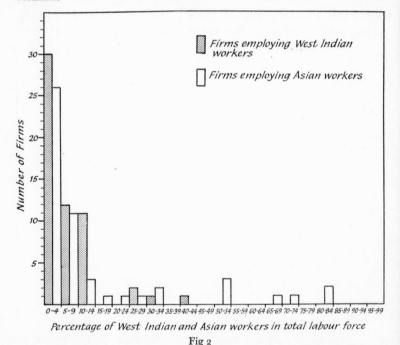

Percentage of West Indian and Asian workers in total labour force

Fig 2

This brings us to another way in which employment opportunities for certain, though not all, coloured workers might be restricted. There was a tendency for some firms to employ one coloured nationality at the expense of another. This was most marked in the case of West Indians and the broad category of Asian workers. Occasionally, a firm would, say, employ Indians at the expense of Pakistanis or vice versa, but, on the whole, firms would employ both if they employed Asians at all.[1] On the other hand, firms often employed either Asian workers or West Indians rather than both groups. In the interview and questionnaire surveys, as can be seen in Table 3, there were thirty-six firms employing a preponderance of Asian or of West Indian workers, compared with twenty-nine with an appreciable proportion of both.

TABLE 3   *Ratios of West Indian to Asian Workers (Interview and Questionnaire Surveys)*

Firms with an Asian to West Indian ratio of more than 10:1	19
Firms with a West Indian to Asian ratio of more than 10:1	17
Mixed Firms	29
Total	65*

* Firms with less than five coloured workers and others with inadequate employment statistics are omitted.

Some indications of the reasons for this tendency were found in the interview surveys. In some cases, it represented a preference on the part of management for one nationality or group rather than another. Central Glass Works,[2] the Ensign Spring Co., Drop Forgings Ltd., the Trafford Iron and Steel Works, and the Hamilton Engineering Co., for example, would only employ West Indians. Bradfield Foundry, Brierley Metal Works, Westwood Foundry, Muirhead Foundry, and Omega Metals Ltd., on the other hand, preferred Asian workers and employed only five or six West Indians at the most.

In other firms (Steel Bars Ltd., Sterling Metal Co., Ridgeway

[1] Providing of course that both were available. In certain towns in the North of England, there are relatively large numbers of Pakistanis, but very few Indians.

[2] In this firm, the fact that the white employees were much less prepared to accept Asian workers was another factor contributing to the employment of West Indians only. (See page 71.)

Steel Co., and the Castle Iron Co.) the preponderance of coloured workers of one group had occurred largely by chance: Asian workers had been the first to apply for jobs and the firm had continued to employ them. The Personnel Manager of the Castle Iron Co. stated: 'We don't have any preferences with regard to the different coloured nationalities. It's just that once you get one race in, you tend to get their pals and relations too.' In one case, however, although it had been a matter of chance which nationality had first been employed, continuing to employ only that nationality had been a deliberate policy decision on the part of the firm. Steel Bars Ltd. employed only Arab workers, not because they were preferred to other nationalities, but because they were afraid that friction might result were another coloured group to be employed. The Works Director stated: '. . . it worked out that way because we had these people (the Arabs) and we didn't want to mix them up. Because that was where we thought we might have trouble. If we were going to employ West Indians, we would employ West Indians and nothing else.' This question will be examined further in Chapter Seven.

A further possibility is that the preponderance of one coloured group rather than another may have resulted, in some cases, from a preference for certain types of jobs on the part of the coloured workers themselves. As will be seen in Chapter Six, very few of the Asian workers interviewed during the present research made any complaints about the nature of their work, whereas complaints about dust, dirt, heat, and fumes were relatively common amongst the West Indians. One West Indian at Hamilton Engineering Co. who had previously worked in a foundry said of his present job: 'It's not a lot of money, but it's not mucky, that's the best part. If I could get a job closer to (the city), I wouldn't mind, but I don't want to go back to the foundry—it's a bit mucky.' Thus the fact that firms in the present sample with a high proportion of coloured immigrants tended to employ Asian workers may have resulted partly from the fact that they were largely foundries and others engaged in the dirtier type of work which the West Indians, and of course white workers, prefer to avoid if possible.

However, the reservation 'if possible' is very necessary. The suggestion sometimes made that coloured immigrants will *refuse* to do heavy or dirty work[1] is hardly justified. The evidence of the present research is that this is just the kind of work which coloured workers, including West Indians, have tended to obtain because of the limited alternatives available to them.

Whatever the reasons for this tendency of firms to employ a preponderance of certain coloured groups, it will be seen that employment opportunities for West Indian and Asian workers were very similar in the firms studied during the present research. The number of firms employing mainly Asians and the number employing mainly West Indians are approximately the same (Table 3), and the tendency for some firms to employ a high proportion of Asian workers is balanced by the larger number of firms employing West Indians where the proportion of coloured workers is smaller (Figure 2). On the other hand, it would be inadvisable to generalize too widely on the basis of this data in view of the relatively small number of firms involved and the fact that the number of coloured workers in the areas concerned is not known with any degree of accuracy. It is necessary, therefore, to rely on other sources of information to provide a general picture of employment levels amongst the different coloured groups.

Writing in 1960, Wood claimed that: 'Almost certainly the (unemployment) rate is higher amongst Indians and Pakistanis than amongst West Indians.'[2] Similarly, Sheila Patterson[3] states that the Indians and Pakistanis were the chief groups to suffer when coloured unemployment doubled from about 7,500 in Autumn 1957 to 15,000 in March 1958, West Indian unemployment rising only from 4,500 to 6,000 during this period. On the other hand, in a survey carried out in 1961, the Economist Intelligence Unit found the *highest* rate of unemployment (9 per cent) amongst West Indians, the figures for Indians and Pakistanis being 5 per cent and 3 per cent respectively. However, the fact that only 3 per cent of the Pakistanis were in unskilled jobs suggests that the sample was not representative in their case.

Probably the most conclusive evidence concerning unemployment rates amongst the different coloured groups is that of

---

[1] For example, a writer in the correspondence columns of the *Edinburgh Evening News*, 15 January 1962, stated that he 'could provide a long list of jobs which coloured immigrants will not look at because the work is heavy, dirty and hard.'

[2] D. Wood, op. cit.

[3] Sheila Patterson, op. cit.

Davison.[1] On the basis of official statistics, he estimates that between August 1961 and February 1963, the average rate of unemployment was 9·5 per cent for West Indians, 5·7 per cent for Indians and 15·6 per cent for Pakistanis. Thus it would appear that unemployment is most acute amongst Pakistanis, but *less* acute amongst Indians than West Indians.

If this is the case, then it is impossible to generalize, as both Wood and Patterson do, about unemployment amongst Indians and Pakistanis as a group, at least as far as the country as a whole is concerned. However, it seems likely that one of the main causes of the high rate of unemployment amongst Pakistanis is their geographical location. They tend to be more numerous in the North of England where unemployment rates in general tend to be higher than the rest of the country. In Bradford, for instance, where coloured workers constituted nearly two-thirds of the total unemployed in the first half of 1962, there are relatively few Indians and West Indians. Thus the effect of their geographical location would go some way towards explaining why Pakistanis have a higher rate of unemployment than Indians, when firms tend to accept both Indians and Pakistanis if they employ Asians at all, and often do not distinguish between the two groups for employment purposes.[2]

Finally, employment opportunities for coloured workers are sometimes restricted because they are not accepted in certain departments or sections of firms, although management as a whole is prepared to employ them. In the Ridgeway Steel Co., it was left to the departmental managers to decide whether they would employ coloured workers or not. Some employed Pakistanis, some employed no coloured workers whatsoever, none employed West Indians and some employed Pakistanis but refused to accept Irish. At Polton Rolling Mills, the Labour Officer claimed that the preponderance of Asian workers em-

---

[1] *Commonwealth Immigrants.*

[2] Davison states that the high rate of unemployment amongst Pakistanis 'may be due in part to their different geographical location . . . but is far more likely to be due to the language difficulties they experience. The fact that an immigrant cannot speak English, complicated by religious and cultural differences, (e.g. in diet, clothes and customs) tends to inhibit employers from offering employment unless they are desperately short of labour.' However, this explanation fails to account for the fact that Indians, who also have language difficulties, different customs and different religions, have a *lower* level of unemployment than West Indians who do not.

ployed by the firm was not an indication of a preference for
these workers on the part of management: it was just that
these workers were the ones who had applied for jobs. Whilst
this may have been an expression of official policy, conflicting
evidence was found elsewhere. The Manager of one of the
departments stated: 'I wouldn't have a West Indian or a Somali:
they are bone idle and arrogant. The Personnel Manager sent
a Somali up here for a job and I told him (the Somali) that
there wasn't one and sent him away. I just wasn't having him.'
In other firms, coloured workers were not accepted in certain
departments because of resistance from the white workers:

We had consultation with the Shop Stewards Organisation. There
was some reluctance, but no great difficulty. We still have some
departments that won't have them. (Personnel Manager, Major
Castings Ltd.)

We sounded out the white workers before we employed coloured
labour. The odd element of the hot workers resented the idea so they
weren't introduced there. (Personnel Manager, Pentland Alloys
Ltd.)

We had no serious difficulties when coloured workers were first
employed. Certain departments refused them for a time: some still
do—certain skilled trades such as building. We had great difficulty
getting them accepted in the machine shop, but by and large they
have been accepted, except in the building and electrical trades.
(Personnel Manager, Sovereign Steel Works)

Finally, at Central Glass Works, not only did the white
workers play an important part in deciding where the coloured
workers were to be employed and in what numbers, but they
also had considerable influence in determining the nationality
and sex of the coloured workers to be employed. The Personnel
Manager stated that in 1954, when it was found necessary to
employ coloured workers, the white workers were consulted by
the management. He claimed that the white workers were prejudiced against Asian workers, because they were afraid of disease
being spread, and against female coloured workers. As a result,
only West Indians had been employed and of these only one
was a woman.

The coloured workers in this firm were employed mainly in

unskilled jobs on the production side. Most of the workers employed on washing scrap glass (which is used for fusing purposes) were West Indian, the remainder being mainly Poles. This job is so distasteful, according to the Personnel Manager, that the British workers tend to avoid it. There was also a preponderance of coloured workers in one of the production shops where there is a repetitive redundancy pattern. 'Men tend to get laid off,' the Personnel Manager said, 'and the local type of workman won't stand for it, so more coloured workers are employed.' In the other production department where there was no redundancy pattern, there were fewer coloured workers because their numbers were limited by the white workers who had their own quota system. No coloured workers were employed in the skilled shops and there was also none in the maintenance department because the white workers would not accept them.

It will be apparent that, in both Central Glass Works and the Sovereign Steel Works, the resistance of certain departments to the employment of coloured workers limited not only the number, but also the 'quality' of jobs available, in that the white workers concerned tended to be in the more skilled and desirable trades. Before turning to the question of employment levels, however, we will first examine the question of redundancy.

(c) *Redundancy and the Coloured Worker*

It is obvious that unemployment amongst coloured workers will be high, not only if they find jobs more difficult to obtain, but also if they lose them more easily in times of unemployment. Richmond[1] states that during the 1930s, coloured seamen became resigned to the fact that they would be 'last to be hired and first to be fired'. This does not appear to have been the case in post-war industry. Wood states: 'The principle "last in, first out" seems in general to apply impartially to coloured workers in those industries where it is an accepted criterion of dismissal in times of redundancy.'[2] Although limited data were obtained on redundancy procedures in the present research, the general impression gained during the interview survey was that, with one major exception, the 'last in, first out' policy was largely accepted.

[1] *The Colour Problem.*
[2] D. Wood, op. cit.

How then are we to account for the fact that unemployment tends to be particularly acute amongst coloured workers during times of redundancy? Wood states that some coloured workers suspect that they are not always treated fairly with respect to redundancy. Whilst this may be so in some cases, three other plausible explanations can be advanced.

Firstly, some of the unemployed coloured workers during recessions have undoubtedly been new arrivals who had not yet obtained employment in Britain and found it more difficult than usual to do so during these times.

Secondly, coloured workers are relative newcomers to British industry. In many cases, therefore, and especially if only recently arrived in the country, they have shorter service records than British workers and, quite legitimately, will be the first to be dismissed when redundancy occurs. The Labour Officer of Edge Tools stated, for example: 'The firm operates on a first in, last out basis, but the coloured workers are genuinely last in. Thirty employees became redundant recently—mainly Pakistanis. They were all given a week's notice and a week's compensation.'[1]

Thirdly, there tends to be a higher proportion of coloured workers in unskilled jobs than white workers. As unskilled labourers are the least indispensable members of a firm's labour force, they are more likely to be made redundant in times of falling production. Thus, the fact that large numbers of coloured workers are in unskilled jobs may be due to discrimination, but the fact that a high proportion of them, as labourers, become redundant may not be the immediate result of any unequal treatment.

Paradoxically, the one firm in the interview survey where discriminatory treatment with respect to redundancy was encountered, provides a good illustration of this point. The Personnel Manager of the Castle Iron Co. stated that when coloured workers had first been employed, the white employees had insisted that they would be the first to go should there be any redundancy. An understanding ('a sort of gentlemen's agreement') to this effect was reached between management

---

[1] A foreman at the same firm stated that, during a fall off in production, the manager had kept coloured workers on sweeping floors and cleaning windows just to avoid having to make them redundant.

and the union. This agreement was still in force at the time of the interview and had been implemented on one or two occasions. On two occasions, however, semi-skilled coloured workers had been retained and white 'floaters'[1] had been 'dispensed with'. 'It does cost money to train a man,' the Personnel Manager said, 'so it would be uneconomic to dismiss a coloured man once he had been trained.'

3. The Occupational Level of Coloured Workers

We have noted that, when first employed, coloured workers tended to obtain the jobs which the white worker found too arduous, distasteful or unrewarding. In the firms visited during the interview survey, this was often still the case at the time the research was carried out. For example:

The kinds of jobs coloured workers do are the knocking out and quenching of castings. Neither job is relished by the white worker. Knocking out is a sledge-hammer job. It's outside work, so it's cold in winter and in summer the bits of sand stick to you when you're sweating. (General Manager, Stainless Steel Ltd.)

Coloured workers are employed mainly on the lower-paid repetitive and semi-repetitive jobs such as electrode cleaning. This is the sort of job that if a white man took it, he doesn't really want a job at all. The West Indians are mainly employed on scrap-crushing, a sledge-hammer job. They also do the loading and unloading of pitch. The highest job done by any coloured worker is fork-lift truck operator. (Personnel Officer, Grange Graphite Co.)

In four of the interview survey firms coloured workers were employed only in unskilled jobs.[2] In another ten firms, the majority of coloured workers were in unskilled occupations, but there were also one or two who had obtained positions such as crane-driver, slinger, fettler, driver, fork-lift truck operator, and in one case skilled positions on the rolling teams.[3] Amongst the remaining seventeen firms, coloured workers were employed in both unskilled and semi-skilled jobs in appreciable numbers in nine cases,[4] and employed in some skilled jobs as well as unskilled and semi-skilled work in a further seven

[1] Workers who only take jobs for short periods of time.
[2] Firms 5, 21, 26, 30.
[3] Firms 8, 11, 15, 16, 17, 18, 22, 23, 25, 27.
[4] Firms 1, 10, 13, 19, 20, 24, 28, 29, 31.

cases.[1] In the remaining firm, insufficient data were obtained to stipulate the occupational level of the coloured workers employed.[2]

Coloured workers usually obtained semi-skilled jobs (and often skilled jobs), not by being employed on them when they first joined the firm, but by being trained and promoted from lower grades of work within the organization. In the Hamilton Engineering Co., for example, some 50 per cent of the West Indian workers, initially employed as unskilled labourers, had progressed to semi-skilled jobs such as slinger, crane-driver, and machine operator in this way. In another firm, Edge Tools Ltd., the steps by which coloured workers eventually obtained semi-skilled jobs was described as follows:

The first coloured workers we employed were Indians and Pakistanis. They were put on labouring jobs because of their lack of capabilities. It was thought that they were not capable of fast piece work on skilled jobs, so we put the coloured workers on labouring jobs and moved up the people they had displaced. Eventually, however, they had to be put on the better jobs because there weren't even enough white workers for these. . . . The firm's policy has been to put the coloured workers on the easiest and most menial tasks and then to select those who shaped well for the better jobs.

A remarkably similar policy was found in Pentland Alloys Ltd. Here the coloured workers (West Indians on this occasion) were first employed as machine shop labourers. Later, however, some of them were promoted to such jobs as grinder, crane-driver, and slinger. According to the Personnel Manager: 'We have never taken a man on as a slinger or a crane-driver. We have taken them on as a labourer and they have fitted in and we have liked them, so they have been promoted.'

The jobs of slinger and crane-driver were specially selected for the coloured workers when the question of promotion arose, because they were not jobs which would lead to a position of authority. Although of a higher grade than the ordinary labouring job, they were still in effect 'dead-end', because they did not lead any further. The Personnel Manager said: 'We have made it a policy never to employ a coloured man in a position, such as part of a team in hot rolling, where in the course of events he

---

[1] Firms 2, 3, 6, 7, 9, 12, 14.
[2] Firm 4.

would rise to a position where he would have to give orders to a white man.' It will be noted that in the list of semi-skilled occupations on which coloured people were employed given above, most of them were the same type of 'differentiated' job, and perhaps for the same reason.

As noted in the previous section, Pentland Alloys Ltd. employed coloured workers not out of necessity but as a matter of policy. It would appear that the firm wished to be altruistic, but did not wish to take any risks whilst doing so. Only West Indians were employed because of the language difficulties which arise with other coloured nationalities, and even then only in limited numbers (thirty-five out of 4,000, or less than 1 per cent) and in limited occupations because they were afraid that trouble might arise should a coloured worker rise to a position of authority over a white worker. To what extent was this fear justified?

As will be seen in Chapter Seven, there is a tendency for resistance to coloured workers on the part of white employees to be greater the higher the grade of job the coloured worker obtains, and the greatest resistance arises in the case of supervisory posts. Nevertheless, coloured workers were employed in jobs of a higher status than white workers in some of the interview survey firms. Whilst walking round one of the department in Precision Engineers Ltd., the writer noted two identical jobs, one with a coloured worker assisting a skilled white worker and the other with a white worker assisting a skilled coloured worker. In another firm, the Sterling Metal Co., the Personnel Manager stated that there had been some trouble over skilled men. On one job, coloured workers were assisting white workers, and one or two were so good that management had wanted to up-grade them. However, the union had objected and the plan was dropped. Yet, on another job in the same shop (bar reeling), a coloured worker had been made a skilled man and was assisted by white workers. The white workers wanted to work with him because his rate of production was so high.

At Drop Forgings Ltd., a similar example was given. The firm employed fifty-five West Indians, about forty-eight of whom were employed on the forges in one capacity or another. The majority of them were on unskilled jobs such as sweeping up, general labourer, fitter's mate, oiler, and so on. Others, however, had higher status jobs; one was a truck driver, another a weigh clerk, two were welders (a skilled job, the men having been trained in Jamaica), one was a tool setter (also a skilled job), and about half a dozen were stampers. The stamper is the only skilled man in a four man team, and on a short trip round the factory the writer observed a number of such teams working. Several consisted of a white stamper assisted by West Indian labourers, one team was entirely West Indian, and one consisted of a West Indian stamper assisted by three white labourers. With respect to the latter, the Personnel Manager suggested that jealousy might arise because the West Indian earned more money than his white assistants, but as the earnings of the team depended upon the skill of the stamper, who controlled the rate of production, the men liked to work with a good stamper irrespective of skin colour.

In other firms visited during the directive interview survey, coloured workers had been employed on precisely the job which Pentland Alloys Ltd. had thought inadvisable, that is as part of a rolling team. Such a team, or set as it is called, usually has six or seven members, and forms a hierarchy from the roller at the top to the 'spare man' at the bottom. Under normal conditions the lowest member of the set is a boy who is being trained, and who, as his training proceeds and as vacancies occur, works his way up the hierarchy. It was on these jobs that coloured workers had been employed in the Quality Steel Co., but here they apparently had not progressed very far. At Sovereign Steel Works, on the other hand, the coloured workers had risen as far as third hand melter, and the firm had obtained acceptance from the men that coloured workers would be promoted higher than third hand should the situation arise. The Personnel Manager added, however, that it was doubtful whether this would happen in the near future because of lack of skill. Similarly, in Steel Bars Ltd., coloured workers were employed as part of rolling sets and had risen to the more senior positions on the 'back side',[1] the lower grade jobs being done by white youths. Again, however, the Works Director stated: 'Mind you, we

[1] The billet of steel is passed through the rollers a number of times until it is of the required size and shape. Thus once the billet has passed through the rollers from the 'front side' to the 'back side' it must be returned again for the next run through. Positions on the 'back side', though on the promotion ladder, are of inferior status to those on the front and it was on these jobs that coloured workers were employed in this firm.

would never put them forward to be a roller. They would have to converse daily on that job and they could not do this yet. We feel that there is a level beyond which they can't go.'

Here, perhaps, is the crux of the matter. At Pentland Alloys, only West Indians were employed whereas the coloured workers on the sets in the above firm were all Asian (mainly Arabs, in fact). Thus there was, in effect, little danger that they would rise to the most senior positions because they lacked the necessary language and literacy qualifications. Were West Indians to be employed on this job, however, the coloured worker might eventually rise to a position where he could claim promotion to roller as his right, having gone through the intermediate stages in the hierarchy. This might lead to objections from the white workers as management in Pentland Alloys feared. Granted that the white workers in the Sovereign Steel Works had consented to the promotion of coloured workers above third hand level, but they knew as well as management that this was unlikely to happen in the near future.

Apart from the above examples, it was rare for coloured workers to obtain jobs directly above white workers in the job hierarchy. Where coloured workers did obtain semi-skilled and skilled jobs, they tended to be of the 'differentiated' type. Whilst the jobs were of higher status than others in the factories concerned, they did not entail authority over other workers. In addition, there was a tendency for white workers not to do jobs at a lower status level than coloured workers irrespective of whether the jobs were differentiated. In other words, whatever level the coloured workers reached, there was a tendency for coloured workers to do the jobs below that rather than white workers. Thus, with the exception of Drop Forgings Ltd., the firms where coloured workers were employed on skilled jobs in significant numbers (Bradfield Foundry, Brierley Metal Works, Westwood Foundry, Muirhead Foundry, and Omega Metals), were also those in which the largest numbers of coloured workers were employed. In these firms, most of the white workers were in the higher status jobs, whilst the coloured workers tended to do the majority of the lower status work in addition to some of the higher status jobs. Thus, there tended to be a mixture of white and coloured workers at the top of the job hierarchy with the lower end of the scale consisting mainly of coloured workers.

The fact that four of the above firms are foundries may also be of significance. This industry was particularly hard hit by the post-war labour shortage, and in the Midlands at least, this shortage seems to have extended to the skilled as well as the unskilled jobs. A foreman at Bradfield Foundry claimed that during the 1930s working at the foundry had been regarded as a very good job. He stated: 'It was almost impossible to get a job here; you practically had to wait for someone to die before you could get in.' In the post-war years, foundry work became less popular and labour became increasingly difficult to obtain. In the early 1950s, advertisements such as 'moulder wanted—prepared to train willing man' were common. According to the foreman, management would bring in a new man, supposedly to assist a moulder, but in actual fact to learn the trade from him. In 1953, one naturalized Italian (an ex-prisoner-of-war) and one Pakistani were employed. By 1962 foreign workers constituted some 75 per cent of the total labour force. The remaining British workers, with few exceptions, were on the staff and in the higher skilled trades. Though quite a few coloured workers were also in skilled jobs, none of them were on the staff.

In Omega Metals Ltd. on the other hand, a coloured worker had been promoted to a supervisory post. This firm, a small engineering concern, also employed a high proportion of coloured workers. Apart from the staff, there were eleven British workers, one West Indian and fifty-one Pakistanis. The British workers were again mainly employed in higher status jobs, such as shot-blasting, fitting, and welding. The one West Indian was a fitter's mate and the majority of Pakistanis were unskilled labourers. All unskilled work in the firm, in fact, was carried out by Pakistanis. Some, however, had obtained higher status jobs. Three were shot-blasters, several were painters, and one was a chargehand. Nevertheless, none of the Pakistanis in higher status jobs had any authority over the British workers. Where the skilled worker had an assistant, the assistant was also coloured, and the authority of the chargehand extended only to the Pakistanis, and not to the white workers or the West Indian.

In the only other firm in the interview surveys in which a coloured worker had obtained a supervisory post, the position was remarkably similar. At Sterling Metal Co., a Somali had been made chargehand 'over his own people' in the boiler house.

7

Thus in both cases the job of chargehand was, in effect, a 'differentiated' one, in that it was part of a separate status hierarchy in which there were only coloured workers. The men concerned were coloured chargehands rather than chargehands who happened to be coloured. This question will be examined further in Chapter Five.

We now turn to the occupation level of coloured workers in the postal questionnaire firms. It was possible to obtain adequate data on the level at which workers, both white and coloured, were employed in thirty-eight cases. These data are presented in Table 4.[1] The same data are presented diagram-

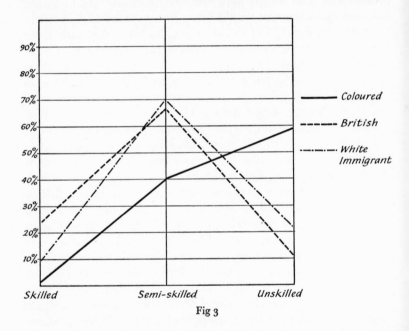

Fig 3

----

[1] One case, a bus company, was omitted because it was thought to be atypical:—

   (a) Although large employers of coloured workers, there were only two bus companies in the area under study and therefore to include one of them in such a small sample would produce a disproportionate effect on the results.

   (b) We are mainly concerned with industry and the occupational structure of a bus company differs from that of an ordinary industrial concern in certain respects: (1) a very high percentage of the employees are in skilled and semi-skilled jobs, (2) there is an equal proportion of skilled to semi-skilled jobs (one driver to a conductor), (3) the main category of skilled job (driver) does not require apprenticeship training.

matically in Figures 3 and 4. It will be seen in Figure 3 that the occupational level of coloured workers was considerably lower than that of British workers, with that of foreign white workers, in general, falling between the two.

TABLE 4   *Occuptional Level of British, Coloured and White Immigrant Workers (Questionnaire Survey)*

	Skilled %	Semi-skilled %	Unskilled %	No.
British Workers	24	66	10	50191
White Immigrants	9	70	21	214
Coloured Immigrants	2	40	58	2307
West Indian	2	40	58	1356
Pakistani	1	39	60	784
Indian	11	39	50	127
Arab	9	65	26	23
African	12	70	18	17

In Figure 4, the occupational levels of the different coloured groups are presented separately. It would be of considerable interest to compare these data with the actual skill level of the coloured workers concerned. However, this involves several difficulties. It is impossible to obtain adequate data on this question from a questionnaire directed to management. Any information from this source would have to be treated as beliefs rather than statements of fact and is, in fact, examined as such in Chapters Four and Five. We must therefore rely on data from the literature. But this has two main drawbacks: firstly, it is not very reliable, being scarce in the case of Asian workers and contradictory in the case of West Indians: and secondly, we do not know how representative these data are of the coloured workers employed in the firms in the present sample. Nevertheless, such a comparison may be of some use providing the limitations of the data are kept in mind.

We suggested in Chapter Two that the estimate of 13 per cent skilled, 22 per cent semi-skilled and 65 per cent unskilled given

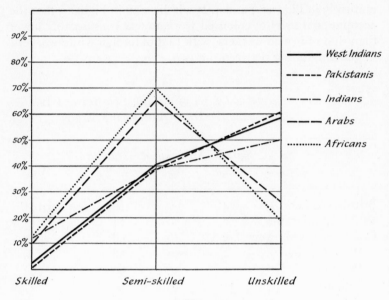

Fig 4

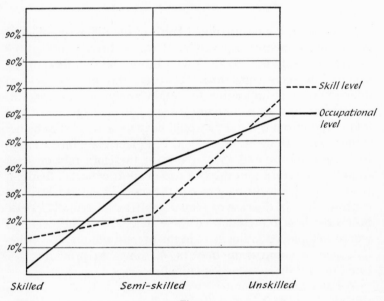

Fig. 5

in the *Civil Service Argus*[1] probably represents the most realistic assessment of the skill level of West Indian manual workers. In Figure 5, these data are compared with the occupational distribution of West Indians in the present sample of firms. It will be seen that although there are fewer West Indians than would be expected in the skilled jobs and unskilled jobs, there are more in the semi-skilled jobs. This would suggest that resistance to coloured workers is greater in the more skilled jobs, which is consistent with other data in the present research. On the other hand, it would appear that some unskilled coloured workers have been accepted and trained for semi-skilled posts, and several examples of this were found in the interview surveys. Thus, on balance, it would appear that the West Indians in the present sample of firms have experienced relatively little occupational down-grading.

However, two points must be noted. Firstly, a large number of West Indian migrants are 'white collar' and not manual workers. Because of the greater resistance to coloured workers in 'white collar' jobs, many of them may have had no alternative but to take manual jobs. Although such workers may technically be unskilled as far as manual work is concerned, to be placed in the position of having to accept such work undoubtedly represents down-grading. Secondly, if the statements of West Indians concerning their own skill level (which are to be found in several studies reported in Chapter Two) are accepted as representing their level of aspiration, then it is apparent that the occupational level attained falls below that expected and will probably be *perceived* as down-grading.

On the other hand, if the estimates of Desai,[2] Alavi[3] and Kathleen Hunter[4] are accepted as representing the skill levels of Indian and Pakistani immigrants, then Asian workers have, in general, achieved considerable occupational *up-grading*. On this basis, one would expect Asian workers to have a considerably higher level of job satisfaction although their occupational level is, in fact, little different from that of the West Indians. As will be seen in Chapter Six, when we come to examine the

---

[1] Op. cit.
[2] R. Desai, op. cit.
[3] H. A. Alavi, op. cit.
[4] Kathleen Hunter, *History of Pakistanis in Britain*, Norwich, 1963.

question of job satisfaction, this was actually the case amongst the Asian and West Indian workers interviewed during the present research.

The lack of correspondence between the skill and occupational levels of the different coloured groups is perhaps the most surprising thing to emerge from Figure 4. The skill levels of Pakistani, Indian, Arab, and African groups are probably lower, and in the case of the Pakistanis much lower, than that of the West Indians. However, the occupational level of the Pakistanis is only fractionally lower than that of the West Indians and in the case of the Indians, Arabs, and Africans is actually *higher*. In view of the small sample of Arabs and Africans and the limited data concerning their skill levels, it would be unwise to place too much confidence in the findings. Nevertheless, this still leaves us with the problem of explaining the disparity in the case of West Indians, Indians, and Pakistanis.

Part of the answer may lie in the conditions under which coloured workers tend to gain employment. Because firms prefer not to employ coloured workers, their occupational level as a whole tends to vary not so much with their skill level but with the number and type of vacancies which cannot be filled by white workers. If white workers can be obtained for skilled jobs, then coloured workers tend not to be employed in them whether they are skilled or not. On the other hand, if white workers, whether already skilled or capable of being trained, cannot be obtained for semi-skilled and in some cases skilled jobs, then coloured workers will be employed and if necessary trained up to the requisite standard. As we have already noted, however, coloured workers tend to be employed at first on unskilled jobs, and skill is only one of the factors which determine managerial preferences when deciding which coloured group should be employed as labourers. Thus whether a coloured worker obtains a skilled job or not may depend more upon whether he happens to be employed in a firm where skilled or semi-skilled workers are desperately needed than upon his own skill level.

A further interesting point arises from Figure 4. It will be seen that the occupational level of the different coloured groups tends to be inversely related to the size of the sample. It may be, therefore, that the fewer coloured workers there are in a group, the greater their opportunities for obtaining the more skilled jobs. If, as we have suggested, there is a tendency for firms to employ one group of coloured workers rather than another, it follows that there is a relatively stable number of jobs available to each national group. As a result, coloured workers will tend to be in competition not so much with coloured immigrants in general, but rather with other members of their own group. Thus, the fewer immigrants there are in the group, the smaller the competition for the better jobs and the greater their opportunities for obtaining them. On the basis of the present evidence, this explanation must be treated as no more than a tentative hypothesis, but it is perhaps worthy of further research.

4. *Summary and Conclusions*

In this chapter, we concluded that employment levels amongst coloured workers were, in general, lower than amongst white workers. Amongst the different coloured groups, employment levels appear to be lowest in the case of Pakistanis, but higher in the case of Indians than West Indians. During times of recession, unemployment amongst coloured workers has tended to rise more rapidly than amongst white workers and to go down again more slowly when trade recovers. However, there has been no hard core of coloured unemployed suggesting that coloured workers tend to have longer periods between jobs rather than to be permanently unemployed. The occupational levels of coloured workers in general were found to be lower than those of native British and foreign white workers, but there was remarkably little difference between the occupational levels of the three major coloured groups.

What then of the future? As far as occupational levels are concerned, it will be apparent that coloured workers have made some progress towards industrial integration during the time span covered by the present research. When first employed, coloured workers were given unskilled jobs in the main, but many were later given semi-skilled and in some cases skilled jobs. However, this progress seems largely to have been dependent on a shortage of white workers in these trades and there is a limit to the number of skilled jobs which can be obtained by workers without apprenticeship training, or even with such training if white workers are always given first choice.

To a large extent, therefore, the future integration of coloured workers depends upon coloured children obtaining apprenticeships and gaining acceptance into the skilled trades. On this subject, Sheila Patterson states:

A minority of exceptional individual migrants have begun to move up from the bottom of the industrial ladder and to undermine the British workers' notion of coloured workers as Lascars, coolies and cane cutters in far away lands. Such progress is limited by the low industrial capacity of the majority of to-day's migrants. It could be speeded up when the locally educated second generation enter the labour market. The latter will no longer be strangers, but they will still have to strive against the 'class' notion that coloured workers are on the whole suitable only for unskilled and semi-skilled work, just as their parents have had to combat the 'stranger' notion to win acceptance as a permanent part of the local labour force.[1]

Relatively little data was obtained on occupational opportunities for coloured children during the present research as the emphasis was mainly upon the employment of adult migrants. Such information as there is, however, does not paint a very optimistic picture. The Personnel Manager of Ensign Spring Co. stated that trouble might arise soon because of coloured school leavers; there was still resistance to employing coloured workers in skilled jobs and one could not employ school leavers as labourers. In the Regal Manufacturing Co. two Indian youths had been employed, although the firm did not usually employ Asian workers because of the language difficulties involved. The Personnel Manager stated that language difficulties did not arise in the case of the youths because they had been to school in this country, but it was difficult to find jobs for such people; they were too old for the type of jobs usually given to school leavers and not old enough for labouring. Finally, at Tool Steel Ltd. the Personnel Manager stated:

The time is coming when, if you employed a young lad from school and he learned his trade in a particular shop, the chances are they would accept him as a skilled man. But if we employed a coloured man in a skilled job who had been trained at another firm and they hadn't had a chance to get used to him, then he would almost certainly be rejected.

[1] Sheila Patterson, op. cit.

Whether these managers are correct in their assumptions or not is to some extent irrelevant: what is important is that they represent beliefs of the managers concerned, and as long as it is believed that difficulties might arise, then firms are likely to be reluctant to employ coloured school leavers. In the latter case, the respondent stated that *the chances were* that a coloured school leaver would be accepted. However, if there is no desperate shortage of apprentices, as there was of unskilled labourers, then it is questionable whether firms will be willing to take this chance.

At the same time, lack of employment in skilled occupations may in the future seriously limit the number of jobs available to coloured workers. In one of the interview survey firms, Blackford Rolling Mills, coloured workers had originally been employed in the hot-rolling mills because of the shortage of unskilled labourers. Since then, however, the hot-mill had been shut down and the firm had turned entirely to mechanized cold rolling which required mainly skilled workers. Some of the skilled workers had been transferred from hot rolling to cold rolling, but all the coloured workers had become redundant, and at the time the present research was carried out were only employed as casual labour during the annual 'shutdown'.

Similarly, at Westwood Foundry, there was a possibility that the firm's requirements for coloured workers would be reduced by mechanization. A new, fully mechanized, moulding plant was being built. According to the Labour Officer, the number of workers needed would probably remain the same, but the 'quality' would be different; they would be button pushers and dial watchers rather than unskilled gangers. This being the case, it is unlikely that Asian workers (who constituted 53 per cent of the firm's labour force) would be employed in these jobs because of language and literacy difficulties. Moreover, the jobs concerned would be less arduous and have more prestige than the type of work they replaced, and would probably, therefore, be more attractive to white workers. This would further decrease the coloured workers' opportunities for obtaining such jobs even if they possessed the necessary qualifications.

Thus although the present generation of migrants have made some progress towards industrial integration, serious problems may still arise with regard to both the employment and occupational levels of succeeding generations unless this progress is maintained. The few examples given in this chapter show that, in spite of some resistance on the part of white workers, coloured workers can be employed on skilled jobs. The danger lies in the fact that many firms may decide to 'leave well alone', or simply never really consider the wider implications of not employing skilled coloured workers in their own particular cases.

CHAPTER FOUR

Managerial Beliefs and Attitudes Concerning the Employment of Coloured Workers: Skill and Training

1. *Introduction*

During the next two chapters we shall consider managerial beliefs and attitudes towards the employment of coloured workers. The available 'objective' data concerning the skill level of coloured immigrants and the vacancies available to them in British industry during the 1950s have already been examined in Chapter Two. It was concluded that coloured immigrants tended to be less skilled than their British counterparts and that there was a considerable shortage of labour during much of this period, especially in the less skilled occupations. The extent to which these two factors complement each other might be expected therefore materially to have assisted the industrial integration of the immigrants.

However, it would be unrealistic to assume that human beings react solely to the objective situation. They react rather to their 'definition of the situation' and the same objective situation may yield two radically different subjective ones. The shortage of labour which management sees as a knotty problem may be regarded as a positive factor by the workers to whom it gives added security and perhaps increased earnings through overtime. Similarly, the immigrant who views himself as adequately qualified for a skilled job may not be so perceived by an employer who 'knows' that all coloured workers are completely unskilled. Thus, it will be not so much the facts about coloured workers, so much as what managers and to some extent white workers, *believe* to be the facts which will determine whether a particular firm employs coloured workers, and if so, in what numbers, of which nationality and on which jobs. As Myrdal says:

It is the popular beliefs, and they alone, which enter directly into the causal mechanism of interracial relations. The scientific facts of race and racial characteristics . . . are only of secondary and indirect importance . . . they are only virtual but not actual social facts.[1]

However, one must be careful not to pursue this line of argument too far. When faced with a complex phenomenon, it is undoubtedly easier to study what people *say* are the facts (their 'definition of the situation') than to determine what these 'facts' actually are. It is tempting, therefore, to use this method as an 'easy way out'—to use popular beliefs as an alternative or substitute for the facts rather than as a different, though equally valid, set of data. To do so, however, seriously limits the use to which the data can be put. Whilst a study of popular beliefs may yield the immediate social cause of a phenomenon, both the popular beliefs and the 'facts' are necessary to provide an adequate basis for action.

This can be illustrated by means of a hypothetical example. We have already shown that coloured workers tend to obtain jobs lower in the occupational scale than white workers. Let us suppose, for the sake of argument, that we discover that this is because managers believe that, coming from an agricultural background, coloured workers lack the manual dexterity for skilled industrial jobs. Irrespective of whether coloured workers do in fact lack the manual dexterity for skilled industrial jobs, this managerial belief would represent the immediate cause of the phenomenon in question. However, this does not tell us what steps to take should we wish to raise the occupational level of coloured workers. If the belief could be shown to be invalid, then attempts to persuade managers that their assessment is inaccurate would be in order. On the other hand, training schemes designed to increase the manual dexterity of coloured workers or something of this nature would be necessary if the belief were shown to be valid. Thus a knowledge of the 'facts' about the manual dexterity of coloured workers would be vitally necessary in order to determine which course of action to take.

Nevertheless, it *is* more difficult to determine the 'facts' than to examine the beliefs systems. To carry out an adequate objective study of, say, manual dexterity amongst coloured workers

[1] G. Myrdal, op. cit.

would have been a major research undertaking in itself, and even this would have been a comparatively straightforward matter compared with the objective study of other, more intangible, subjects such as diligence and amenability to discipline. In the course of a three-year research project, such as the one on which the present work is based, it would have been possible to examine in this manner only one, or at the most perhaps two, of such factors. On the other hand, it proved possible to examine a wide variety of beliefs concerning these factors during the same period. There is a strong argument, therefore, for examining the belief systems first, especially in an under-developed field where there are a number of factors involved. Firstly, it enables the research worker to present a general out-line of the whole field, thus providing a frame of reference to which it would be possible to relate subsequent more detailed studies. Secondly, to analyse the facts without first examining the beliefs would not allow the research worker to discover which facts were the socially relevant ones and might lead to a large amount of time being wasted on the collection of relatively unimportant data.

For this reason, the writer has mainly concentrated upon the study of the beliefs of managers and workers concerning the employment of coloured workers. Where possible, however, some attempt has been made to check the validity of these beliefs by comparing them with the available data in the literature, with the actual employment conditions of coloured workers in the firms concerned, and by comparing the beliefs expressed by different respondents. In this chapter we will be concerned with skill and training, but we will turn to such factors as diligence, flexibility, supervision, labour turnover, and so on in later chapters.

2. *Managerial Beliefs Concerning the Skill of Coloured Workers*

In the non-directive survey, only three managers expressed beliefs concerning the skill level of West Indian workers. Their opinions varied as much as did those of the academic authorities quoted in Chapter Two. The Personnel Manager of Ensign Spring Co. said: 'We get a lot of coloured people coming for jobs and we have to turn them away. Experience is needed and Jamaicans haven't got the experience.' This firm employed only twenty to twenty-five West Indians out of a total of 800 to 900 employees, all of them in unskilled work.

On the other hand, Brierley Metal Works, which also employed few West Indians (about six out of a total labour force of 2,300, of whom about 30 per cent were Asians) apparently did so for the opposite reason. The Labour Manager said:

> The firm employs very few West Indians—about half a dozen. . . . Most of the Jamaicans are very well educated; much too highly educated to accept labouring jobs. Employing West Indians just doesn't work out: they soon want to be boss and they can't all be boss.

In both these cases, it seems likely that the opinions expressed were rationalizations, either conscious or unconscious, for the small number of West Indians employed by the firms. At Ensign Spring Co., as we have already noted, several of the jobs, in fact, required very little previous experience. Similarly, the other respondent's claim that West Indians were much too highly educated to accept labouring jobs, whether he himself believed the statement or not, was simply not a statement of fact. West Indians were employed on labouring jobs in many of the other firms visited by the writer and in several cases, for instance, Central Glass Works, on the most menial of labouring jobs. On the other hand, the firm in question employed a high proportion of Asian workers, compared with whom West Indians are more 'educated'[1] and also perhaps more eager to obtain higher status jobs (hence the respondent's claim that they 'wanted to be boss'). Thus it seems likely that the basis of the Labour Manager's assessment was not the fact that West Indians were completely unwilling to accept labouring jobs, but that they were less content than Asian workers to remain in labouring jobs and therefore, from the firm's point of view, made less satisfactory workers.

At Drop Forgings Ltd., a firm employing fifty-five West Indians out of a total labour force of 450 men, the assessment of the skill of West Indian workers was somewhat similar to that in the Ensign Spring Co. The Personnel Manager claimed that, in general, West Indians were not skilled enough for the skilled

---

[1] If only in the sense that they speak English as their native language, an 'educational' criterion found elsewhere in the present research (see page 191).

jobs, especially the highly skilled jobs requiring apprenticeship. He stated: 'Most of the Jamaicans we employ are completely unskilled: about half of them were cultivators.' However, this case differs from the previous one in several respects. Firstly, the firm was prepared to employ a much higher proportion of West Indians (12 per cent compared with about 2.5 per cent); secondly, the firm employed two skilled men who had received their training in Jamaica; and thirdly, a number of West Indians had been trained for skilled positions by the firm.

In the directive interview survey, managerial assessments of the skill level of West Indian workers were obtained in ten firms. In eight cases it was stated that West Indians were, in general, less skilled than British workers.[1] In one of the remaining two firms, Sovereign Steel Works, the respondent evaded the question by saying that most of the coloured workers had had some experience before coming to work at the firm. By this he meant that they had not come 'straight off the boat', but had worked in other firms in Britain first. However, he said later that the firm had no skilled coloured workers and those who worked on semi-skilled jobs had been trained by the firm. Finally, the Personnel Manager of Pentland Alloys stated that West Indian workers had experienced no difficulty with the unskilled and semi-skilled jobs which they had been given, but he did not think that they could be employed on skilled jobs because they lacked the necessary apprenticeship training.

In three firms, it was stated that by British standards West Indians were sometimes less skilled than they claimed to be.

In general, they are less skilled. We have had a number who claimed skill, but were tested and didn't come up to standard. If they have had a little experience, they tend to think they are skilled. (Labour Officer, Hamilton Engineering Co.)

The bloke who claims to be a tradesman is generally of a lower standard than we would expect. They have not had the experience of complicated work in big firms: they are not capable of a variety of work. We haven't had one who could pass the trade test we set for English applicants. We had one who had good references from a small firm, but who wasn't good enough for us. If they had some sort of post-graduate apprenticeships, they might do all right, but we

[1] Firms 15, 17, 18, 19, 20, 21, 22, and 27.

have had no reason to do this. (Personnel Officer, Grange Graphite Co.)

We have never been able to put a West Indian on electrical or engineering jobs because the qualifications claimed do not come up to our standard. (Personnel Manager, Sterling Metal Co.)

Codable answers concerning the skill level of West Indian workers were obtained from thirty-nine firms in the questionnaire survey. They were said to be less skilled than British workers in twenty-two cases and 'about the same' in seventeen cases. In none of the firms was it stated that West Indians were more skilled than British workers.

We now turn to managerial beliefs concerning the skill level of Asian workers. In the directive survey, managers in fourteen firms out of fifteen stated that Asian workers were less skilled than native British workers. The one exception was Sovereign Steel Works, where the manager again avoided the question by saying that most of the coloured workers had previously had some experience in other firms. In six cases, comparisons between the skill level of Asian and West Indian workers were obtained. In Annerley Iron Foundry and Tool Steel Ltd., it was said that West Indians were slightly more skilled. The Personnel Officer of Grange Graphite Co. stated that West Indians were always of a higher skill—he had never come across an Asian worker who claimed to be anything other than a labourer. In Quality Steel Co., Sovereign Steel Works and Polton Rolling Mills, however, no difference had been found between the skill level of Asian and West Indian workers.

The results of the questionnaire survey with regard to the skill level of coloured workers are presented in Table 5. It will be seen that the majority of respondents described Asian workers as less skilled than British workers and that Asian workers, especially Pakistanis, were assessed as being less skilled in a higher proportion of cases than West Indians.

TABLE 5   *Managerial Assessments of the Skill Level of Coloured Workers (Questionnaire Survey)*

Nationality	More skilled than British workers %	About the same as British workers %	Less skilled than British workers %	No. of firms responding
West Indians	0	44	56	39
Pakistanis	0	21	79	19
Indians	0	37	63	33
Arabs	0	23	77	13
Africans	0	27	73	11

Thus far we have been concerned only with formal training in skilled trades. With Asian workers, however, the level of industrial sophistication is also an important consideration. Not only did Asian workers tend to be considered less skilled than British workers, but some managers further suggested that they often lacked even the most elementary knowledge of industry and industrial techniques, knowledge which would be regarded as almost axiomatic by anyone brought up in an industrialized society whether they had actually worked in industry or not.[1]

At Bradfield Foundry, for example, several Arabs had been

[1] This question was touched upon by Wood (op. cit.) in connection with the allegedly slow work tempo of coloured immigrants. He states: 'The most common complaint about coloured people of both sexes and all nationalities is that they are often slow workers to begin with, and we have heard this in almost every town from a variety of sources. The immigrants were not brought up in an industrial atmosphere where the child picks up almost unconsciously the attitudes and unspoken assumptions of factory life. They have to accustom themselves to the tempo of work and alien environment of industry . . . all this cannot be learned in a day by immigrants with a rural background who are not used to gadgets and machinery.' Although this coincides to some extent with the findings of the present study, two points need to be made. Firstly, not all managers said that coloured workers were slow at first; some, as will be seen in Chapter Five, stated that they were fast at first but slowed down later. Secondly, at least three factors seem to be involved in the work tempo of coloured immigrants: (1) level of industrial sophistication; (2) speed of learning; and (3) attitude towards work, once trained. In general, complaints about factors (1) and (2) occurred mainly with respect to Asian workers and in relation to factor (3) mainly with respect to West Indians. Although undoubtedly relevant, therefore, the question of industrial sophistication cannot be advanced as the sole explanation for the slow work tempo sometimes found amongst coloured workers.

8

employed, none of whom had ever worked in a factory before. When first employed, according to the Works Superintendent, they had to be taught how to use a broom, which they held near the head instead of at the end of the handle; how to use a wheelbarrow, which they pushed along with the legs scraping on the floor; and how to put on protective gloves (used when working at the grind wheels), which they were incapable of doing unassisted. In other words, they had to be taught how to be labourers.

Similarly, the Labour Manager of Edge Tools stated:

Asian workers do not know many things which are just taken for granted with whites. This causes a strain on supervisory time. The firm employs more supervisors than usual and pays them higher wages than normal. It is an invisible cost of employing Pakistanis.

The respondent claimed that the Pakistanis' lack of industrial sophistication not only caused difficulties in training, but was also a danger to themselves. They had been told not to touch moving parts of machinery, he stated, but they did not realize the danger. One Pakistani, for example, had been told to stop a grind-wheel and had attempted to do so, not by switching it off, but by putting his hand on the wheel. Fortunately he had not been badly hurt, and, according to the Labour Manager, there had as yet been no major acidents.

In the directive survey, Asian workers were said to be 'accident prone' in seven[1] of the fourteen firms in which they were employed. Some of the managers' comments were as follows:

Our product looks the same when it is hot as when it is cold. Asiatics are prone to pick it up and touch it when it is still hot. We haven't had any serious accidents, but minor accidents, they are prone to. (Personnel Officer, Grange Graphite Co.)

There is a tendency for coloured people to be accident prone. It's probably due to lack of industrial experience. It may also be the fact that they aren't in a position to read all the safety propaganda.[2] We

---

[1] Firms 22, 23, 25, 26, 27, 28 and 30.

[2] In this firm, danger notices in foreign languages had been put up in certain hazardous areas. Because of the relatively high illiteracy rates amongst Asian immigrants, however, this could be no more than a partial solution to the problem.

take industrial experience far too much for granted; it's not lack of intelligence. (Personnel Manager, Sovereign Steel Works)

We have found this (accident proneness) ourselves in the Hot Mill. There seems to be a lack of appreciation of danger. Also, they see our blokes doing things and try to do the same, although they are not as experienced. (Production Services Manager, Blackford Rolling Mills)

The unskilled (Asian workers) have been more accident prone than our own people. We have made our own assessment of this. We think that it is due to the change of environment. They are surrounded by mechanical things of which they have no knowledge whatsoever. (Personnel Manager, Castle Iron Co.)

It will be seen that, as in Edge Tools, 'accident proneness' tended to be attributed to the Asian workers' lack of industrial sophistication. In none of the firms was it suggested that West Indians were accident prone.

Apart from lack of industrial sophistication, another difficulty which often arises in the employment of Asian workers is that of language. In the questionnaire survey, one respondent stated:

You appear to have missed out one very important factor, at least as far as Pakistanis are concerned. I refer to the barrier of language.[1] We have employed up to eight Pakistanis in this factory and have found that, although they are good workers, we are necessarily limited in our use of them due to the difficulty in getting over to them what is wanted with regard to any particular job. This means, of course, that we have to teach them thoroughly on one job and leave them on that, although some of them would have the ability to carry out a slightly more skilled job than the labouring jobs they are doing.

This example suggests that, in some cases, the ability to speak English can be regarded as the equivalent of an industrial skill in the immigrant workers, in that language difficulties may lead to training being necessary where simple order giving would have been sufficient in the normal course of events.

The question of language was mentioned in several firms visited during the interview surveys. In the non-directive survey, one firm[2] gave the lack of ability to speak English as the reason why Asian workers were not employed, and in two further

---

[1] It was assumed that respondents would refer to the language problem, if relevant, in relation to the questions on training and supervision.

[2] Regal Manufacturing Co.

firms[1] this reason was advanced as a contributing factor. In Components Ltd. Asian workers who could not speak English were not employed. The Personnel Officer stated: 'At first the coloured workers were employed mainly on labouring jobs and sign language was used. Now it is a matter of selection. The Personnel Office selects those who can speak English.' Finally, in Edge Tools, a firm which did employ non-English speaking Asian workers, the Labour Manager stated that the language difficulties were 'almost impossible' until a sign language was evolved.

In sixteen of the seventeen firms visited during the directive interview survey, language difficulties were mentioned in relation to either training or supervision. The one exception was Torrington Cutlers where no Asian workers were employed. In the two other firms in which there were no Asian workers, language difficulties were advanced as a reason for not employing them. Pentland Alloys had decided to employ only West Indians after hearing of the problems encountered by other firms. Hamilton Engineering had employed Indians and Pakistanis in the past, but had found West Indians to be 'the better type of applicant, especially with regard to their command of the language'. Moreover, they had never employed Asian workers who could not speak English with a reasonable degree of fluency. Similarly, in Leigham Cannery, where Asian workers were employed and in this case highly thought of, the ability to speak and read English was a necessary qualification for obtaining a job. The Personnel Officer stated:

All coloured workers are literate: illiteracy is a bar to employment. They must be able to read and speak English up to four letter words. We test prospective employees with a newspaper: we ask them to read a simple piece.

At this stage, we will not examine the question of language difficulties further, but merely note that it is a problem which often arises with respect to the employment of Asian workers but does not occur in the case of West Indian or, of course, British workers. However, it is a question which will require more detailed examination when we come to consider the training and supervision of coloured workers.

[1] Drop Forgings Ltd. and Central Glass Works.

3. *The Training of Coloured Workers*

As might be expected, managers tended to find Asian workers more difficult to train than either British or West Indian workers. Managers in several firms visited during the non-directive survey commented upon this. For example, the Labour Manager of Edge Tools stated that the promotion of Pakistanis to semi-skilled jobs had 'only been half-way successful' because they were 'not very bright'. He described the introduction of Asian workers (mainly Pakistanis in this firm) into one of the semi-skilled jobs as follows:

The Polishing Shop was the hardest to staff. Pakistanis were tried there. It looked at first as if it wasn't going to work. It is impossible to put them straight on piece work because they wouldn't earn anything. We had to pay them a reasonable rate and hope for the best whilst they were being trained. It was a costly business to begin with —only about one-fifth were trainable on semi-skilled jobs at first— but once half a dozen were established, they helped the newcomers and things became easier.

Other comments were as follows:

Pakistanis are very slow at first. For the first month they are a dead loss to the firm. You have to be prepared to lose a month. (Works Manager, Omega Metals)

If there are opportunities for up-grading and the man is suitable, the coloured worker gets his chance the same as anyone else. But this is the principle rather than the rule, because, in general they are incapable of being up-graded. (Personnel Officer, Components Ltd.)

In general, Arabs are a bit slow on the uptake. (Works Superintendent, Bradfield Foundry)

The latter statement was contradicted by the Labour Manager at Brierley Metal Works who stated that although Arabs were, in the main, absolutely unskilled they were very quick to learn and made very good welders and oxy-acetylene cutters.

In the directive interview survey, managers in seven firms[1] stated that Asian workers tended to be slower to learn their jobs than British workers. A variety of reasons were given. In Grange Graphite Co. the Personnel Manager stated:

[1] Firms 16, 22, 23, 25, 26, 27, and 28.

Initially coloured workers are much slower. With Asiatics it is largely physique. Except on the simplest jobs they never get to full capability. West Indians will eventually, but Asiatics never. Beyond a certain point we just have to let them be. Language is the first difficulty with Asiatics and this is just insurmountable I'm afraid. We have to use the demonstration technique and this limits the jobs they can be trained for to those with a short cycle.

On the other hand, the General Manager of Stainless Steel Ltd. stated: 'They are a bit slow, but once they've got it, they understand the job thoroughly. It could go both ways, inadequate training as well as slowness.'

At Quality Steel Co. difficulties had arisen because the job on which coloured workers were mainly employed (the lower grades of set work) had to be taught in stages. The Personnel Officer stated:

You don't want to push them too much so you give them the basic essentials first. Then when you try to teach them more, they think they are being given more work for the same money, and they won't move on to the next stage without a lot of persuasion from the Departmental Manager. If they lose their temper, they revert back to their own tongue and you can't argue with them.

At the Castle Iron Co. the Personnel Manager stated:

The main (initial) difficulty was training from unskilled to semi-skilled. They are slower to learn due to the language difficulty and the adjustment to mechanization as opposed to manual labour. They seem to be the kind of people who are not mechanically minded and they have had no training whatsoever in using their hands. Some of them we have been able to train to semi-skilled jobs, but out of the whole number we have employed, not more than 10% have been trained and have proved to be useful workers.

Finally, at Polton Rolling Mills the Labour Officer suggested that accident proneness contributed to the slower rate of learning of the Asian worker.

They are a bit slower than the average Englishman. There is the language difficulty and also they are accident prone. They drop things on their toes. They are less quick on the draw than the Englishman if you know what I mean, less quick to get out of the way of things.

However, it will be seen that a recurring problem was that of language. Language difficulties in the training of Asian workers had been encountered in all seven firms, and in one case it was suggested that this was the only reason for their slowness. The Personnel Manager of Sovereign Steel Works stated: 'Provided you can get hold of the language problem, they are no slower (to learn than the British worker). However, they usually are slower due to language difficulties.'

In two other firms, Major Castings and Leigham Cannery, managers stated that there was no difference between Asian and British workers *providing difficulties with language did not arise*. Both respondents stated that Asian workers took a pride in learning their job. The Personnel Officer of Leigham Cannery went into some detail on this question:

There is no difference between the Pakistani and the local bloke providing he can speak the language. In fact, the Pakistani is better than the average white worker under present conditions. The majority of available whites are part of the floating population. The majority (i.e. the non-floaters) can get a good job and stick to it. The West Indians are reasonable—not an embarrassment—but not as good as the Pakistanis. The Pakistanis feel they *have* to succeed, even more than the West Indians. It may be that they have some incentive behind them. Their country is recently independent and possibly they feel that they must not let their country down.

By contrast, the Personnel Manager of Sterling Metal Co. claimed that Pakistanis were very slow to learn and were 'strictly limited' in the type of job they could be given. Arab and African (mainly Somali) workers, on the other hand were described as 'very adaptable and quick to learn'. In this firm, according to the respondent, jobs requiring more skill were given to the Arabs and those requiring less skill to the Pakistanis.

This again is in direct contrast to Blackford Rolling Mills, where Arabs and Pakistanis were classed as members of the same group, and management had noticed no difference between them in relation to either skill or performance. The Production Services Manager said that both Arabs and Pakistanis picked up unskilled jobs and manual work very quickly. He added that it was very difficult to evaluate their potential ability because of the communication problem, but having overcome that, he had no doubt that some of them could be trained for skilled work.

In Steel Bars Ltd. the above assessments of the Arabs' ability to learn industrial jobs was strongly endorsed. The Works Director stated: 'We have five Arabs working in the mill and they have picked up handling tongs like shelling peas. They're experts. They are as good as whites who have had 20 to 30 years experience.'

The respondent stated that, in general, the initial skill level of the Arab workers had been 'very poor', but with a couple of exceptions, they had been very quick to learn. Originally, they had been employed on the lowest jobs in the sets, but they had been very keen to obtain promotion to the more skilled jobs.

After they have been here for about four months, the Arabs are straining at the bit. It's best not to hold a man back when he is trying to better himself, so we've let them have better jobs and it's always paid off. They have gone up to the top jobs on the back side in both mills. We haven't got an Arab on a low job now; white youths do these jobs.

The Arab workers, the respondent claimed, had a different attitude towards work from the white worker. When an Arab took over the lowest job in the set, he would try the job above when he had the opportunity, so that when a vacancy occurred, he could do the job. The English worker, on the other hand, did not learn the job above in this manner and therefore was unable to step straight into the next job without further training.

As a result of this attitude towards the job, the Works Director stated, the training of Arab workers had involved no problems whatsoever.

They virtually don't need training. The bottom job doesn't require any training and they pick up the next job on their own. When he's got a minute, he has a go at the job above. He's been watching the man who does the job.

However, two reservations need to be made about the assessment of Arab workers at this firm. Firstly, the Works Director said that the coloured workers employed by the firm were probably not representative of Arab workers as a whole:

We have sifted them over eight years. To say that they are above the average is putting it mildly. I would say that the eight we have are superior to the white worker. Mind you, we have had one or two that were plain bloody awkward. You literally couldn't tell them to sweep the floor.

Secondly, notwithstanding his claim that the Arabs did not require training, the Works Director stated that the firm's biggest problem had been the language barrier. One Arab had been dismissed because they were unable to communicate with him, and the Arabs' lack of facility with English was given as the reason why they could not be promoted to the position of head roller.

In general, then, managers interviewed during the directive interview survey thought that language difficulties, lack of industrial sophistication or lack of apprenticeship training would prevent Asian workers from obtaining skilled jobs. In seven firms,[1] it was stated that they could do semi-skilled jobs, but in a further four firms there were some reservations even about this level of work. In three cases,[2] it was stated that some Asian workers could do semi-skilled but the remainder only labouring work, and in the other case[3] the respondent claimed that Asian workers could only do certain types of semi-skilled jobs. In Stainless Steel Ltd. the General Manager assessed the situation as follows:

There is a small percentage who could be skilled and a small percentage who could be semi-skilled and then you've got the workers and the drones. You get the same categories with white workers, but the percentages are not so good with coloured workers. You get more at the lower end of the scale and less at the upper end than you do with white workers. We have had about twenty to twenty-five coloured workers at the firm altogether. Only two could have made skilled workers, four semi-skilled, about ten labouring and the rest no good.

Finally, the Personnel Manager of Sterling Metal Co. again differentiated between Pakistanis and Arabs. He stated that whereas the Pakistanis were strictly limited, the Arabs could go as far as they were permitted.

Comparatively little data were obtained on the training of West Indian workers. This, in itself, would suggest that it was

[1] Firms 19, 20, 22, 23, 25, 27, and 30.
[2] Firms 16, 18, and 28.
[3] Firm 15.

not perceived by managers as being a serious 'problem' as was often the case with Asian workers. What data there are tend to support this contention.

The Personnel Manager of Drop Forgings Ltd. stated that only about half a dozen of the fifty-five West Indians employed by the firm had been made stampers (a skilled job), but added that 'you wouldn't get any more out of the same number of whites'. Similarly, the Personnel Manager of Trafford Iron and Steel Co. said that there had been isolated cases of men finding jobs too difficult, *but this had not been associated with colour.*

When asked about the training of West Indian workers, the Personnel Manager of Pentland Alloys Ltd. stated:

They've always had a good name. We have never had any trouble on the jobs we've given them. They have done well and been indistinguishable from the white man in performance. In fact some of them have been a good deal better.

He said that he had no doubt that West Indians could be trained for semi-skilled jobs, although he was dubious about skilled work because five years training was necessary.

In Hamilton Engineering Co., on the other hand, the Personnel Manager thought that, on the average, West Indians were slower to learn than the British workers, although there were exceptions: 'It depends entirely on their background. If the Jamaican has spent some time in a factory he is reasonably fast. If he has been a plantation worker, then he is slow.' Nevertheless, the respondent was of the opinion that the majority of West Indians were capable of being trained for semi-skilled jobs and, in fact, some 50 per cent of the West Indian employees had progressed to semi-skilled jobs such as crane driver, slinger, and machine operator. Moreover, the firm had employed Asian workers in the past, but West Indians were preferred. The Personnel Manager stated:

We have employed Pakistanis and Indians. Jamaicans have been the better type of applicant especially with regard to their command of the language. We used to get the 'uncle' coming in with four men trying to get them a job. He could speak English but didn't want a job and the ones that did want a job couldn't speak English.

Where comparisons were made between the different coloured groups, West Indians tended to be found easier to train. The

Personnel Manager of Major Castings Ltd. stated that West Indians showed more initiative than the Pakistanis: 'I don't think they (the Pakistanis) are as adaptable. They can't do all the semi-skilled jobs. The West Indians are rather ahead of the Pakistanis in this respect.' In Torrington Cutlers, the Works Director claimed that the West Indian worker was easier to train than the Pakistani and compared favourably with the local unskilled worker.[1] He stated that West Indians could be trained on semi-skilled jobs and many could be trained for skilled work. Finally, the Personnel Officer of Grange Graphite Co. stated that although both Asians and West Indians were much slower workers initially, West Indians would eventually reach full capability whereas Asians never did:

Asiatics are almost all on labouring and semi-skilled work. Language, education and physique hold them back. The better West Indian has the potential to be trained for skilled jobs. We have never tried it, but I think we could do it.[2]

There were, however, two exceptions. Firstly, as noted above, the Personnel Officer of Leigham Cannery stated that although West Indians were 'reasonable' at learning their jobs, Pakistanis were better. And secondly, the Personnel Manager of City Transport claimed that all coloured workers were slow to learn and that Pakistanis and West Indians were no different in this respect. The respondent noted, however, that they all got through the training course all right.

4. *Methods used in the Training of Asian Workers*

Given that certain difficulties arose in the training of coloured workers due to the language barrier, what methods were employed to overcome this problem? By far the most common was the 'demonstration technique': the white workers already employed on the job showed how it was done by means of sign

[1] However, it should be noted that the respondent thought that the local worker was of a very low standard, and that the West Indian workers would not compare as favourably in other areas.

[2] The respondent stated: 'As far as the West Indians are concerned there is no real difficulty, except for the fact that they think they can do the job as well as the man who is training them. They don't like you to start with the fundamentals: they are insulted. But you've got to start with the fundamentals. This limits them and it's their own fault. They are like stubborn children.'

language and the Asian workers learnt by imitation.[1] This method was summed up by one manager as 'demonstration of movement'.[2]

The demonstration technique has, of course, its limitations. The Personnel Officer of Grange Graphite Co. stated that the foreman had been put through T.W.I. (Training Within Industry) mainly with a view to the fact that many people could not be trained by ordinary methods. Nevertheless, he thought that Asian workers, because of the language difficulty, were limited to jobs with a short cycle which could be demonstrated. Similarly, one of the foremen at Bradfield Foundry thought that some jobs were more susceptible to the demonstration technique than others. He was somewhat dubious about training Asian workers to be moulders (he had been a moulder himself before being promoted), partly because of the language difficulties involved:

Moulding is the kind of job you must grow up with. Although it is mechanized, there is still a lot of skill in it. The human element makes all the difference between a good mould and scrap. This is where the difficulty arises with foreign workers. In the Fettling Shop, you can show a grinder a well ground casting and a badly ground casting and say: 'This one is bad, do it like this.' But this is not possible in moulding where there is no finished product. Two moulds may look alike, but one will produce a bad casting and the other a good one. If the sand is pressed too tight, the metal won't run and if it is packed too loose, the casting swells. It is difficult enough to teach an Englishman to do it just right, but it is doubly difficult with a foreigner because he can't understand you. The fact that they say they understand you is no guarantee. They may say they understand, but when you leave them to it, they do it wrong. If you could solve the language difficulty, you would solve half the colour problem in industry.

Nevertheless, it should be noted that foreign workers, Italians as well as Indians and Pakistanis, had been trained as moulders, so obviously the language difficulties were not insurmountable in this case.

Another quite common method of training Asian workers

---

[1] This method of training was mentioned in eight firms altogether (2, 15, 22, 23, 24, 27, 28, and 30).
[2] Personnel Manager, Castle Iron Co.

was the use of instructors who could speak their language. In one case (Major Castings Ltd.) the instructor was a white foreman who had lived in Pakistan and, according to the Personnel Manager, knew the language and the country. More usually, however, Asians themselves were used as instructors. At Annerley Iron Foundry, for example, the Works Manager said: 'The Arabs train each other. When we are a man short we ask one of the Arabs we already have to bring a man in. He trains him.' Other examples include Bradfield Foundry, where it was a policy to put someone who was just starting with a member of his own nationality so that he would receive help with learning his job; Edge Tools where the established Pakistani workers in the Polishing Shop assisted the newcomers, thus considerably easing the firm's training difficulties; and Omega Metals where an English speaking Pakistani chargehand undertook the training of all his fellow countrymen irrespective of the job on which they were employed. Further details of the latter case will be given in the next chapter.

Finally, in two cases firms went so far as to modify the jobs concerned to make them more suitable for Asian workers. In Muirhead Foundry the Personnel Manager stated: 'Coloured workers (mainly Indians) work on every operation in the foundry except fitting. We have reduced the elements of the jobs to really simple pieces of work so that they can't go wrong.'

In the other case, Bradfield Foundry, an ingenious method had been evolved to overcome the language (and also literacy) barrier in order to enable Asian workers to be employed on a particular job. The Technical Controller had trained four Indians to charge the furnace. In essence, the job was a relatively simple and menial one: it consisted merely of wheeling barrow loads of the necessary raw materials from the stock piles and loading them into the furnace. However, the difficulties arose because it was necessary to weigh the barrow loads before emptying them into the furnace and the Indians were illiterate as well as being unable to speak English. The situation was further complicated by the fact that the necessary ingredients varied according to the type of metal being produced; grey pig iron, grey scrap, Durham coke and limestone was required for grey iron, and malleable scrap, malleable pig iron, Welsh coke and limestone was required for malleable iron. In addition, the proportions also varied according to the type of metal being produced; for instance the proportion of grey iron scrap needed for grey iron was not the same as the proportion of malleable iron scrap needed for malleable iron.

According to the Technical Controller, it took six months constant supervision to evolve an infallible system. This was eventually done by coding the various ingredients. Grey iron was given a red code and malleable iron a blue code. The various ingredients were designated by shape, for instance, scrap by a square and pig iron by a triangle. Thus malleable scrap would be a blue square, grey scrap a red square, grey pig iron a red triangle and so on.

The various stocks of raw materials were sign-posted so that when, say, grey iron was being produced, the Indian knew that he had to obtain coke from the pile marked with a red circle, scrap from the pile with the red square and so on. He then filled the wheelbarrow and wheeled the load on to the weigh-scale. To obtain the correct proportion of the ingredient, he simply had to ensure that the pointer came to rest opposite a particular mark on the face of the weigh-scale. For each grey iron ingredient there was a red mark on the dial and for each malleable iron ingredient a blue mark, each corresponding to the correct amount of the ingredient to be charged into the furnace for the type of metal being produced. These marks, it should be added, signified the weight of the raw materials *plus* the weight of the barrow, so that it was not necessary to subtract the latter.[1]

By this means, the Indians were able to 'weigh' the various ingredients without being able to speak English, read English or calculate in terms of the British system of weights and measures. The Technical Controller concluded:

The attitude used to be: 'You can't train them because they are Indians.' I feel that they should be treated like intelligent children. Intelligent children can be taught and so can Indians, because they are keen to learn. I could put an intelligent Indian in the foundry laboratory and have him doing chemical analysis in three months, not by teaching him the chemical formulae, but by training him with a colour code system.

[1]All the barrows used on this job were, of necessity, of a standard weight.

The success of this method of training suggests that, if firms were prepared to go to some trouble, Asian workers could be trained for many jobs now thought to be beyond their capabilities. Nevertheless, even apart from the lengthy training period required, this method, in common with the other techniques we have discussed, suffers from a major drawback both for the Asian workers and the firms concerned. It involves the learning of a particular job by rote, as it were, and transfer of training to other, similar jobs may be negligible. Thus the Indian workers in the above example were perfectly able to 'weigh' materials at Bradfield Foundry, but would have been unable to do so at another firm unless the same colour coding system were used. Similarly, an Asian worker trained to do a semi-skilled job by the demonstration technique may require almost complete retraining if the firm introduces a modified version of the machine or wishes to transfer him to another semi-skilled job. This brings us to the question of the flexibility of coloured workers, which will be examined in greater detail in the next chapter.

5. *Summary*

We noted at the beginning of this chapter that managerial assessments of the skill of coloured workers varied considerably. It will be seen that this applies equally to the question of training. Occasionally, diametrically opposed views were encountered. Thus one manager claimed that West Indians were too unskilled for anything other than labouring jobs whilst another stated that they were 'too educated' to accept such work. Similarly, one manager claimed that Arabs were 'slow on the uptake' whilst others reported that they were very quick to learn.

Nevertheless, certain patterns could be discerned. Although generally regarded as less skilled than British workers, West Indians tended to be found more skilled and easier to train than Asian workers. Several reasons for the Asian workers, comparatively slow rate of learning were suggested, including inferior physique, inadequate training, difficulties involved in teaching a job in stages, lack of industrial sophistication and accident proneness. However, the main problem appeared to be that of language.

Various methods of overcoming the language and other problems had been evolved. Most common was the demonstration technique, but job modification and the use of instructors, white or coloured, who could speak the language of the trainees, were also encountered in some cases. These methods had met with varying degrees of success in different firms. Two respondents claimed that language difficulties limited to a considerable extent the range of jobs which Asian workers could be taught. However, the fact that they had been trained as moulders and furnace chargers in Bradfield Foundry strongly suggests that an equally important factor is the amount of time and trouble management is prepared to take, which is again related to the difficulty of obtaining British workers to do the jobs concerned.

CHAPTER FIVE

Managerial Beliefs and Attitudes Concerning the Employment of Coloured Workers: Diligence, Flexibility, and Supervision

1. *Introduction*

In the previous chapter, with its emphasis on skill and training, we were concerned, in effect, with attitudes towards the coloured immigrant as a potential rather than an actual worker. We now turn to a consideration of managerial attitudes concerning the 'standard' of coloured workers once they have become trained and fully functioning members of the labour force. In their assessments of coloured immigrants as workers, managers seemed mainly to be concerned with two sets of factors, which, for the sake of convenience, we will call 'diligence' and 'susceptibility to supervision'. Diligence includes both the willingness and the ability to work hard, and susceptibility to supervision refers not only to amenability to discipline but also to the ability to understand and comply with orders. A further topic mentioned by some managers, mainly in relation to Asian workers, was the question of flexibility. We are partly concerned here with amenability to discipline in that one of the factors involved is the willingness of coloured workers to be transferred from one job to another. However, the coloured workers' *capability* of being put on different jobs is another important factor, and the question will, therefore, be discussed in a separate section. At the end of the chapter we will also examine various methods which have been evolved in order to overcome language difficulties in supervision, and in particular the use of bi-lingual 'go-betweens'.

9

2. *Diligence*

In the non-directive survey, the majority of managers thought that West Indians were slow workers. However, explanations as to why this should be the case varied somewhat.

According to two respondents, West Indians were lazy. At Westwood Foundry, sixty West Indians had been employed in 1954 because workers were needed at short notice. The Labour Officer stated:

> Within a month, there were only three left. . . . The main trouble was that they did not come here to work. . . . We have employed a few West Indians since, but none have been much good. Those we have now are all in menial jobs that won't break their backs.

Similarly, the Works Manager at Omega Metals was most vehement in his condemnation of West Indian workers. He stated:

> West Indians are just no good. They just won't work. 'No-hopers' we call them. We have tried employing them periodically and it is always the same. They start off 'red hot' during the first week and by the end of the next week, they are fast asleep. Some of the West Indians we employed didn't even last a fortnight.

On the other hand, some managers seemed to think that West Indians were slow workers, not so much because they were lazy, but because they were incapable of working at a fast tempo.

> The Jamaicans are naturally slow. We only have one on the production side. He is O.K. because he has to keep up with the conveyer, but he would be terribly slow if we put him on a job on which he could go at his own pace. (Works Superintendent, Bradfield Foundry)

> Fifty per cent of the Jamaicans we employ have been used to a very slow tempo. Some of the young ones can buckle down and keep up with the pace, but some have great difficulty keeping up. (Personnel Manager, Drop Forgings Ltd.)

> We only employ a few Jamaicans—you have to sort them out a bit more. They are not in the same class of worker (as the Asians)—a bit slower. (Personnel Manager, Muirhead Foundry)

> We prefer to employ Indians and Pakistanis because the West Indians tend to be happy go lucky. (Personnel Officer, Components Ltd.)

In all the firms so far mentioned, with the exception of Drop Forgings Ltd., West Indians were compared unfavourably, either directly or indirectly, with Asian workers with regard to diligence. At Drop Forgings, on the other hand, Indians had been employed during World War II, but subsequently only West Indians had been employed because, according to the Personnel Manager, they worked harder and had the advantage of being able to speak English.

In the remaining firms, the attitude towards West Indians was also somewhat more favourable, but no comparisons were made between West Indian and Asian workers as far as diligence was concerned. The Personnel Manager at Ensign Spring Co. stated that West Indians were: 'Jolly good workers; not such fast workers, but jolly good plodding workers.' In Central Glass Works, the Personnel Manager claimed that West Indians were better time keepers and, according to some standards (for instance, labour turnover and absenteeism) more keen than British workers.

Finally, at Edge Tools, management had not been favourably impressed with the first West Indians they had taken on, and for a time had ceased to employ them. Later, however, mainly at the instigation of the local Employment Exchange, West Indians had been employed once more and the firm had developed a much more favourable attitude towards them. The Personnel Manager stated: 'The West Indians we have now are all first-class people. It's not true that they won't work. If you give them a job where they can earn good money, they will have a go.'

In the directive interview survey, assessments of the diligence of West Indian workers were obtained in six firms. On the whole, more favourable views were expressed than in the non-directive survey, but again there was some variation.

In Pentland Alloys Ltd., Hamilton Engineering Co. and Leigham Cannery, West Indians were said to be as hard working as British workers, although in the latter firm Pakistanis were thought to be even better. In Leigham Cannery and Hamilton Engineering Co. respondents stated that West Indians were capable of working at high speed on piece work, but in Pentland Alloys the Personnel Manager was somewhat dubious. He stated that although they had done very well on the jobs they had been given (unskilled and semi-skilled), he had gained the impression that they were not capable of working at speed—they seemed to be more phlegmatic.

In the remaining three firms, West Indians were described as 'steady workers' in one case[1]; in another the respondent claimed that, in general, they were not hard workers, although there were exceptions[2]; and in the third, it was stated that Trinidadians were hard workers whereas Jamaicans were lazy.[3]

The results of the questionnaire survey for all nationalities are presented in Table 6.

TABLE 6   *Managerial Assessments of the Diligence of Coloured Workers (Questionnaire Survey)*

Nationality	More hard working than British workers %	About the same as British workers %	Less hard working than British workers %	No. of firms responding
West Indians	0	52	48	42
Pakistanis	10	61	29	31
Indians	0	64	36	14
Arabs	0	67	33	12
Africans	0	64	36	11

In just under half the firms responding, West Indians were said to be 'less hard working' than British workers. Asian workers, on the other hand, and in particular Pakistanis, were so described less often than the West Indians, and in the only three cases where a coloured group was described as 'more hard working', the workers concerned were Pakistanis.

In the non-directive survey, Asian immigrants were highly regarded as workers in most of the firms in which they were employed. At Bradfield Foundry in particular, several members of management spoke very highly of the firm's Asian employees.

[1] Personnel Manager, Major Castings Ltd.
[2] Works Director, Torrington Cutlers.
[3] Works Manager, Annerley Iron Foundry. The respondent was under the impression that both the West Indians employed by the firm were from Trinidad, but one later informed me that he came from Grenada.

The Works Superintendent stated that the Indians were good workers and quoted several examples of their diligence. A Sikh, he claimed, had set a production record for moulding which had previously been thought impossible to attain,[1] and another Indian had been told to start work early at 6 a.m., but had clocked in at 5 a.m. and got so much work done that the firm decided to pay him for the extra time even though he had not been told to do it. In the same firm, the Technical Controller stated:

With coloured workers you have a different kind of problem from the one you have with white workers, but I'm not so sure I don't prefer this kind of problem to that you have with British workers, with organized unions and all that. These (i.e. the Asians) will work and that's a great advantage.

Similarly, the Production Manager said: 'I'd rather have these workers than British workers. It makes me ashamed of my own race, honest. British workers don't come here to work: they want something for nothing.'

The Works Manager of Omega Metals was equally enthusiastic about Pakistani workers.

Once they have been trained, they are very diligent and never late. . . . It is worth putting up with the stupidity of the Pakistanis for two months because once they are trained, they work hard and go on working hard . . . they work a sixty hour week and just love it.

Similarly, the Labour Officer at Westwood Foundry said that Indians and Pakistanis worked hard and earned good money, and in Muirhead Foundry it was said that Indians did 'hard graft'.[2]

However, there were some anomalies in the data. At Brierley Metal Works, the Labour Officer described Indians as 'excellent workers', but claimed that Pakistanis were a little more educated—which they played on—and unless on piece-work were

---

[1] The respondent claimed that there was no restriction of output on the piece-work jobs; if one worker could set a higher rate, the others did not object but tried to equal it.

[2] In the latter case, however, the Personnel Manager did not think that Indian workers were as good as British workers. He said that Indian workers were getting greedy: they wanted exactly the same as British workers and they were not up to their standard. He then quickly added that, of course, they did get exactly the same as British workers—there was no difference in rates—and this wasn't fair because they did not deserve to get as much as the British worker when they were not as good as he was.

less satisfactory than Indians. As a result, when a Pakistani left, the firm tried to replace him with an Indian because the Indians 'have an edge'. Conversely, the Personnel Officer of Components Ltd. said that East Indians applied themselves better than West Indians, but of the East Indians the firm preferred Pakistanis because the Indians tended to be more highly educated and therefore less likely to accept menial work and stick to it. These contradictory statements are even more surprising when it is taken into account that the two firms were situated on adjacent premises on the same street.

In two firms it was stated that Arabs were not strong enough for heavy work.

They are much smaller in stature . . . not quite suitable for heavy manual work and therefore quite limited. (Labour Manager, Brierley Metal Works)

Arabs don't fit the bill for heavy industry. (Labour Manager, Westwood Foundry)

On the other hand, the Works Superintendent of Bradfield Foundry stated that, whilst Arabs might be a bit 'slow on the uptake',[1] they were exceptionally good workers once they got to know the job.

Finally, the Personnel Director of Precision Engineers stated that coloured workers in general could not work as hard as white workers, mainly because of malnutrition (they did not eat properly even in Britain), but perhaps also because they were used to just sitting in the sun at home. It was unusual, however, to find both these stereotypes applied to both Asian and West Indian workers. More commonly, it was the West Indians who were said to be lackadaisical, and the Asians (in particular Arabs) who were said to be incapable of hard work because of physique.

The following article in the Sheffield *Star* indicates that the latter stereotype at least has gained quite wide currency:

Steel mills proving too tough for coloured immigrants
Sheffield's forges and rolling mills are proving too tough for many of the coloured workers who two years ago were flooding into the city looking for work. This is the view of Ministry of Labour officials who report a big exodus of coloured folk, mainly Arabs, from

---

[1] 'Cf. training difficulties in this firm.

Sheffield. The number of coloured workers registered as unemployed is down to 294, the lowest figure for a considerable time. A year ago the figure was around the 600 mark.

Said a Ministry spokesman: 'The bulk of these workers are Arabs, Pakistanis and Indians, usually fairly slight in build. They mostly come from peasant communities and just aren't strong enough for doing our heavy work. Also, whilst there is nothing in the nature of a colour bar, unskilled workers are picked on their merits and in many cases the merits of the coloured workers are not good enough.'

An official of English Steel Corporation told the *Star* that although they had noticed no significant trend, the coloured men they employed were chosen because they were strong, hefty and suitable for the work they would be required to do.[1]

In the directive interview survey, only one respondent suggested that Asian workers were not strong enough for heavy work, and even he did not think that this meant that they were unemployable. The Personnel Officer of Grange Graphite Co. stated:

Asiatics are physically incapable of really hard work, of course. But some have been really good workers. On the most unpleasant, lowest paid jobs they are better than the Englishman who would want to be away from the job.

In Steel Bars Ltd., on the other hand, the Works Manager spoke very highly of the Arabs' willingness to work extremely hard and of their capability of doing so. Some examples of his remarks on this subject are as follows:

I don't like to use the term 'machines' for human beings, but as far as work is concerned they are like machines. Before we got mobile (that is, mechanized), the older men had got too old for man-handling and the younger men would not do the job, and this is where the Arabs came in. Now we are mobilized, but before, the Arabs did this job and they had about 50 per cent more capacity than the white worker. If some heavy work was to be done, where the white worker would look for his mate to help him, the Arab will do it on his own. His attitude would be: 'Let's get on with it, there isn't time to mess about.'

One backer (that is, one of the Arabs working on the back side of the rolling mill) left because the team finished working after they had done what they call their stint, instead of working time out.

If you ask a white worker to do a double shift, he will do it but he

[1] 9 December 1959.

won't do another one that week. But if you asked an Arab to do a double shift every day for a week, he would go down on his knees and kiss your feet.

They are quite capable of working as fast as the white worker will let them. If we could get the white man to step up his speed, the Arab would match him. The white man is the brake to him on this particular job.

Similarly, in Annerley Iron Foundry, Arabs were described as fast and hard working, once trained. The General Manager of Stainless Steel Ltd., on the other hand, thought that Asians, though willing workers, were not particularly fast. However, he did not appear to regard this as a serious disadvantage.

They are more like the tortoise. They are plodders and plodders always have their place in industry. They keep on plodding and they get there in the end. The white worker tends to work faster in short bursts with rests in between and by the end of the day, you might find that the coloured worker has done more.

As one of the Asian workers (an Arab) employed by this firm worked on a sledge-hammer job (knocking out castings), I asked the General Manager whether he thought Asian workers in general were capable of doing heavy work. He replied that they were like the British worker—some could and some could not. He described the worker concerned as 'very strong—not big, but wiry'.[1]

The other managers' assessments of Asian immigrants as workers were on the whole favourable.

I think the Pakistanis are all regarded as excellent workers. They will do as they are told until the cows come home. (Personnel Manager, Major Castings Ltd.)

In my opinion, once he has absorbed the job, you get a good stint of work out of him. (Personnel Officer, Quality Steel Co., re Arabs and Pakistanis)

There's nothing special about coloured workers, good or bad. Eighty per cent of coloured labour is no trouble and gives a fair day's work. (Personnel Officer, Tool Steel Ltd. re Pakistanis and Arabs)

[1] The respondent stated that he had no preferences with regard to the different Asian nationalities. ('Mankind is the same everywhere, there's "good uns" and there's "bad uns", and as long as I get the "good uns" I don't care about colour.' However, he added: 'Mind you, I prefer these to the pure black: we had a couple of Africans who made a great show of doing nothing.')

Providing they satisfy us within the six weeks training period, we will probably be satisfied with them. Pakistanis are a much better proposition than West Indians. (Personnel Officer, Leigham Cannery)

They are no different from the white worker—they vary. In the rolling mills their output is the same as the others. Generally speaking, however, they are more anxious to please. (Personnel Manager, Sovereign Steel Works, re Arabs, Pakistanis and Somalis)

All the men are on piece work and bonus and they will work like hell for money. (Personnel Manager, Sterling Metal Co., re Arabs, Pakistanis and Africans)

They work hard once they have been trained. (Personnel Manager, Ridgeway Steel Co., re Pakistanis)

Once they have got hold of the job, they get on with it. Given a repetitive job, they get on with it and don't waste time. They need very little supervision. (Labour Officer, Polton Rolling Mills, re Arabs and Pakistanis)

They are good workers—you will see Arabs lifting bars of metal that a white man would leave for the crane. There's very little to choose between Arabs and Pakistanis, but on the whole, I think that the Arabs just have it. Mind you, you get good Pakistanis and bad Arabs: there's not all that much in it. (Departmental Manager, Polton Rolling Mills)

As usual, however, there were certain anomalies in the data. In two firms it was suggested that Asian workers worked very hard at first, but slowed down within a short period of time. The Personnel Manager of Castle Iron Co. stated with respect to Indians and Pakistanis:

Initially, they were jolly good workers—they would work twice as hard as an English bloke—but after six weeks or a couple of months 50 per cent degenerated into lazy, good for nothing slackers. We weeded these out pretty quick. . . . We have had one or two Arabs, but they've not lasted long. They really have been idle devils.

The only way to keep coloured workers 'on their toes', the respondent claimed, was constant supervision; without constant supervision they were inclined to be lazy. However this question did not arise in the case of coloured workers on semi-skilled jobs because they had to work 'willy-nilly' at the same speed as their team mates.

In the other firm, Blackford Rolling Mills, Arabs and Pakistanis were employed as casual labourers during the yearly shut down. The Production Services Manager stated: 'For the first two or three days they are faster than our own men, but they quickly slow down, although not to an unreasonable rate.'

Unlike the previous respondent, however, he regarded Arabs and Pakistanis as being, in general, satisfactory workers. In fact, at another point in the interview he stated: 'They are very good workers: two Pakistanis could do in a day what five of our own engineering staff could do in a week.'

Finally, there was some disagreement between the Labour Manager and the Personnel Manager of Sovereign Steel Works. The former claimed that Arabs were good workers, but Somalis were inherently idle. The Personnel Manager, on the other hand, stated that it was very difficult to generalize: a lazy Somali was the same as a lazy Englishman, just one representative of his race.

3. *Flexibility*

The question of flexibility was mentioned only occasionally during the non-directive survey. This would suggest that it is one of the less important factors in the determination of managerial attitudes towards the employment of coloured workers. Nevertheless, the few comments which were made are interesting in two respects: firstly, they referred only to Asian workers, and secondly, they were completely contradictory.

Two respondents claimed that Asian workers were highly inflexible. In Bradfield Foundry the Technical Controller stated:

Foreign workers, Asians in particular, like to have one job they can consider their own. They like to come into one place where they can hang up their hat and coat and think: 'This is my office.' I used to wonder what they wanted when they came up to me and said 'steady job, steady job, all time one place', or asked for 'all time casting', but it was simply the fact that they wanted the same job all the time. For example, that bloke over there (pointing to an Indian) is very good at his job: if he was off for any length of time we would have to replace him with two men. But if we were to change him on to another job, he would quit just like that.

In Brierley Metal Works, the Labour Officer stated that Indians were excellent workers and caused no trouble as long as you put them on a job, told them what to do and did not mess them about: 'If you change jobs, you've had it. They cannot adapt themselves to more than one job. The firm employs a few hundred Indians and not more than half a dozen can do more than one job.' Similarly, he stated that Arab workers were put on one job, taught that job, and that was the only job they knew.

On the other hand, two respondents, both in Bradfield Foundry, stated that they had found coloured workers to be flexible. When I asked the Production Manager how many people were general labourers, he replied that it was very difficult to say because a man might be doing a semi-skilled job one day and labouring the next. Pointing to a Pakistani who was shovelling sand for a bench moulder, he said: 'That man is on general labouring now, but he was on grinding a couple of weeks ago.' He continued: 'We have a very fluid labour force here. Frankly, I don't think our blokes would stand for so much messing about, but they are glad to get any job.'

The Fettling Shop foreman stated that, if pushed, most of the workers in his department (Indians and Italians) could be put on different jobs.

One or two can only do one job, but there are also one or two who can do any job in the department. An Italian drill operator and the Sikh who is on Progress will do any job. If they are left on their own and finish one job, they will find another. The Sikh can not only do every job in this department, he can also operate the core machine, and he is sometimes 'borrowed' to do this during lunch time.

He concluded:

Foreign workers are very helpful. They will come in early or work over when asked. The main thing is that they will always try to do something if asked, where our blokes would probably say it was too much.[1]

[1] The above statements of the Foreman and the Production Manager in the Bradfield Foundry provide us with an interesting example of the same 'facts' being given an entirely different interpretation. Whereas the Production Manager saw the Asian workers' willingness to do any job as arising from their low employment status, the Foreman saw this as being helpful. Conversely, the Production Manager regarded the British workers' refusal to try any job as a justifiable resistance to being 'messed about', whereas the Foreman thought that they were simply unhelpful.

Finally, in Edge Tools Ltd., a supervisor stated that it was best to put coloured workers on one job, where they couldn't wander. However, whilst walking round the factory I noticed a Pakistani hitting a block of wood with a succession of knife blades. As he neither looked at the block of wood nor, apparently, inspected the blade afterwards, I asked what he was doing. The supervisor replied that he was usually a grinder, but that day he had been put on testing the blades to see whether the cutting edge turned over after striking the wood. This provides us with another example of an Asian worker being taken off his normal semi-skilled job and put on labouring work.

In view of these discrepancies, it was decided to follow up this question in greater detail in the directive interview survey. Two factors seemed to be involved: the capability of coloured workers to be transferred from one job to another and their willingness to be transferred. Separate questions were therefore asked on these topics. Several managers stated that they could not answer either question because transfer did not occur or because they usually involved promotion. Such information as was obtained, however, was again contradictory.

With regard to Asian workers, respondents in Stainless Steel Ltd., Polton Rolling Mills and Quality Steel Co. thought that they would resent being transferred from one job to another. In the latter firm, as we have already noted, difficulty had been experienced in persuading Asian workers to learn the more complex aspects of their jobs after being taught the basic essentials. This problem had also been encountered occasionally in Tool Steel Ltd. The Personnel Manager stated:

There has been some resistance to introducing new elements of the job. Having taught the basic essentials, some supervisors run up against a brick wall when they try to teach them something else. Their reaction is 'not my job'.

On the other hand, five respondents[1] stated that Asian workers did not object to being transferred and one claimed that they actually liked it. According to the Personnel Manager of Sovereign Steel Works, they were always looking for something new; they had their eye on the main chance.

Similar inconsistencies were found with regard to the capa-

[1] Firms 18, 19, 22, 23, and 24.

bility of Asian workers to be transferred from one job to another. Four[1] respondents claimed that Asian workers could not be put on different jobs and another[2] stated that Arabs were adaptable whereas Pakistanis had to be put on one job and kept on it all the time. One of these respondents, the Personnel Manager of Castle Iron Co. stated that the Asian workers' flexibility depended to some extent upon how different the two jobs were. He stated:

We have transferred them from one semi-skilled job to a similar semi-skilled job in the same department, but we have never tried putting them on a different type of job. With coloured workers, putting them on a different type of job would entail retraining. White workers are more flexible: if a white worker can do one semi-skilled job, then the chances are he can do another.

In the Ridgeway Steel Co., on the other hand, a Furnace Supervisor claimed that difficulties had arisen even when Pakistani workers had been transferred between very similar jobs. In this firm, Pakistanis were rarely put on different jobs, a fact which the Personnel Manager suggested was probably an indication that they were not considered flexible. However, they were sometimes put on the same job on a different shift. This, according to the Furnace Supervisor, was where the difficulties had mainly occurred: 90 per cent of the job was the same, but each shift supervisor had a different way of doing the last 10 per cent. Once Pakistanis had been trained to do a job one way, he claimed, they objected to doing it another, and it was very difficult to get them to change their methods.

Nevertheless, managers in five other firms[3] claimed that Asian workers could be transferred between different jobs. Furthermore, the Personnel Manager of Castle Iron Co. stated that although Asian workers in general were less flexible than white workers, Pakistanis had been found more adaptable than the others.

Data concerning the flexibility of West Indian workers were obtained in four firms.[4] All four respondents stated that they

[1] Firms 15, 17, 25, and 28.
[2] Firm 24.
[3] Firms 16, 18, 19, 22, and 23.
[4] Firms 19, 20, 21, and 22.

could be transferred from one job to another and three[1] claimed that they would not resent being transferred. In Hamilton Engineering Co., according to the Labour Officer, only five of the firm's fourteen West Indian workers had never been employed on more than one job. The respondent claimed, moreover, that they had been 'quite happy' to accept a different job, even when they were given one at a lower rate of pay, because of redundancy.[2] Similarly, the Works Director of Torrington Cutlers Ltd. stated that West Indians seemed just to take any job they were given. The Personnel Officer of Grange Graphite Co., however, thought that there might be some resentment if the West Indian thought that being transferred was a reflection on his skill.

In the questionnaire survey, only one question was included on flexibility in order to economize space. Respondents were simply asked to state whether they had found the various coloured groups to be 'more or less flexible (i.e. capable of being put on different jobs) than British workers, or about the same'. The following answers were obtained:

TABLE 7   *Managerial Assessments of the Flexibility of Coloured Workers (Questionnaire Survey)*

Nationality	Less flexible than British workers %	About the same as British workers %	More flexible than British workers %	No. of firms responding
West Indians	59	33	8	39
Pakistanis	65	32	3	31
Indians	57	43	0	14
Arabs	77	23	0	13
Africans	69	23	8	13

[1] Firms 12, 20, and 21.

[2] Hamilton Engineering Co. carried out several different types of industry on the same premises, so it was rare for a lapse in trade to occur in all departments at the same time. Instead of making workers redundant, therefore, the firm's policy was to transfer workers from departments where work was slack to others where there were vacancies. However, it was not always possible to transfer at the same level, so this sometimes involved accepting lower wages.

It will be seen that over half the respondents thought that coloured workers were less flexible than white workers and that, in general, Asian workers were regarded as being slightly less flexible than West Indians.

4. *Supervision*

In the questionnaire survey, managers were asked whether they had found that coloured workers required more supervision than white workers, less supervision or about the same amount. Their responses are presented in Table 8.

TABLE 8   *Managerial Assessments of the Supervisory Requirements of Coloured Workers (Questionnaire Survey)*

Nationality	Less supervision than white workers %	About the same supervision as white workers %	More supervision than white workers %	No. of firms responding
West Indians	2	42	56	41
Pakistanis	6	35	59	34
Indians	0	50	50	16
Arabs	0	44	56	13
Africans	0	44	56	13

It will be seen that, in a little over 50 per cent of cases, coloured workers were thought to require more supervision than white workers, and rarely were they thought to require less. The writer would suggest, however, that different factors are involved in these assessments as far as Negroes (West Indians and Africans) and Asian workers are concerned.

Broadly speaking, the supervisor in industry has two main functions: firstly, to give instructions concerning the work to be done, and secondly, to ensure that the worker maintains a satisfactory level of performance. For the instructions to be carried out, two things are necessary: firstly, the worker must be able to understand the instructions, and secondly, he must be prepared to carry them out. Thus the supervision of coloured workers (or any nationality of worker, for that matter) is likely to be more difficult:

(a) if the workers cannot understand instructions,

(b) if the workers are not amenable to discipline, and

(c) if the workers do not maintain a satisfactory level performance without constant supervision.

In relation to the latter question, much of the ground has already been covered in the section on managerial beliefs concerning the dilgence of coloured workers. It was concluded that, in general, managers tended to believe that Asians were more hard working than West Indians. It would seem to follow, therefore, that they would also be regarded as requiring less supervision in this respect. One further point requires attention, however. Some managers suggested that Asian workers often lacked the initiative to proceed to other tasks when they had finished the one on which they were working, and therefore required closer supervision.

> If anything goes wrong or they run out of work, the Asiatics just stand there—they don't tell anyone. The West Indians are more likely to do something about it. (Personnel Officer, Grange Graphite Co.)

> They don't appear to exercise any initiative. They will do the job they are told to, but they will not go on to anything else when they've finished it. (Production Services Manager, Blackford Rolling Mills)

> Coloured workers (mainly Indians in this firm) need a lot more supervision, especially on day work—they can't think for themselves. (Personnel Manager, Muirhead Foundry)

Nevertheless, certain reservations need to be made in respect of the above belief concerning Asian workers. Firstly, it was only mentioned in the above three firms. Secondly, it is only relevant to certain jobs, principally day work. It would apply to a much lesser degree in the case of piece work or team work. Thirdly, some managers were of the opposite opinion with regard to Asian workers. For example, in Polton Rolling Mills it was stated that Asian workers required very little supervision and in Stainless Steel Ltd. the General Manager said that, once they had mastered the job, Asian workers could be left to it. And fourthly, one manager expressed the same belief about West

Indian workers. The Labour Officer of Hamilton Engineering Co. stated that the majority of West Indians needed to be 'chased up' after each job had been finished on routine work.

We now turn to the question of communication. Language difficulties with respect to supervision were mentioned in several firms[1] in both interview surveys. Some examples are as follows:

Pakistanis have to be spoon-fed. All their booking has to be done for them. Giving orders is a more complicated business. For example, there are many different sizes and shapes of tool blade and handle. Instead of merely saying, 'Put such and such a blade on such and such a handle', the supervisor must take the coloured worker to the pile of blades, show him the relevant pile of handles, and then demonstrate that he wants *this* handle fastened to *this* blade. Even then, mistakes are made, and a coloured worker will happily go on fastening the wrong handle to a blade, when, apart from the fact that they each have three holes through which he can put rivets, they obviously don't fit. (Labour Manager, Edge Tools Ltd.)

The main difficulty is with language. They say they understand an order, but then when you go and check what they are doing you find that they have got it all wrong. (Furnace Supervisor, Ridgeway Steel Co.)

The Personnel Office selects those (coloured workers) who can speak English. It is the foreman who have to give the orders and this can lead to difficulties if there are workmen who cannot speak English. They can always say 'Me no understandee' if anything goes wrong. (Personnel Officer, Components Ltd.)

At Blackford Rolling Mills communication difficulties had been experienced, not so much with supervision of work, but with administrative details such as National Insurance and Government Graduated Pensions, and with the settling of domestic difficulties.[2]

---

[1] Firms 1, 8, 10, 13, 14, 15, 16, 17, 18, 19, 23, 24, 25, and 26.

[2] Another administrative difficulty occasionally mentioned where large numbers of Asian workers were employed, was the fact that many of them had the same name. Bradfield Foundry, for instance, employed about fifty Indians, forty-two of whom were called 'Singh'. This difficulty was overcome by referring to the men by their clock numbers, e.g. '181 Singh' or '42 Singh'. Similarly, at Sovereign Steel Works the Labour Manager stated: 'We have a lot of trouble with names. They often have the same name. I had to take a phone call for a coloured man to say that a relation was in hospital. We had six men all of the same name working for us, none of whom lived at the address given.'

In some firms, it was suggested that the supervision of Asian workers became less difficult, the longer they worked for the firm.

Initially, they require more supervision. In the later stages, they adapt themselves pretty similarly to the white worker in the same grades, but still finding language a difficulty. (Personnel Officer, Quality Steel Co.)

In the early days they were more difficult to supervise. Now we've had the experience, it's easy. In the early days we used to have difficulty with language. We used sign language and we sent them to school in their spare time to learn English. We don't notice the language difficulty now: we understand them better and they understand us better. (Personnel Manager, Sterling Metal Co.)

Finally, at Castle Iron Co. it was stated that no difficulties with language had been experienced even when coloured workers were first employed. The Personnel Manager was asked whether any initial difficulties had been encountered in the employment of coloured workers. He replied:

Like the language difficulty, you mean? No, not really. We rapidly picked up a few words and we found we could make ourselves understood. We had a bloke who had been in India and could speak a bit of Hindi who helped us with this. Then gradually these blokes (the Asian workers) picked up English.

However, the above case was exceptional, and even here language difficulties were encountered in the training of Asian workers.

In the case of the West Indians, of course, the question of language hardly arises. There were occasional complaints concerning the difficulty of understanding dialects, but, in the main, the West Indians' ability to speak English was regarded as one of their major advantages over the Asian group. The West Indians' attitude towards supervision, on the other hand, was often regarded as one of their major disadvantages. Three firms (Bradfield Foundry, Westwood Foundry, and Omega Metals) had ceased to employ West Indians as a matter of policy, and in each case, an adverse assessment of their amenability to discipline had been a contributing factor.

The Labour Manager of Westwood Foundry stated that West Indians had 'caused trouble with their arrogance' and had 'wanted quite a bit of their own way'. The Indian, he claimed, was proud of his heritage whereas the West Indian wanted to be 'bleached' and felt strongly about the colour bar. Similarly, the Works Manager of Omega Metals Ltd. stated: 'They are colour conscious from the word go and have a chip on their shoulder from the word go. No matter how you try to nurse them along it comes out.'

At Bradfield Foundry, the Technical Controller stated that, as opposed to Indians who did as they were told, West Indians tended to be 'barrack-room lawyers'. The Production Manager in the same firm stated:

They are truculent and troublesome. They expect preferential treatment. If you do not employ them, they say it is because of the colour of their skin. If you give them a job no-one else wants, they say they are being picked on because they are coloured. But some-one has to do these jobs and they came last, so what do they expect.

The general attitude towards West Indians in this firm was summed up by a foreman who said: 'If there was any trouble, they would say "colour bar", but if there was, it was of their own making.'[1]

In Brierley Metal Works the Labour Manager's attitude to-wards West Indians was somewhat more favourable: he thought that they were too highly educated for labouring jobs. Never-theless, very few West Indians were employed. The Labour Manager stated: 'Employing Jamaicans doesn't work out. They soon want to be boss and they can't all be boss.'

In Polton Rolling Mills, where there were also very few West Indian workers, the Labour Officer claimed that this state of affairs had occurred by chance—it was just that Arabs and

---

[1] The West Indians' claim that this firm operated a colour bar is understandable perhaps, but somewhat inaccurate. As over 50% of the firm's employees were Asian immigrants, 'shade bar' would be a more apt term. According to the Produc-tion Manager, the Gateman tells West Indians, when they come for jobs, that there are no vacancies. He continued: 'Then the Jamaican will say we have a colour bar and we will not employ him because of the colour of his skin. That's a laugh—they say outside the works that all the white men here have their own football sweep—all twelve of them.'

Pakistanis had been the ones who had applied for jobs. On the other hand, one of the Departmental Managers stated that he would not accept West Indians or Somalis because they were, he claimed, 'bone idle and arrogant'.

Even in some of the firms in which West Indians were employed, there were complaints concerning a 'chip on the shoulder' attitude.

West Indians have a chip on their shoulder about a colour bar which does not exist.[1] (Personnel Manager, Central Glass Works)

On the average, West Indians are a little more difficult to supervise because you do have to tread on thin ice. Supervisors have found that if they have to reprimand a coloured worker, they tend to claim that they are being picked on because of their colour. (Labour Officer, Hamilton Engineering Co.)

They tend to have a man-sized chip on their shoulder. Our greatest problem is with West Indians who look for insults where there aren't any. (Personnel Officer, Grange Graphite Co.)

In Drop Forgings Ltd. the 'chip on the shoulder attitude' was also mentioned, but here it was apparently regarded as the exception rather than the rule. The Personnel Manager stated:

We have had isolated spots of trouble with coloured workers: one sat on a box and smoked cigars all day and thought he should be paid for it. We sometimes get a Jamaican with a chip on his shoulder and we have to get rid of him. He then turns round and claims he is the victim of a colour bar. During the late fifties, when there was a boom in the industry, a Jamaican would turn down a job at £12.10.0. to £13 because it wasn't enough money. They would turn down jobs that white men were doing.

However, the respondent concluded:

There has been some trouble, but you get the same kind of thing with whites. We know housing conditions are sometimes bad, but it doesn't seem to reflect on their attitude to work.

---

[1] In this case, the West Indians' claim that there was a colour bar had considerable justification. According to the Personnel Manager, Asian workers were excluded and the West Indians' employment and occupational levels were limited as a result of restrictions on the part of the white workers. Under these circumstances, it is difficult to see how he could maintain that the colour bar about which the West Indians were concerned did not exist. Nevertheless, he did so.

In another firm, it was suggested that West Indians had tended to become less amenable to discipline as the immigration to Britain had progressed. The Personnel Director of Precision Engineers Ltd. claimed that the better type of immigrant had come first. They were grateful just to have employment and the height of their ambition had been to own a bicycle—usually a very fancy machine with lots of accessories. The later people, he said, were not so grateful: they were more aggressive and arrogant.[1]

Conversely, in Edge Tools, an initially adverse assessment of the West Indians' amenability to discipline eventually gave way to a much more favourable attitude towards them. The Labour Manager stated: 'They had a chip on their shoulder at first— they argued with the foreman and perhaps were awkward—but now they have got to know us better and some of them are quite pleasant.'

In only two cases was it said that West Indians were more amenable to discipline than white workers. The Personnel Manager of Pentland Alloys stated: 'I'm told by the foremen that they are no trouble at all. In fact they are less difficult—less argumentative. Still you must take into account the fact that they are happy to have a job.' Similarly, in Torrington Cutlers, the Works Director stated:

Within the limitations of their activity, they are a little easier to supervise. They are a little less worried about working conditions. On the type of job they do, where they just do as they are told, they will go on doing as they are told and are less likely to swing the lead. However, they don't look for work.

In the latter firm, however, another member of management disagreed with the Works Director's assessment. He claimed that the West Indians not only did not look for work, but actively avoided it. The respondent stated:

They don't like work, apart from in the Silversmith section. They are terribly lackadaisical and if they are not watched all the time, they disappear. I went into the storeroom once and found three of them sitting in the dark, two asleep and one awake. Their supervisor has a terrible time with them. He sometimes has a lorry to unload in

---

[1] The respondent also stated that the foremen did not like West Indians because they required more supervision.

a hurry: the big lorries can't get into the yard so they have to stay in the lane blocking the road until they are unloaded. Then he can't find his coloured workers to do the job so he has to make do with what he's got. And they don't like being told what to do: they resent being given orders. I don't know why they have to put with them for so long.

Finally, in City Transport it was stated that West Indians were more amenable to discipline than Pakistanis. The Personnel Manager stated that West Indians were 'easier to get along with' than Pakistanis, the latter tending to be more aloof. Pakistanis, the respondent claimed, were more argumentative than West Indians—they would not take 'no' for an answer. It must be remembered, however, that as this firm was a bus company and the majority of coloured workers were conductors, the supervisory position was quite different from that found in the normal industrial concern. Presumably, therefore, the respondent's attitude was based upon his experience of the behaviour of coloured employees in the Personnel Office.

The majority of managers in the interview surveys found Asian workers very amenable to discipline. As we have already noted, one manager described them as 'more anxious to please' than the British worker and another stated that they would 'do as they were told until the cows came home'. Other comments were as follows:

The Indian soon learns and is amenable to discipline. (Labour Officer, Westwood Foundry)

The Pakistanis are a very impassive people. I have never seen one of them get het up about anything or lose his temper. (Labour Manager, Edge Tools Ltd.)

Pakistanis are more polite than the British worker. (Works Manager, Omega Metals Ltd.)

West Indians are more difficult to supervise. With Asiatics, it's easy enough. If you say 'Run round the car park', they will run round the car park all day. (Personnel Officer, Grange Graphite Co.)

Pakistanis are more amenable to discipline than white workers. They do as they are told, if they understand, more quickly than white workers. (Personnel Manager, Ridgeway Steel Co.)

I think they are easier (to supervise). It may be that we have a good crowd here—they were handpicked. They will work all hours of the day if you ask them. They sometimes bring in a nephew or a brother if you need more labour. (Labour Officer, Polton Rolling Mills)

In the Grange Graphite Co. amenability to discipline was apparently the key determinant of managerial preferences with regard to the different coloured groups. The Personnel Officer stated that West Indians tended to be more skilled than Asian workers, were easier to train and, because of their superior physique, capable of working much harder. Nevertheless, the respondent said that he would rather employ Asian workers because they were more *tractable and easy to control*.

Some evidence that Pakistani workers were regarded as being more amenable to discipline than West Indians was also found in the questionnaire survey (Table 9).

TABLE 9   *Managerial Assessments of the Amenability to Discipline of Coloured Workers (Questionnaire Survey)*

Nationality	Less amenable to discipline than white workers %	About the same as white workers %	More amenable to discipline than white workers %	No. of firms responding
West Indians	9	62	29	45
Pakistanis	9	51	40	35
Indians	17	61	22	18
Arabs	13	67	20	15
Africans	13	60	27	15

However, this was not so in the case of other Asian groups and, in contrast to the interview surveys, few managers reported that West Indians were less amenable to discipline than white workers. Of the two sets of data, studies reported in the literature provide more support for the interview findings. Banton[1] and Patterson[2] for example, note the existence of a 'chip on the shoulder' attitude amongst many West Indians, and Banton

[1] *Coloured Quarter.*
[2] Sheila Patterson, op. cit.

comments upon the great docility of Asian workers. It seems likely, therefore, that the interview survey data presents a more reliable picture of the situation, but the further possibility that the apparently anomalous results of the questionnaire survey reflect a change in the behaviour of West Indian workers or in the attitude of management cannot be ruled out on the basis of the present evidence.

5. *Methods Used in the Supervision of Asian Workers*

As was the case with training, several methods were evolved to overcome the language difficulties involved in the supervision of non-English speaking workers.[1] Sometimes the same methods were used in both training and supervision, but the emphasis placed on these methods was not necessarily the same in both spheres. Sign language, for example, was commonly used in training, but more rarely encountered in supervision. The reason for this, the writer would suggest, is the fact that whereas training is a relatively short term matter, supervision is a permanent necessity. Training may take longer when sign language is employed, but if the job is capable of being taught by sign language, then it is possible for the Asian worker eventually to become proficient. On the other hand, if only sign language is used, supervisory efficiency is likely to be permanently impaired.[2] For this reason, other methods have tended to be evolved.

In two firms, Stainless Steel Ltd. and Castle Iron Co., supervisors had learnt 'a few words' of the language of the Asian workers concerned.[3] Conversely, in Sterling Metal Co. an attempt was made to teach the coloured workers English. This, however, was the only firm in which such an attempt was made in a systematic manner, although it was stated in other firms (for instance, Components Ltd. and Tool Steel Ltd.) that individual white workers would sometimes help those Asian immigrants who wished to learn English. Both these methods

---

[1] As we have already noted, some firms avoided the problem altogether by not employing Asian workers or only employing those whose English was adequate. However, we are not concerned with these cases here, but with those in which non-English speaking Asian workers *were* employed.

[2] See, for example, Edge Tools Ltd. (page 127).

[3] The General Manager of Stainless Steel Ltd. stated: 'The supervisors have learnt a few words in their language such as, "up", "down", "left", "right", "stop", "go".'

suffer from the same drawback. A vocabulary of a few words in the language concerned may be of some help, but of necessity it is of limited value except for the simplest of orders. Becoming fully conversant with the language, on the other hand, is a laborious and time consuming matter, a factor which has no doubt deterred most firms from employing either of the above methods.

A more common method of solving language difficulties in supervision was job placement; that is, the placing of coloured workers in jobs in which the supervisory requirements were minimal. On some piece work jobs, for instance, moulding in Bradfield Foundry, the necessity for order giving was virtually non-existent. The workers concerned were on the same job each day and, providing the necessary raw materials were available, could carry on doing their job without needing to communicate with anyone, supervisors or other workmen. The fact that they were on piece work also meant that they were highly motivated and therefore it was not necessary for the foreman to be present in order to maintain a satisfactory level of performance. The foreman in question spent relatively little of his time within sight of the workers and only rarely, during my visits to the firm, communicated with any of them.

Similarly, the Asian workers employed as members of rolling teams required little or no supervision. The machine was set by the roller (who was invariably British) and once the process had been begun, the Asian worker (and other members of the team) merely had to feed the strip back and forth through the rollers until it was the required size and shape. Thus no communication was required during the operation except perhaps for a sign to start and a sign to stop. Again, supervision in order to maintain a satisfactory level of performance was not necessary either; the pace was set by the head roller and by the machine. In Steel Bars Ltd., for example, the Works Manager said: 'There is no supervision involved. They are part of a team. The roller is responsible for his men.'

In some firms it was suggested that Asian workers were easier to supervise in a group rather than individually. For example:

Language is a problem. We had to sack a Pakistani last year because we could not understand him and he could not understand us. They seem terribly thick, but this is largely because they don't speak the language. However, we can deal with them in teams. (Personnel Manager, Ridgeway Steel Co.)

They seem to work better in a team. By a team, I mean a team of their own people. (Production Services Manager, Blackford Rolling Mills, *re* Pakistanis and Arabs)

The obvious advantage of employing Asian workers in a group is that any order has to be 'got across' only once. Were they on different jobs throughout the works, on the other hand, the language barrier would have to be surmounted with each individual worker. In addition, where Asian workers are in groups, the order has to be 'got across' to only one worker (the most alert or the one who has least difficulty with language) and he will translate for the rest. From this, it is but a short step to using the 'go-between' system.

The use of bi-lingual 'go-betweens' as interpreters was perhaps the most common method of overcoming the language problems where large numbers of Asian workers were employed. Examples are as follows:

Often the Pakistanis cannot speak English, and orders have to be given through the few who can. Usually there is one Pakistani per shop who can speak English and he is used as a 'go-between'. New Pakistani employees tend to live in one of three houses in the district owned by one or other of the 'go-betweens'. (Personnel Director, Precision Engineers Ltd.)

The coloured workers (mainly Indians) cannot speak English, so one or two interpreters are used. (Personnel Manager, Muirhead Foundry)

Because of the language difficulty, we used one of the Arabs to interpret for the rest who have only a smattering of English. (Works Manager, Annerley Iron Foundry)

The firm used to use a Somali as an interpreter. He also used to help the police. He has just left the firm to go back to Somaliland. He was the chief of the Somalis in (the city). He sometimes wore the full regalia of a chief—for example, during the independence celebration. (Personnel Manager, Sovereign Steel Works)

In Ridgeway Steel Co., according to the Personnel Manager, the first coloured worker employed by the firm had become 'a kind of unofficial labour officer'. He had selected the Pakistani workers who were later employed and had 'sorted out their problems' at the shop-floor level.

In the above cases, the 'go-betweens' had no official standing other than that of an ordinary workman. In two firms, however, 'go-betweens' had been promoted to the position of chargehand. At Sterling Metal Co. most of the early employees had been Somalis. The Personnel Manager stated:

> The first one was an admirable man, a very good worker. He could speak good English and could always be relied upon to introduce good men. He wouldn't let the firm down by bringing in people who weren't much good. He eventually became a charge-hand over his own people in the boiler house.

Similarly, the Pakistanis in Omega Metals Ltd. were supervised by a chargehand of their own nationality. Although technically speaking a chargehand, however, the man's position was more that of an officially recognized 'go-between', in that his authority extended to all the Pakistani employees irrespective of their jobs, but not to any of the British workers nor to the one West Indian employed by the firm. Nevertheless, as the only man in the works who could communicate verbally with both the Pakistani and the British members of the firm, he was in an extremely powerful position. All orders from management to the Pakistanis had to go through him, as had all communications from them to management. According to the Works Manager, all hiring of Pakistani workmen was left in his hands: management simply told him how many men were required and he supplied them. He also undertook most of the training of the Pakistanis, even though their jobs might be quite dissimilar from his own. Eight out of the ten Pakistanis I interviewed, including three shot-blasters, a fork-lift truck operator and a painter, stated that the chargehand had taught them their jobs.

Management seemed to be highly satisfied with this arrangement and not without reason from their point of view.[1] By the

---

[1] The two British supervisors employed by the firm were, however, less satisfied with the situation. Both found language a difficulty and both thought that coloured workers required more supervision. The Works Engineer said that the language barrier had caused a lot of trouble: as a result of not understanding orders, the Pakistanis 'did things they shouldn't and sometimes smashed things up.' The Foreman said that Pakistanis required a little more supervision because they had never worked in industry before, but the longer they had been in the country the less

employment of a bi-lingual chargehand, the language difficulties in training and supervision of Asian workers so often found
in other firms, had largely been avoided. The chargehand himself stated that it was because of the language difficulty that
Pakistanis only obtained labouring jobs in the big firms. He
stated: 'They can do every (that is, any) job, but they cannot
learn because of language. If I tell them, they can understand
and they can do the job.'

How far the success of this system resulted from the mere fact
that the chargehand was bi-lingual and how far it was due to the
personality and capabilities of the chargehand, it is difficult to
say. The Works Manager spoke very highly of him both as a
workman (he was a painter by trade, and 'red-hot' at it according to the respondent) and as a supervisor. As an example of his
efficiency in the latter capacity, the Works Manager told me of
an occasion when the firm had needed four men to do some con-
tract work at a large steel works. The chargehand was simply
informed that four men were required, that they would need to
know shot-blasting, and that they would need lodgings near the
steel works. The chargehand got the men, had them trained
within a month, and when asked what he had done about
accommodation, he informed the Works Manager that he had
obtained lodgings for them across the road from the firm concerned.

The chargehand would appear to have made himself indispensable to the firm. When he wanted to go back to Pakistan
for a holiday, the firm not only granted him three months leave,
but paid his air fare there and back. Furthermore, whilst he was
away, there was considerable unrest amongst the Pakistani
workmen. According to the Works Manager, they split up into
two groups which 'were practically at war with one another'.
When the chargehand returned, he was told of the situation. He
immediately lined up all the men and, in the words of the Works
Manager, 'played hell with them'. Apparently, what he told

supervision they needed. He also stated that it was *easier* to give orders to Pakistanis,
providing one could make oneself understood. One of the white workers also claimed
that the language barrier caused difficulties: 'If you want anything done, you go to
their chargehand and he arranges it. The trouble is, you keep having to go to him.'
Another white worker claimed that the chargehand used the fact that he was the
only Pakistani who could speak English to his own advantage: he would not bring
in anyone who could speak English.

them was, in effect, that there were plenty of men who would be glad to work there, and that if they didn't behave, he would get rid of the lot of them and get in some new men who would. The Works Manager said that he had never seen a supervisor play hell with workers to such an extent before. There had been no trouble since.

The Works Manager stated that the chargehand was also useful to the firm in other respects. On one occasion, for example, the management wanted a rate cut to provide more incentive. They simply told the chargehand that the rate was to be cut and 'that was that'. They did not exploit the coloured workers, the Works Manager quickly explained. They couldn't even if they wanted to: it would have been possible at one time, but it wasn't any more, which was a good thing.

In spite of the apparent success of this method, Omega Metals and Sterling Metal Co. were the only firms in the interview surveys in which 'go-betweens' had been given official supervisory posts. In the other firms, the possibility of using Asian supervisors was hardly even mentioned. In one firm, the respondent merely stated: 'We have never contemplated supervisory jobs for these people.' (Personnel Officer, Grange Graphite Co.) In two firms, however, respondents explained why they thought it would be unwise to promote Asian workers to such positions. In one case, it was stated that promotion was open to all workers, irrespective of nationality, but only as far as skilled jobs and no further. The respondent did not believe in promoting Asian workers to supervisory posts or even giving them any knowledge of supervisory methods. The reason given was that bribery and corruption had been rife in their own countries for hundreds of years and there would be a grave danger of an Asian supervisor receiving gifts for services rendered.[1]

In the other firm, Ridgeway Steel Co., a Shop Manager stated that the firm had once tried to train a Pakistani as a supervisor, but it had been a mistake. The man had been 'all on

---

[1] In Omega Metals the chargehand is, of course, in an ideal position for taking 'kick backs'. The Works Manager stated, however, that he had suggested to the chargehand that he was taking graft and the man had denied it. He told the respondent that he owned two houses and charged the boarders who worked at the firm only fifteen shillings per week, all the boarders putting something in a common pool for meals. He claimed that he had no need to take graft because he had no intention of going back to Pakistan.

the management's side', and had treated the Pakistani labourers under him 'like dirt'. It would have been quite a problem, the respondent stated, but fortunately the man in question had gone back to Pakistan. Since then, he had drawn the line at promoting Pakistanis to supervisory positions. The respondent also stated that there had been rumours that one of the Pakistanis had been taking a 'rake off' from the rest, but management had been unable to prove anything.

In some firms not even unofficial 'go-betweens' were used. A variety of reasons were given. In Components Ltd. the Personnel Officer stated that the interpreter system was not used because it would have necessitated the segregation of Asian workers into their own work groups, which was against the firm's policy. In Major Castings Ltd. the Personnel Manager stated:

> There is a leaning towards Jamaicans because of language. The Ministry of Labour suggested that we should use an interpreter to overcome the language problem, but what happens if the interpreter leaves? You are left with twenty to thirty people, none of whom can speak English.

In Grange Graphite Co. the Personnel Officer said that they had never used unofficial 'go-betweens' because they would not want anyone usurping the supervisor's position. It would appear that one of the Asian immigrants had attempted to act as a 'go-between' in this firm, but had been stopped. The respondent stated:

> You occasionally get one Asiatic who can understand the language who then capitalizes on the situation. We had one who set himself up as the Arab shop steward. We put a stop to that. We pointed out that if we had a shop steward to represent every different nationality we employ, we would have more shop stewards than members of staff and we weren't having that.[1]

---

[1] The respondent also stated that there had been cases of Asian employees taking bribes from their fellow countrymen. 'We have had trouble with ten-percenters—people who take a cut from their work mates. One man brought in eleven men and took £1 a week from them. We had to stop him. We couldn't reason with him; he thought it was natural. We had to threaten him with the sack, but he didn't see why. He seemed to think I was a lucky fellow because I was getting a pound a week from 625 men. I have also had offers from West Indians. One West Indian landlord offered me a cut if I would get work for the men in his house. But it seemed more vicious with the West Indians—more like gangsterism. With the Asiatics, it just appeared to be the natural thing to do.'

Before leaving the subject of 'go-betweens', it is worth noting that they were sometimes used for purposes other than supervision. In Omega Metals, for example, the duties of the Pakistani chargehand exceeded those usually carried out by the industrial supervisor in that he also obtained workers for the firm when they were needed. Managerial policy towards the recruitment of workers in this manner varied somewhat in the firms visited during the interview surveys. In Precision Engineers Ltd., for example, 'go-betweens' were used in order to facilitate order giving, but not for recruitment purposes. The Training Officer said that all labour requirements were obtained through the Labour Exchange: there was no hiring on the job. He stated: 'If we didn't use the Labour Exchange, there would be one long queue at the works gate. The Labour Exchange method saves their time and ours.'

In Edge Tools, on the other hand, 'go-betweens' were not used for order giving, but were used for recruitment. The Labour Manager stated that it was easier to obtain new employees by asking a workman to bring in a friend than by obtaining them from the Ministry of Labour. The reason was that the friends were helped by workmen already employed by the firm whereas those from the Ministry of Labour were not. The respondent stated, however, that the drawback to this method was that it lent itself to bribery. The firm had investigated rumours of bribery in the factory, had threatened some people thought to be responsible and begun employing coloured workers through the Employment Exchange. This, however, had not worked (presumably for the reason mentioned above) and the firm had gone back to employing friends of existing employees.

The recruitment of Asian workers through friends and relatives already employed by the firm was also mentioned in Major Castings Ltd., Annerley Iron Foundry, Polton Rolling Mills, and Castle Iron Co.[1] In Steel Bars Ltd. a 'go-between' was also used for recruiting purposes, but in this case the man did not himself work for the firm. The Works Director stated that they had a contact man, an English speaking Arab, who brought men in when they were needed. A foreman in the same firm suggested

[1] This method was also used for the recruitment of West Indian workers in Hamilton Engineering Co. The Labour Officer stated: 'When we are short of men, we contact one of our existing employees who brings along some applicants.'

that this method of recruitment was one of the reasons why the employment of Arab workers had been so successful. He stated:

> It's like this, if they're no good to us we don't keep them. We told their 'father'—he's the bloke who gets them their jobs (he doesn't work himself)—that we won't have the bad types. So he doesn't send the bad ones down: he knows we won't have them. So maybe these places that you hear about that have trouble aren't as selective as we are.

In both Hamilton Engineering Co. and Leigham Cannery, it was reported that there had been cases of English speaking Pakistanis bringing round several of their fellow countrymen in an attempt to obtain jobs for them. In neither firm had coloured workers been employed in this way, but in Leeds it appears that a formally organized Employment Agency of Asian workers has been set up. The following report appeared in *The Guardian:*

The man who sells jobs to immigrants

The Commonwealth People's Employment Agency (Mohammed Abdul Aziz, director) has been founded in Leeds to find and sell jobs to immigrants. According to his forms, Mr. Aziz charges immigrants £12 for this service. 'I have not yet charged more than £10 a head,' he said yesterday. 'I am very generous, you know. I feel for these people. At the same time, I feel for British industrial supremacy.'

Anyone who has seen unemployed Pakistanis trailing hopelessly from factory to factory could not help sharing his feelings for them. They are often illiterate and have little or no English. Mr. Aziz, on the other hand, is resourceful, business-like and articulate. Using his home in Abbot View, Armley, as an office, he sends forth messages to industrialists declaring his readiness 'to throw myself heart and soul in providing the employers with hard working and punctual workers absolutely free of cost'. It is this charging of the workers instead of the employer that makes Mr. Aziz's agency so unusual in an area which has full employment. A man who is not only unskilled, but also a coloured illiterate immigrant soon finds himself in a buyer's market for labour. Or, as Mr. Aziz puts it: 'If I charged a fee to employers they would say: "Look Mr. Aziz, I can get labour from my factory gate. Why should I take it from you?"'

Mr. Aziz says he wants to see immigrants getting jobs 'through proper discipline and manners', rather than being picked from the factory gate irrespective of their merits. His method, he claims, also eliminates the danger of such 'irregularities' as an immigrant being obliged to bribe a foreman to get a job. And he makes sure that his Commonwealth clients are equipped with proper cards, or have applied to the Ministry of National Insurance for them.[1]

Finally, it is interesting to note that in several firms 'go-betweens' owned houses in which their fellow workers lived. This was reported in Precision Engineers and Omega Metals, as we have already noted, and had also been the case in Stainless Steel Ltd. In the latter firm, the General Manager stated:

The coloured workers are confined to the Foundry and Forge mainly, but about six years ago we had one bloke, an Indian, acting as furnaceman. He was very intelligent, the ringleader of the coloured people who worked here. He bought himself a house and sub-let it to his fellow countrymen.

Similarly, a Pakistani interviewed in Ridgeway Steel Co. stated that he owned a house and had recently obtained a job with the firm for one of his lodgers. This would suggest that the 'go-between' in industry may tend also to be a leader in the community, and the fact that the interpreter in Sovereign Steel Works was said to be the leader of the Somalis in the district and the contact man in Steel bars Ltd. was referred to as the 'father' of the Arabs, lends some support to this conclusion.

Thus, to summarize, the Asian 'go-between' is an extremely powerful position as far as his fellow countrymen are concerned. Often he is the sole, or at least one of the very few, representatives of management to these workers. He is in a position, if he wishes, to claim more power than he actually has because it would be difficult for his non-English speaking workmates to check on the validity of his claims. In addition, the 'go-between' who has a lodging house in which his fellow workers live may use his authority in one sphere to support his authority in another. There is very little, therefore, to prevent him from abusing his power, for instance by accepting bribes for obtaining jobs or simply by being autocratic, and the indications are that this sometimes does happen.

As far as the firm is concerned, management is left in the position of being able to treat the Asian worker as an 'economic man'—that is, controllable by the simple application of reward

[1] 3 February 1964.

and punishment—to a much greater extent than is possible with British workers. There is very little the Asian worker can do about this, since his one representative is likely, through self-interest, to be on the side of management. It must be said, however, that most managements do not appear to take full advantage of this situation, although there are, of course, exceptions, one of which will be examined in the next chapter.

6. *Summary*

As in the case of training and supervision, managerial beliefs and attitudes concerning the diligence, flexibility, and supervision of coloured workers varied considerably. Thus, when making any generalizations, one must take into account the fact that there may be a considerable number of exceptions. Nevertheless, it does appear that, in the main, Asian workers were regarded as being more hard working and more amenable to discipline than the West Indians. On the other hand, the supervision of Asian workers, apart from the question of amenability to discipline, was often made more difficult by their lack of facility with English. Various methods had been evolved, principally job placement, employment in teams and the use of bi-lingual 'go-betweens', in an attempt to overcome this problem.

For some firms, language difficulties were sufficient to deter them from employing Asian workers or at least from employing those who could not speak English with a reasonable degree of fluency. In other firms, however, the Asian workers' greater diligence and amenability to discipline were regarded as more than compensating for the difficulties encountered in training and supervision. This division of opinion, I would suggest, provides one explanation for the tendency of firms to employ either Asian workers or West Indians rather than an appreciable proportion of both groups, and for the relatively high employment level of Asian workers in the present sample of firms in spite of their lower level of skill and industrial experience.

CHAPTER SIX

Equality of Treatment, Job Satisfaction, and Labour Turnover

1. *The Treatment of Coloured Workers by Managers and Supervisors*

We suggested in Chapter One, that apart from employment and occupational levels, another important aspect of the work integration of coloured immigrants was the way in which they were treated by managers and supervisors. Unfortunately, this is also an area in which it is extremely difficult to obtain accurate data. It is not to be expected that managers will volunteer information concerning their ill-treatment of coloured workers. There seemed little point, therefore, in asking direct questions on this subject: at best one would obtain mere platitudes and at worst completely ruin the rapport. Similarly, in the interviews with coloured workers, the absence of complaints about the way in which they had been treated might mean that they had received fair treatment or simply that they were wary of providing information which might have unpleasant repercussions should it come to the knowledge of management.

In some cases, however, it proved possible to obtain the necessary information from the white workers and in others it was provided inadvertently by the managers themselves. Little systematic data could be collected in this way—sometimes, for example, management representatives were present during interviews with white workers—but it may still be of some value providing its limitations are kept in mind.

In only two firms was it possible to determine with any degree of certainty, that coloured workers were not receiving fair treatment. The first was Omega Metals Ltd. where, it will be remembered, the Works Manager claimed that coloured workers were not exploited. His claim was not, however, supported by other white respondents. The Foreman stated that coloured workers were very much exploited by the employer, which was very bad for the British worker. He claimed that Pakistanis stood for much more pushing around by management: 'There are jobs which I ask Pakistanis to do that management would not even expect men to ask British workers to do. There are one or two that get the same rates as British workers, but not many.' When asked whether the Pakistanis expected equal treatment, he replied: 'They don't get it: whether they expect it or not, I don't know, but they put up with it.' The Works Engineer stated: 'They stand more pushing around: there's no doubt about it. They don't hold it against you though; they are not a malicious people.' However, he claimed that coloured workers received equal treatment, although he did not think that they expected it.

All five white workers interviewed in this firm said that (a) coloured workers stood for more pushing around, (b) they did not expect equal treatment, and (c) they did not get equal treatment. One white worker said that they did the jobs no-one else would do. Another, in answer to a question concerning how he felt about working with a firm which employed coloured workers, said:

It doesn't make much difference to me: or at least it wouldn't if they were all on the same rate. If I'm on one rate and they're on another, it's bad for us. If they (that is, management) can get work done cheaper than us, then we get kicked out.

A third white worker, when asked how he felt about a coloured worker doing the same job as himself, replied:

I don't mind him doing the same job, but if he gets paid less money than me—and there are coloured workers doing my job and working just as hard for two shillings an hour less—I can't go to the gaffer for a rise. He's got a Pakistani who will do the job.

The same respondent also claimed that the manager sent the Pakistani workers home 'when he felt like it'. 'If there's no work to be done, he sends them home at any time of the day. They just do as they're told. That's why he likes them so much.'

Finally, certain comments of the Works Manager himself concerning, for example, rates being cut and the chargehand 'playing hell' with the Pakistanis[1] provide further indications that discrimination occurred.

Thus, drawing together statements and innuendos from various sources, it is possible to build up a picture of the kind of treatment received by coloured workers[2] in this firm: Firstly, they were given the worst and most menial jobs to do; secondly, they were ordered about more, both by management and the supervisors, including their own chargehand; thirdly, they were paid less than white workers on the same jobs; and fourthly, although this only came from one source, they were sent home when there was no work for them to do. This scarcely supports the Works Manager's claim that there was no discrimination.

It is worth noting, however, that management's behaviour did not appear to arise from prejudice. The Works Manager had a very favourable attitude towards the Pakistani workers with respect to both their diligence and amenability to discipline. It may be, of course, that the prejudices were latent and did not manifest themselves because the Pakistanis behaved in the manner in which coloured workers were expected to behave.[3] Nevertheless, the main causes of discrimination in this firm appeared to be economic. The second case of discriminatory treatment, on the other hand, involving as it did not only stereotyping and sexual jealousy but also the ability to hold contradictory beliefs without even realizing it, presents an almost classical example of racial prejudice.

After interviewing the Personnel Manager of Sterling Metal Co., the writer also interviewed two Departmental Managers. In one department, the coloured workers were employed in the rolling teams. A union representative told me that on one shift a Somali was employed as middle man—that is, third in seniority from the roller—and had white men working under him. The Shop Manager compared the coloured employees very favourably with white workers. He stated: 'They're good workers. We used to have some riff-raff, but they've drifted away now. We

---

[1] See Chapter Five.

[2] That is, the Pakistanis. None of the above comments applied to the one West Indian employed by the firm.

[3] Cf. the belief of some white people in the Southern States of the U.S.A. that 'the Negro is all right in his place'. Prejudice therefore, is more likely to be manifested against those Negroes who step out of their 'place' rather than those who remain in it.

used to have some trouble, mainly between different coloured people, but we haven't had any recently.'

In the other department, the coloured workers were also Somalis, but here they were employed only as sweepers up. Immediately the manager was informed of the nature of my work, he stated that he couldn't stand coloured people, that he hated the lot of them, and that they all ought to be sent home. When asked what he had got against them, he asked me what I had got *for* them (implying by his tone that there could not possibly be anything in their favour). When I replied non-committally, he said that the trouble was that they were 'an idle set of black bastards who sat on their arse all day and did nothing'. They couldn't understand you when you wanted them to do something, he continued, but they were as sharp as anything when they thought they had been underpaid. The respondent told me that he had been all over the world and seen them in their own countries. They were uncivilized and dirty, and then they came over here, put on a white shirt, and started going out with white women. He stated that he could not stand the idea of coloured men and white women, but was not so averse, however, to discussing his own experiences with coloured women.

The Shop Manager said that his foreman would back him up in his opinions about coloured workers. The foreman was then introduced to me and the Shop Manager then left the room to find some coloured workers. When asked how he had found the coloured workers, the foreman merely stated that they were all right for sweeping up jobs, but no use for anything else because they were not intelligent enough. However, he displayed none of the virulent prejudice of his superior.

Two Somalis were brought in to be interviewed. The first answered questions without difficulty. The second, however, was a little slow in answering: he stated that he did not understand. The Shop Manager stated that the man *did* understand and was deliberately pretending not to. He then tried to elicit answers by asking the same questions over and over, but each time shouting them louder and louder. The Somali became more and more flustered, but eventually the Shop Manager was able to ascertain that the man had landed in London and had worked in Manchester before obtaining his present job. After the man had left, the respondent turned to me and said: 'You see how evasive they are, he understood all along.'

Finally, just before I left, the respondent asked me how the other Shop Manager had found the Somalis. I replied that he had said that they were good workers. The respondent then said: 'Ah, but I never said that they weren't good workers.'

In most of the other firms visited during the interview surveys, the writer gained the impression that, on the whole, coloured workers were reasonably well treated by management, although it was not always possible to verify this. Similarly, it was suspected in one or two cases that management was perhaps more demanding towards coloured workers—there were for example, the comments in Bradfield Foundry that they stood for more 'pushing around' and in Muirhead Foundry that it was unfair that Indians should receive equal pay because they were not as good as British workers—but again it proved impossible to obtain confirmatory evidence.

However, it may be significant that in such cases, the coloured workers concerned were usually Indians or Pakistanis. As we have noted, the white workers in Omega Metals claimed that the Pakistanis did not *expect* equal treatment. In the interviews with the Pakistanis themselves, none of them had any complaints about the treatment they had received, in spite of the overwhelming evidence of discrimination and the fact that they were specifically asked about the way management behaved towards them. Of course, it is quite probable that they would not have been so reticent had they been interviewed outside the works by a fellow Pakistani who had no connection with the firm. On the other hand, it also seems to be the case that Indian and Pakistani workers tend to accept unfair or unequal treatment with much less protest or sense of discrimination than either West Indian or British workers. In Edge Tools, for example, one British worker claimed that whereas Pakistanis expected to be pushed around, West Indians seemed to want the same treatment as white workers. Similarly, the stress often placed on the amenability to discipline of Asian workers compared with the 'touchiness' of the West Indians would seem to represent the same situation seen from the management viewpoint. Further evidence that Asian workers have, as it were, a lower level of aspiration with regard to working conditions is to

be found in the next section when we come to examine job satisfaction.

2. *Job Satisfaction*

Data concerning job satisfaction amongst Asian workers were
obtained in twenty-one formal interviews and in two informal
interviews on the shop-floor. In the latter two cases, both respondents stated that they did not like their jobs. The first, a
Pakistani crane driver in the Ridgeway Steel Co., simply said
that he wanted a job with more money. The other, an Indian
moulder's mate in Stainless Steel Ltd. stated:

> It's not very nice work; the money is not very much. I don't stay
> here because of the money. I stay here because of Mr.—(the moulder
> whom he assisted) and Mr.—(another moulder). The people here
> are very nice so I stay. The Shop Manager, he is very nice too.

In the formal interviews, on the other hand, all twenty-one
respondents[1] stated that they liked their jobs. In Edge Tools in
particular, they seemed highly satisfied. Some comments were
as follows:

> I like everything: anywhere, anytime, I like. (Interviewer:
> 'Would you prefer a better job?') This job better. All England better
> job! (Pakistani labourer)

> Here everything good, very good. Nothing I don't like. (Pakistani
> labourer)

> I like it very much; anytime job like. The Foreman is very nice—
> very good man. (Pakistani testing machine operator)

All the respondents said that there was nothing about their
jobs they disliked and only one said that he would prefer to do a
different type of work. A Pakistani general labourer in Polton
Rolling Mills stated that although he liked his present job very
much, he would have preferred 'something mechanical'. All the
other Asian workers wanted to continue doing the same jobs.

Of the twenty-five West Indian workers who were inter-

[1] Five Pakistanis and one Indian in Edge Tools, eleven Pakistanis in Omega
Metals, a Pakistani in Major Castings Ltd., an Arab in Annerley Iron Foundry, a
Pakistani in Polton Rolling Mills and an Arab in Steel Bars Ltd.

viewed,[1] only seven stated that (a) they liked their jobs and (b) that there was nothing about them that they disliked. Even amongst these respondents, however, five said that they would have preferred another job if they could have found something better. A further two respondents stated that they liked their work in general, but there were aspects of it which they did not —the wages in one case and the heat in another. Both would have preferred a better job than they had.

Nine of the West Indians described their jobs as 'all right' or said that they neither liked nor disliked their work or words to that effect. Five respondents said that there were aspects of their work which they disliked and five that they would have preferred something better.[2] Finally, seven respondents said that they disliked their work, two of them stating that they only continued with it because it was 'better than the Labour Exchange'.

In all, eighteen of the twenty-five respondents would have preferred a different job from the one they had. Eight gave no clear indication of the work they would have liked, and the preferred occupations of the remaining ten respondents were as follows: mechanical engineering, diesel engineering, 'something mechanical' (two cases), electrician, builder, painter, crane driver, pipe fitter, and operator for the Midland Gas Board. Only three respondents had had previous experience in the fields they chose.

Fourteen respondents gave details concerning the aspects of their present jobs which they did not like. Four stated that the wages were too small and another that the opportunities for advancement were limited. Three respondents, all polishers in Edge Tools, found the work too arduous; three stated that they did not like the dust; one that the job was too dirty; another that it was too hot; and two that they did not like working in acid because of the fumes.

Thus, in general, job satisfaction was much higher amongst

[1] West Indian workers were interviewed in the following firms: six in Edge Tools, one in Omega Metals, one in Annerley Iron Foundry, two in Leigham Cannery, six in Hamilton Engineering Co., five in Torrington Cutlers Ltd. and four in Pentland Alloys Ltd.

[2] There was, however, little overlap between these two groups. Only one of the nine respondents stated both that there was something about his job which he did not like *and* that he would have preferred something better.

the Asian workers than the West Indians. Only in Edge Tools was it possible to interview members of each group in appreciable numbers, and this case is particularly revealing. All six Asian respondents stated that they liked their jobs compared with only one of the West Indians. Two of the West Indians stated that their jobs were all right and the remaining three that they did not like them. This difference was even more striking in view of the Labour Manager's claim that the West Indians had the better jobs. The firm employed only a few West Indians, he stated, because they would only work in the Polishing Shop where the money was good, whereas the Asian workers would accept any job.

3. *Labour Turnover*

Writing in 1955, Banton[1] suggested that there was a relationship between the level of job satisfaction and rates of labour turnover amongst West African and West Indian workers. He stated:

> The ambitious immigrants find (the restrictions on vertical mobility) frustrating, and for a time they cannot believe that all jobs are as unrewarding as those they have tried. This leads them to change from one to another 'in the expectation of getting the right job some day'.

In all but one of the ten firms visited by Banton as representative of the main employers of unskilled labour in Stepney, labour turnover was said to be much higher amongst West African and West Indian workers.

Since Banton's study, however, the situation has changed radically, mainly it would appear as a result of fluctuations in the state of trade. According to Patterson, one consequence of the 1956–8 recession was that West Indians in work ceased to regard their jobs as expendable; their time keeping improved, and many employers who had formerly criticized their nonchalant attitude and high mobility gradually came to regard them as more reliable than most in these respects.[2]

Wood reached much the same conclusion on the basis of a research study carried out in 1959. He states:

[1] *Coloured Quarter.*
[2] *Dark Strangers.*

When coloured workers get permanent jobs they tend to stick to them. No longer are the complaints of a few years ago heard that coloured workers, particularly West Indians and West Africans, leave jobs suddenly when they hear of a factory down the road which offers them a few shillings a week more. The recession had a chastening effect on this kind of restlessness. Employment Exchange managers and personnel officers agree that the turnover is now the same as or often lower than that of white workers in comparable jobs. Only in Cardiff, where there is no great recently arrived coloured population, was it believed that the labour turnover was higher.[1]

A similar pattern emerged from the present research. A few managers still believed that labour turnover rates were higher amongst coloured workers, but the majority claimed that they were as low or even lower, and more often the latter.

In the questionnaire survey, twenty-two respondents (48 per cent) stated that labour turnover was lower amongst coloured workers than amongst white, fifteen (33 per cent) that it was about the same and only nine (19 per cent) that it was higher. In one further firm labour turnover was said to be higher in the case of Pakistanis, but no reference was made to the West Indians also employed by the firm. In no other case was a distinction made between the labour turnover rates of West Indian and Asian workers.

In the interview surveys, data concerning labour turnover was obtained in twenty-six firms in all. It was said to be higher than amongst British workers in four firms,[2] about the same in five firms,[3] and lower in fifteen firms.[4] In the remaining two cases[5] the data did not readily fit into the above categories and must be examined separately.

In Tool Steel Ltd. the Personnel Manager described labour turnover amongst coloured workers as 'not bad', but suggested that it followed a different pattern than amongst white workers. He stated:

Coloured workers stay two, three or four years and then go back home. If a white man is here this length of time, he is usually here

[1] D. Wood, op. cit.
[2] Firms 5, 24, 26, and 30.
[3] Firms 16, 20, 21, 22, and 31.
[4] Firms 2, 3, 7, 9, 10, 11, 12, 13, 15, 18, 23, 25, 27, 28, and 29.
[5] Firms 17 and 19.

for good. So I think you could sum up labour turnover amongst the coloured workers by saying that they have longer short term engagements.

In Leigham Cannery, on the other hand, the Personnel Officer suggested that the labour turnover pattern differed between coloured men and women. In the case of women, labour turnover was about the same as amongst white women, but in the case of the men, it was very low indeed.

Among the men, it would be nil if they had their way. Labour turnover is mainly due to redundancy.[1] Once a coloured man gets over his training period, he tends to stay as long as we will keep him.

Claims that labour turnover was so low amongst coloured workers as to be almost non-existent were found elsewhere in the present research. The Personnel Manager of Muirhead Foundry stated, for example: 'You have to have more Indians in to find a good one, but once you have found him, you don't have turnover. The English workers are continually turning over.' Similarly, the Personnel Manager of Drop Forgings stated: 'There is no labour turnover with Jamaicans; they rarely leave.'

Oddly enough, another example of negligible labour turnover amongst West Indians was found in one of the firms where labour turnover was said to be *higher* than amongst white workers. The Personnel Manager of Ensign Springs Ltd. claimed that although the firm had no colour bar, they would hesitate to employ any more coloured workers than they already had. It would be a bad policy for any industry to employ too many coloured workers, he stated, because they tended to move from district to district. The respondent asked me whether I had found the same thing in the course of my studies. I replied that I had heard conflicting reports, some managers stating that they moved around between districts[2] and others that they tended to remain in the same job because they would not easily obtain another one. The respondent then agreed that, because they were grateful to have a job, West Indians might stick to an un-

---

[1] There was a high rate of seasonal redundancy in this firm.

[2] Only one manager had, in fact, mentioned this question at this stage. The Works Superintendent at Bradfield Foundry stated that Pakistanis (who were not employed in Ensign Springs Ltd.) had at one time tended to move backwards and forwards between the Midlands and Yorkshire, but this no longer happened to any great extent.

skilled job where a white worker would leave. Later, when asked specifically about labour turnover amongst coloured workers, he stated that it was nil. He claimed, however, that this was because they were only employed where necessary; if more were employed, he stated, labour turnover would be 'tremendous'.

In the remaining three firms where labour turnover was said to be higher, Asian workers (mainly Pakistanis and Arabs) were employed. The Personnel Manager of Sterling Metal Co. stated that coloured workers were 'more mobile' than British workers, although not so much now as they used to be. In Stainless Steel Ltd. the Works Manager claimed that coloured workers tended to leave for trivial reasons without giving the job a fair trial. Two coloured workers had left because they were put on outside jobs and another two because it was too wet. The white worker, the respondent thought, would try the job for about three months before he left.

Finally, in Blackford Rolling Mills, the Production Services Manager claimed that both labour turnover and attendance were worse amongst coloured workers. He stated:

> We find that they do not have the attitude of being here five days a week. They will take the odd day off. We also found this with the permanent coloured workers; generally they were unreliable from the attendance point of view. Labour turnover is rather higher than with non-coloured workers, there's no doubt about that. They don't require much provocation to leave one job and get another. It ties in with their attendance. They are far worse than our own workers in both respects.

Little support for this contention can be found elsewhere in the present research. We have already seen that most managers had found labour turnover amongst coloured workers no higher than amongst white. Similarly, although no systematic data were collected concerning attendance, the respondents who mentioned this subject invariably stated that it was better amongst coloured workers. It must be remembered, however, that the above firm had ceased to employ permanent coloured workers some four years previously and patterns of labour turnover and attendance could have changed considerably in the intervening period.

Thus far we have mainly been concerned with labour turnover arising from coloured workers moving from one job to another. In the case of Asian workers, however, several respondents also mentioned the question of coloured immigrants returning to their own countries. In one of the firms in the questionnaire survey, labour turnover was said to be higher amongst Pakistanis 'due to the attractions of returning to their homeland when they have accumulated sufficient money'. In another firm, employing Indians and Pakistanis, the respondent stated:

There is only one criticism we have to make and that is that we find that after they have worked here for a certain length of time and have learnt all we have to teach them, they have a tendency to return to their native land which, of course, places us in an awkward position although we can understand their feelings in this matter.

Further examples were found in the interview surveys. As we have already noted, the Personnel Manager of Tool Steel Ltd. claimed that coloured workers tended to return home after two, three or four years. In Steel Bars Ltd. the Works Director stated:

Labour turnover is negligible. In general, once they are here, they stay. Except for going home that is. With their standard of living, they could save about £1,000 in two to three years and then go back home again and set themselves up in business. Or they might save £400 to £500 and 'plonk' it on my desk and ask me to have it sent home to their father to buy a shop, for example. This has happened. One bought property and set up a 'doss house'. He got £40 to £50 a week in rent, so he gave his notice. He made about £2,000 to £3,000 and went home a rich man. At least, a comparatively rich man by his standards.

In other firms, the question of Asian workers returning home for an extended holiday was mentioned. In Edge Tools, labour turnover amongst Pakistanis was generally low, but the firm had recently lost some workers who had gone back to Pakistan. They had wanted a guarantee that they could have their jobs back when they returned, but the firm had refused to do this. One reason was that it was impossible to predict what the state of trade would be like when they returned, and another that they would have to be replaced and the firm could not simply sack the replacements when the returnees wanted their old jobs back again.

Similarly, during an interview with the Assistant Personnel

Manager of Ridgeway Steel Co., a Pakistani asked the respondent whether the firm would hold his job for him whilst he went back to Pakistan. The respondent said that he supposed that the man would want a month off, but the Pakistani replied that he wanted a year—he couldn't spend all that money going back to Pakistan for just a month. The Assistant Personnel Manager stated that, in that case, he would just have to take 'pot luck' when he came back and suggested that the man should write to the firm about two months before he was due to return and they would 'see what they could do'.

In one of the questionnaire survey firms, on the other hand, Pakistanis were granted up to a maximum of six months home leave after the completion of three years service and subsequently at intervals of five years. The respondent stated that labour turnover amongst Pakistanis was low for this reason.

Finally, the question of Asian workers returning home was also mentioned in Grange Graphite Co., but in this case the respondent was dubious as to whether they always gave the correct reason for leaving. The Personnel Manager stated:

Three coloured workers have been here twelve years. The average length of stay is about three years with a median figure of three years as well. They leave for three main reasons: they leave for Bradford, they leave for Birmingham and they leave for Aden. They can pack up and leave easily, probably due to the lack of personal possessions. You never really know why they are leaving. They say they are going to Aden and three weeks later they are back for a job. Their concept of truth seems to be entirely different from ours. They say they are going to Aden and they know they are not going to Aden and you know they are not going to Aden and they know you know, but they are still going to Aden. I have very rarely had one come in and tell me he is leaving because he has got a better job.

Nevertheless, it should be noted that in the above firm and in Ridgeway Steel Co. it was stated that there was no difference between the labour turnover rates of white and coloured workers. Similarly, in both Edge Tools and Steel Bars Ltd., labour turnover was said to be low in spite of the fact that some Asian workers had left to return home. This, combined with the low rates of turnover found generally, suggests that the number of Asian workers returning to their own countries is insufficient, as yet anyway, seriously to affect labour turnover.

Thus, although there were a few exceptions, the present data indicate that levels of labour turnover amongst both Asian and West Indian workers are remarkably low. How then are we to account for this situation? Can it be suggested for example, that the 1956–8 recession brought about a long term change in the attitudes of coloured workers towards stability of employment? Whilst this may be the case, it must also be remembered that the field work of the present research was mainly carried out in 1962 and 1963 at the beginning of and during another major recession, when coloured workers were once more finding employment scarce.

Several managers, in fact, attributed the low levels of labour turnover amongst coloured workers to the difficulties of obtaining alternative employment. In Central Glass Works, for example, the Personnel Manager claimed that they were 'afraid that if they left one job, they might have to walk the streets for months before they found another'. Similarly, the Personnel Officer of Trafford Iron and Steel Co. stated:

We have had no difficulty with labour turnover. Under present conditions the reverse is the case. The West Indian is anxious not to lose his job, presumably because he would not find another one easily.

Some supporting evidence was found in the interviews with coloured workers, particularly the West Indians. As we have already shown, job satisfaction was relatively low amongst West Indian workers. Nevertheless, several respondents who either did not like their jobs or would have preferred a better one stated that they would remain in their present employment. Examples include:

Well it's hard work and nobody likes hard work, but there's no other, so I've got to stick to it. (Polisher, Edge Tools)

The money's a bit short, but I am quite satisfied until I can find something better. It's a bit tough to get work now and it is better to stick. (Labourer, Torrington Cutlers Ltd.)

I don't like it very much, but I stick to it because it's better than going to the Labour Exchange. (Window Cleaner, Torrington Cutlers Ltd.)

I would really like a different job where I could learn something, but it's very difficult to find a better job now. Jobs are scarce. (Turner's mate, Pentland Alloys Ltd.)

On the other hand, there were also indications that, irrespective of the state of trade, some of the respondents preferred stability of employment. A West Indian sand miller in Hamilton Engineering Co. stated: 'The job carries a lot of dust, but I would rather remain on it. I just love a steady job.'

In two other cases, 'skilled'[1] West Indians had become resigned to the fact that they could not obtain jobs in their own fields. In Edge Tools, a cabinet-maker now employed as a polisher said: 'At first I would have liked my old job, but not now. It's been so long that it doesn't make any difference.' And in Torrington Cutlers, a West Indian who had previously been a painter, said of his present job, stripping silver: 'I've got so accustomed to it now that it doesn't bother me. If I could get a job as a painter, I would accept it, but if I can only get another job like the one I have here, I will continue.'

The respondent had, in fact, tried to obtain a job as a painter, but had been told, he claimed, 'Sorry, no Coloureds'. However, this had occurred some five years previously, and it would appear that since then he had not tried to obtain work in his own field. Similarly, another West Indian employed in the same firm stated: 'I would like to get back to my old trade doing building work, but I would lose a day if I went out to try for another job and it's difficult at week-ends.'

There is little evidence in the above comments of Banton's[2] highly mobile West Indian moving from firm to firm in the hope of finding the right job some day, or of the tendency to leave jobs for trivial reasons reported by Wood.[3] This change may have been brought about partly by the 'chastening effect' of the 1956–8 recession and partly by present trade conditions. However, there were also signs that some West Indians at least had lowered their level of aspiration and, following the disillusionment of the high hopes with which they arrived in this country, were now prepared simply to 'make the best of things'.

[1] That is, skilled according to their own standards. Of one of these respondents a white worker in the same firm (Torrington Cutlers) stated: 'The one in our department was a brush hand, painting corridors in a hospital; he told a firm he was a skilled painter, and he was most upset that they wouldn't take him on.'

[2] *Coloured Quarter.*

[3] D. Wood, op. cit.

CHAPTER SEVEN

Inter-group Relations at Work

1. *Introduction*

One of the first firms to be visited during the present research was Bradfield Foundry. In all, five or six weeks were spent there interviewing management representatives and observing white and coloured employees at work. The labour force consisted of 134 male and 22 female workers. Of the male workers 37 were British, 12 Italian, 4 West Indian, 4 Arab, and 77 Indians and Pakistanis. Of the latter, about 50 were Indians, mainly Sikhs. The female labour force consisted of 19 British women and 3 West Indian. It seemed, therefore, an ideal firm in which to begin observing 'race relations in action', as it were.

By the end of the period of observation, however, I had come to the conclusion that race relations as such just did not exist in this firm. At this time, I had been studying race relations for only a few months and my ideas were still influenced by pre-conceptions which had grown up on the basis of second hand information (newspaper reports and so on). Looking back on it now, I realize that, somewhat naïvely, I was trying to discover whether relations between the races were 'good' or 'bad'. Good race relations, I thought, would show themselves in acceptance of the coloured workers by the white and friendly relations between the races. Bad race relations, on the other hand, would demonstrate themselves in rejection of the coloured workers, prejudice and discrimination against them and friction between the races. Neither, however, was the case in this firm.

In general, interaction between the different national groups was minimal. Whilst actually working, the behaviour of the workers was almost entirely task-orientated. There was little or no social intercourse; such interaction as did occur was mainly concerned with work and there was little enough even of this because the work did not demand it. Admittedly, social inter-action did take place during lunch and tea-breaks, but very little of this was inter-racial. The workers tended to split into groups consisting of one nationality only and there was no interaction between the groups.

Thus, being unable to carry out my original intention of studying 'race relations', I decided to do the next best thing and study the apparent lack of them. The morning tea-break seemed to present the best opportunity of doing this as it was possible to observe the change-over from work to social relation-ships. Accordingly, I went round the factory at this time on several mornings and made a note of where people worked, where they spent their tea-break and what happened before and during the tea-break. The following is a description of what occurred on a typical morning at this time.

All morning there has been the continual noise, vibration, dust and dirt of industrial machinery operating at full pressure. The work is carried out in a brick-walled, corrugated roofed building about one hundred and twenty feet long and sixty feet wide. The floor appears to be packed earth, but there may be concrete somewhere underneath it. It is difficult to tell. The production line begins in the moulding department. There are twenty moulders, eight Indians, seven Italians, four British workers and a Pakistani. The finished moulds, consisting of machine compressed sand in a wooden or metal frame, are placed on the 'track' (a circular conveyor system) and thus carried a short distance to the casting platform. Here, six casters, a Pakistani, a West Indian and four Indians, fill the moulds with molten metal carried manually in ladles from the Cupola. The filled moulds are then carried by the slow moving track, cooling and setting as they go, to the knock-out. Two Pakistanis and an Indian then drag them off the track on to a vibrating grid. The mould breaks up: the sand falls through the grid, the redhot castings are placed on another conveyor system and the frames are placed back on the track to be transported back to the moulders.

After the castings have cooled, they are inspected for flaws by two women, one British and the other West Indian. Some then go to the Grinding and Drilling Deparment where there are six grinders (three Pakistanis, one British worker, an Indian and a West Indian), two drillers (an Arab and an Indian), an assembler (a Pakistani) and two bench workers (both British). Others go to the Fettling Department which is staffed by a British foreman, five Indians, two Italians, a Pakistani, an Arab and a British worker, all on bench work, drilling or grinding. Subsequently, the castings are reinspected, painted and sent to the Despatch Department.

Work is carried out at high pressure as the product in various stages of completion proceeds through the different departments. There is little need for communication about work as the mould or casting is carried from the previous operator and on to the next mainly by means of conveyor systems. As long as the moulds or castings are available, therefore, each operator is able to carry out his operation in virtual independence of the rest. Social communication is minimal and in many cases non-existent. In general, the workers appear to devote their entire attention to the task in hand, having neither the time nor the inclination to interrupt this with social activities.[1]

At about 9.45 a.m., however, the pace slackens somewhat and preparations begin to be made for the morning tea-break. An Indian places a saucepan (later seen to contain curry) on a red-hot casting on the moving conveyor-belt, and then carries on working. Another Indian is heating a saucepan on a similar casting on the shop-floor. A West Indian woman is toasting bread in front of a stove in another part of the factory. Chapatis are being heated over a brazier in yet another part of the factory. An Indian working next to the track leaves his place of work, goes further up the conveyor system, places a billy can of water on one of the freshly filled moulds and goes back to work again. The mould, containing red-hot metal, continues to move along the track. Five minutes later, it has almost reached the Indian's work position.

At ten o'clock an electric bell is rung. The conveyor-belts are brought to a halt, the moulding, grinding and drilling machines are switched off, the casters lay down their ladles and the workers begin to congregate in groups.

The Indian casters and Indians from other parts of the foundry gather round the brazier next to the casting platform. On the brazier billy cans of water are boiled, chapatis are heated and saucepans full of curry are cooked. One of the Indians leaves the group to heat a chapati in a casting ladle which has recently held red-hot metal, then rejoins the group. Tea and sugar, measured out by the handful, are added to the freshly boiled water and the Indians squat or stand around drinking tea and eating pieces of the chapatis dipped into

---

[1] N.B. The majority of employees are on piece work or bonus.

the curry. The group round the brazier is quite lively and boisterous, with much talking and shouting back and forth.

One Indian who does not join this group is the man who was working next to the track. By the time the tea-break bell was rung, his can of boiling water was within a foot or so of his place of work. Having made his tea, he then heats a saucepan of curry on the now stationary mould. Usually he eats alone, but occasionally he is joined by one or two other Indians. He is somewhat older than the Indians who congregate round the brazier and spends his lunch time in a much more quiet and leisurely manner.

The Pakistanis squat together in a group on the opposite side of the casting platform from the Indians. The Italians sit in a group at the end of the line of moulding machines drinking tea and eating sandwiches. Although the two groups are quite close together, there is no social interaction between them.

The rest of the moulders sit in small racially homogeneous groups in amongst the moulding machines. Two Indians (one of whom has the record for mould production) are working on their machine apparently trying to rectify some fault.

The West Indian caster and one of the Cupola attendants (a British worker) spend the tea-break together, sitting on a small bench next to the Cupola, drinking tea and eating sandwiches.[1]

The workers in the Fettling Department spend their tea-break sitting round the only stove in the department. The group consists of two British women, one male British worker, several Indians and an Arab. Whilst the different nationalities are not broken up into separate groups, there is a tendency for people sitting next to each other to be of the same nationality. There is much less social interaction than in the racially homogeneous groups, and what interaction there is, takes place mainly between people of the same nationality. The Indians in this department are eating English food.

On the opposite side of the track from the casting platform, four or five British workers sit drinking tea and eating sandwiches. Two members of this group work in this position, the others coming from different parts of the foundry.

The coloured workers in the Grinding and Drilling Department

---

[1] The Technical Controller stated that although the West Indian caster usually spends his tea-break with the Cupola attendant, he goes and sits with another West Indian in the Dispatch Department during the lunch break. According to the respondent, he could not do this during the morning tea-break because there was insufficient time. The Technical Controller also stated that the West Indian caster was 'not too happy' about the fact that his workmates were all Asians. There used to be two other West Indians on this job, but they have both left and he is now the only English speaking caster.

are gathered together in a large racially mixed group next to the grinding machines. There are several Indians and Pakistanis, the West Indian grinder and one or two Arabs. The two British bench workers in the department sit together at some distance from the coloured workers. At some distance from both these groups sit two British women (both inspectors). Later, they are joined by a West Indian woman, also an inspector, who remains with them for the rest of the tea-break.

At 10.15 a.m., the electric bell is rung once more, signifying the end of the tea-break. The West Indian caster starts up the track, the moulding, grinding, and drilling machines are switched on and the second half of the morning's work is begun.

Further information concerning race relations in this firm was obtained from interviews with management representatives. The Works Superintendent stated:

When we first began employing coloured workers, I envisaged race riots and all kinds of trouble, but by and large they have settled down and been accepted without difficulty. You still get some British workers who will say, for example, 'What else can you expect from a bloody nigger', but it never comes to anything.

On the other hand, the respondent claimed that there had been some friction between Indians and Pakistanis. For example, an Indian would out point to a supervisor that a Pakistani had done a hopeless job on some task, not so much as a means of 'telling tales' on a particular person, but rather to demonstrate that all Pakistanis were hopeless. Similarly, the Fettling Shop foreman claimed that Indians and Pakistanis did not get on well together; if placed on the same job, each would blame the other if anything went wrong. Such friction as there was in the foundry, the Works Superintendent concluded, occurred between Indians and Pakistanis; it did not occur between West Indian and Asian workers who tended to ignore each other, nor between white workers and coloured workers in general, nor between the two groups of white workers, the Italians and the British.

Two main points arise from the foregoing account. Firstly, it is an over-simplification to view race relations in such a context in terms of a white/coloured dichotomy. There is a complex pattern of relationships, and whilst such concepts as a colour bar and racial prejudice on the part of white workers may have some relevance, they cannot provide a full explanation of the situation.

Secondly, even if we isolate the attitude of white workers towards the coloured, this cannot be described in terms of simple acceptance or rejection. The white employees were prepared to accept the coloured immigrants as workers, in the sense that they did not threaten strike action if they were employed, nor did they refuse to work with them. It may be said that they would have preferred white workmates and only accepted coloured workers because white workers could not be obtained, but they accepted them nevertheless. On the other hand, they did not in general accept them in the social context.

We would suggest, therefore, that the study of inter-group relations in the works environment should be approached from three main standpoints:

1. Attitudes of the British workers towards coloured immigrants as work-mates.

2. Social relations between white workers and coloured workers, and

3. Where more than one nationality of coloured immigrants is employed, work and social relations between the different coloured groups.

In the next three sections, we will examine each of these topics in turn.

2. *British Attitudes towards the Immigrant as a Worker*

(a) *Level of Work Acceptance*

As we noted in Chapter Three, opposition from British employees has in some firms prevented or deterred management from employing coloured immigrants. Unfortunately, we cannot estimate from the present data how commonly this occurs as the majority of firms studied did in fact employ coloured labour. In these firms, however, remarkably little opposition to the coloured worker was reported by management.

In the questionnaire survey, it was stated in thirty-six firms out of fifty that no initial resistance to the employment of coloured workers had been experienced. In seven firms there had been some opposition on the part of the white employees and in a further seven firms slight resistance had occurred. In some cases, the earlier resistance was overcome and coloured workers eventually gained acceptance. At the time the survey was carried out, coloured workers were said to be accepted as work-mates in forty-five of the firms. In three, coloured workers were still not accepted and in two cases uncodable answers were received.

A similar pattern emerged from the interview survey. In twenty firms no initial resistance to the employment of coloured workers was reported. Often, the agreement of the white workers was obtained before coloured labour was introduced. In Edge Tools Ltd., for example, the Labour Manager stated:

When it became necessary to employ coloured workers, the position was explained to the whites at a meeting. It was guaranteed that no white man would ever be excluded by the employment of coloured people. The men were left to think it over for day or so. There was no resistance, nor has there been any trouble right from the start.

And according to the Works Manager of Annerley Iron Foundry: 'Management had the union's blessing when coloured workers were employed. All the coloured workers are in the union.[1]

In the remaining eleven firms, some initial resistance to the employment of coloured labour had occurred. In some cases[2], only a certain section of the white workers, usually those in skilled trades, had been opposed to their employment, whilst the remainder had accepted them. In Central Glass Works, for example, coloured workers had been accepted in the production departments, but the skilled shops and the maintenance department had refused to take them. Similarly, in Pentland Alloys Ltd. some of the white workers in the hot rolling department had been reluctant to accept coloured workers so management had employed them elsewhere. In Major Castings Ltd. and Sovereign Steel Works, several departments had refused to accept coloured labour at first, but some had later relented. In Sovereign Steel Works the Personnel Manager stated:

Certain departments refused them for a time, and some still do—certain skilled trades such as building. We had great difficulty

---

[1] Consultation with the white workers with respect to the employment of coloured labour was also reported in Firms 1, 3, 7, 11, 15, 18, and 31.

[2] Firms 11, 15, 17, 23 and 31.

getting them accepted in the machine shops, but by and large, they have now been accepted everywhere except in the building and electrical shops.

In the other firms,[1] there had been a general reluctance to accept coloured labour. Often, however, this was slight and relatively short lived. In Steel Bars Ltd., for example, the Works Director stated:

I suppose if you went right back to the start, we didn't have any difficulty, but we did have some back-chat and grumbling. A sort of mild reproach to management. But they realized that we had to have men and that it was better to have a coloured man than no jobs. After about a year, they discovered that they (the coloured workers) were friendly. And generous—some of the white men kept borrowing money off the Arabs until we put a stop to it.

Similarly, in Stainless Steel Ltd.:

There was some initial difficulty with the white workers. This is a non-union firm . . . so there was an undercurrent rather than an official outcry. They said they weren't going to eat in the same place as the coloured workers, and if they were going to use the showers, well that was the end! When they saw the menial jobs being done and helping them to get their bonus, they soon shut up. (General Manager)

And in Sterling Metal Co.:

The greatest objection was from the economic standpoint—overtime and redundancy. This was easy to overcome—we pointed out that the coloured workers were getting the jobs they didn't want. Now the whites have come round and insist on equality in redundancy—last in, first out, irrespective of colour. (Personnel Manager)

By the time the interview survey was carried out, coloured immigrants had been accepted as workers in the majority of firms visited. Only in Muirhead Foundry was it reported that the white employees in general were still strongly opposed to the employment of coloured labour. In this firm, coloured workers had been employed since it was founded two years previously, and although the white employees were prepared to work with them because, other than leaving the firm, there was no alternative, their presence was still resented. Even here, however,

[1] Firms 20, 24, 25, 26, 28, and 29.

the coloured workers were not completely rejected. According to the Personnel Manager:

The British workers realize that it is impossible to get sufficient white workers, so they just accept them on sufferance. In general the British workers do not like them—although they do like them in certain jobs because they do hard graft.

In the main, however, the attitude of the white workers seemed to be neither favourable nor unfavourable, but rather one of indifference. The coloured workers were accepted, but this did not denote a positive orientation towards them, merely the absence of rejection. Some typical reports by management were as follows:

By and large they accept them, but they don't either like them or dislike them. There is no non-acceptance except by a minority, nor are they favoured except by a minority. (Personnel Officer, Sovereign Steel Works)

They're indifferent: they don't like them, but they're indifferent —they don't actively dislike them. It's like the U.S.A. and Red China: they don't like them, but they try to pretend they aren't there. (Personnel Officer, Grange Graphite Co.)

I don't know . . . I suppose they accept them, but they tend to be indifferent. If you put it to the vote, they'd rather be without them. (General Manager, Stainless Steel Ltd.)

Comparative data from the white workers on this question is somewhat limited; owing to the reluctance of managers to allow formal interviews only twenty-five complete questionnaire schedules could be obtained. What information there is, however, does tend to support the above conclusions. White workers were first asked how they felt about working for a firm which employed coloured labour. The majority of respondents claimed that they did not mind or were not greatly concerned over this matter. Some typical responses were as follows:

Oh, they're all right, they don't interfere with my job. (Edge Tools Ltd.)

I've got nothing against coloured workers. (Omega Metals Ltd.)

I'm not bothered; they don't interfere with me. (Omega Metals Ltd.)

It's immaterial to me what colours they are as long as they work all right. (Leigham Cannery)

If they'll work, if they'll pull their weight as a member of a team, I don't mind what colour they are. (Torrington Cutlers Ltd.)

At this stage only three respondents indicated that they were not prepared to accept coloured workers. However, when subsequently asked whether, other things being equal, they would prefer to work where only white people were employed, fifteen respondents stated that they would. Even amongst those who said that they would not, the attitude seemed largely to be one of indifference. For example, a worker in Omega Metals Ltd. stated:

I get on with them all right; there's good and bad in every race. You just have to accept them. I don't mind working with coloured chaps; they don't interfere with me and I don't interfere with them.

And in Hamilton Engineering Co. another said:

It's difficult to answer because there's only three or four, but if there was a lot . . . I'm not frightened they might take my job you see. Some of the other blokes, if they are labourers, might be worried about losing their jobs because of them, but they don't bother me.

In six cases,[1] however, the white respondents had a positively favourable attitude towards coloured workers. In Torrington Cutlers a white worker stated: 'Both socially and to work with, I've found them very good. They've been hard workers, and they've done everything they've been asked to do. And I don't think we've ever had any trouble.' And in Pentland Alloys Ltd. two skilled white workers indicated that they preferred West Indian labourers:

'I find them just as good as, well in fact better than our own. There's one thing about them, they will work.'

'No I wouldn't (rather work where only white people were employed). I've had some terrible white labourers—laziest buggers under the sun.'

Further examples of favourable attitudes towards coloured workers were also found in the informal, shop-floor interviews

[1] One respondent in Torrington Cutlers, one in Steel Bars Ltd. and four in Pentland Alloys Ltd.

with white workers. In Stainless Steel Ltd. a moulder said of his
Indian labourer:

He's champion. I couldn't hope to get a better mate. I'd rather
have him than any of the white men we've got here. He's a very
willing worker. You just tell him what to do and he gets on with it.
You can leave him on his own and he carries on working. If I had
a white mate and I left him, he would be waiting for me to tell him
what to do when I got back. But not this bloke. He could just about
do my job for me. And he's only been here about a year and he'd
never worked in a foundry before that. Now he knows more about
moulding than any other labourer in the firm. Well he knows more
than some of the moulders for that matter. Some of them have to
ask me which cores go into a particular mould, but he knows them
all.

In Sovereign Steel Works two rollers spoke very highly of the
coloured workers in their teams. The first praised coloured
workers in general for their willingness to work and stated that
in this respect they were much better than white men. If there
was a job to be done, he said, they would get on with it whereas
the white workers would stand around and wait. The number
two man in this team was an Arab. The roller stated that it was
only the language difficulty which was holding him back from
further advancement; if he could read and write English, he
could become a roller with no difficulty. The second roller
stated that the coloured workers were all keen workers and
ready to learn the job above their own in order to gain promotion. They were, he said, prepared to stick to the job, whereas
the white workers had tended to drift out of the rolling mills.

We had a white bloke, a roller, who came in from another firm.
He came in, rolled his first billet, and walked off the job, and we
never saw him again. So that doesn't say much for your white bloke,
does it?

In both teams, the coloured workers were mainly Arabs.

To summarize: the data thus far indicate that coloured immigrants were largely accepted as workers by the white employees
in the firms under consideration. This acceptance, however, was
largely of a negative nature. Few white workers were vehemently
opposed to the coloured workers, but at the same time, few had
a positively favourable attitude towards them. The majority,

other things being equal, would have preferred not to work with coloured workers.

(b) *Variables Affecting the Level of Work Acceptance*

In the previous section, we discussed work acceptance only in general terms. However, a number of factors appeared to affect the general level of acceptance. These included the number of coloured workers employed, the skill level of the jobs they obtained, their nationality, and the state of trade. Most of these topics have already been considered in relation to the employment and occupational level of coloured workers.

We noted in Chapter Three that some managers believed that whilst coloured workers were accepted in a minority, resentment might arise if they were employed in larger numbers. Little additional data on this question were obtained in the interviews with white workers, but if we accept that the majority of respondents would have preferred to work where only white people were employed, then it would seem reasonable to assume that they would be more prepared to accept coloured workers, the fewer were employed.

The interviews with white workers did, however, provide further evidence concerning variations in the level of work acceptance in relation to the level of job obtained by coloured workers. In the first two firms in which such interviews were carried out (Edge Tools and Omega Metals), nine of the eleven respondents stated that they were willing to accept coloured workers in their own job, but only four were prepared to accept coloured workers in a job above theirs. On subsequent interviews, white workers were asked to state whether they would be prepared to accept coloured workers in labouring, semi-skilled, skilled, and supervisory jobs respectively. Of the twelve respondents who replied to this question,[1] eleven stated that they were willing to accept coloured workers in labouring jobs, nine in semi-skilled jobs, seven in skilled jobs, and only one was prepared to accept a coloured worker as a supervisor.

It will be seen that whilst few white workers rejected coloured workers in any job whatsoever, the level of work acceptance tended to decrease the higher the status of job the coloured

[1] The question had to be omitted in two cases due to pressure of time.

worker obtained, and in particular, there was a general reluctance to accept a coloured worker in a supervisory position.

Furthermore, it should be noted that whilst these responses may represent the individual views of the white workers concerned, the general level of acceptance in the higher positions may be lower in a group situation. In Pentland Alloys Ltd. a foreman stated:

> You can't take what they say at face value. They talk like that (on job acceptance) when they are on their own and believe it, but it is a very different story when they get together, say at a Union meeting. A few people, about 10 per cent, will take a much harder viewpoint and the rest will fall into line with the others for fear of being out of step.

Similarly, a Union representative in Sterling Metal Co. stated that, although the majority of white workers did not mind coloured workers obtaining the higher jobs, there was always one trouble-maker who would make a fuss and eventually get the others on his side.

Nevertheless, there were cases in this firm, and in Steel Bars Ltd. where coloured workers had been promoted to the intermediate jobs in the rolling sets with white workers beneath them and had been accepted. Similarly, in Precision Engineers Ltd. and Drop Forgings Ltd. there were skilled coloured workers with white assistants. Thus, as the interviews with white workers would suggest, coloured workers are not invariably rejected in superior positions.

With regard to the nationality of the coloured workers employed, there was a general tendency for West Indians to be preferred as work-mates (see Table 10). The usual reason given was their ability to speak English and the fact that their way of life was more similar to that of British people.

TABLE 10 *National Preferences of White Workers*

West Indians	13
Pakistanis	3
Arabs	1
No preference	8
Total	25

Only in one firm however, did the British workers refuse to work with Asian immigrants.[1] In Central Glass Works, the white workers were consulted before coloured labour was employed. According to the Personnel Officer, the British workers had been prejudiced against Asian immigrants because of their sanitary habits and because of the fear of disease being spread. As a result, only West Indian workers were employed.

Finally, we turn to the effect of the state of trade on work acceptance. The majority of white workers (nineteen out of twenty-five) stated that, other things being equal, white workers should be given preference for jobs in the event of a recession. However, only three respondents claimed that white workers should still be given preference irrespective of the skill or length of service of the coloured workers. Of the remaining twenty-two respondents, nineteen stated that the coloured man should be given preference if he was more skilled or had worked for the firm longer, and three were undecided. This would suggest that white workers would be less prepared to accept new coloured workers in times of unemployment, but would not insist on existing coloured employees being made redundant first. Of course, it may be that the white workers would have been less impartial in a group situation, say at a union meeting. However, the fact that, with the exception of Castle Iron Co., 'last in, first out' seemed to be the generally accepted policy in cases of redundancy tends to support the interview responses.

(c) *Factors Causing Resentment of Coloured Workers*

We noted above that although most white workers accepted coloured immigrants as work-mates, they did so with some reservations. The majority, other things being equal, would have preferred to work where only white people were employed. What then were the reasons given for this preference?

The most common source of complaints concerning coloured workers was the general question of health and hygiene, particularly with respect to their alleged misuse of toilets. Management in thirty-seven out of a total of seventy-eight firms (interview and questionnaire surveys combined) and nine out of the twenty-five white workers interviewed stated that difficulties

---

[1] There was also one firm in the questionnaire survey in which it was stated that West Indians only were accepted.

over the 'toilet question' had been experienced. Such complaints occasionally occurred with respect to West Indian workers, but in the main, the difficulties were attributed to the different sanitary habits of Asians. As will be seen in Table 11, complaints concerning misuse of toilets occurred to a much greater extent in firms employing Asian workers than in those employing West Indians only.

TABLE 11   *Occurrence of Complaints concerning Misuse of Toilets*

	Firms employing Asians		Firms employing West Indians only	
	No.	*Total*	*No.*	*Total*
Reported by management	33 (55%)	60	4 (22%)	18
Reported by white workers	9	18	0	7

The Labour Officer of Westwood Foundry summed up the problem as follows: 'Asians wash rather than wipe, squat rather than sit. The result is feet marks on the seat and milk bottles being taken into the toilet.' A further difficulty reported in other firms was that the Asians would refuse to clean toilets because of religious taboos. This naturally caused resentment amongst the cleaning staff. The Labour Officer of Edge Tools Ltd. stated:

The firm has had some trouble on this question. If they cause a mess you cannot order an Asian to clean it up because he would leave. On the other hand, it is not fair to expect the cleaners to clear up after them.

Periodically the cleaners complain. I try to placate them the best I can and promise to do something about it. I then make a fuss about it to the Pakistani workmen, but there isn't anything I can do really. It is a very difficult problem.

In Omega Metals Ltd. hygiene was described as 'the biggest bug-bear' in the employment of Asian workers, and in Regal Manufacturing Co. the Personnel Manager stated that, in general, East Indians were not employed because they were 'not too clean in their personal habits'. The Labour Officer of Brierley Metal Works stated that the toilet problem was a most important question: 'If a man doesn't settle down, you can sack him. It is more difficult to find out whether he is using the toilet properly or at all.'

In Precision Engineers Ltd., according to the Personnel Director, the sanitary habits of Pakistanis were 'the only major factor causing friction between white and coloured workers'. An employee representative on the Workers' Council stated that the toilet question was beginning to cause trouble amongst the men and suggested that a note should be put in the wage packets of the coloured workers explaining the situation. This would hardly have had the desired effect; the majority of Pakistanis in this firm could not speak let alone read English and amongst the West Indians it would simply have caused resentment. A Personnel Officer in the same firm stated that management were at their wits' end to know what to do: the only logical solution was to provide separate toilets, but they did not want to do this because they were strongly opposed to segregation.

In other firms, however, this dilemma had been avoided. The Labour Officer of Westwood Foundry stated:

Because of the expansion of the labour force, new conveniences were needed. A new ablutions block was built to cater for the Easterner without segregation or discrimination. Asiatic toilets were provided as well as the ordinary British ones. The rule is that anyone can use anything provided he uses it properly. Anyone, white or coloured, not using them properly goes up the drive.[1]

Similarly, the Labour Officer of Brierley Metal Works said that Asian-type toilets had been provided because the coloured workers had different habits. There was no restriction on the use of European-type toilets, but the Asian workers preferred their own kind. This he stated had improved race relations considerably.

In all, Asian toilets had been installed in six[2] firms and were about to be installed in another firm[3] at the time the interview

---

[1] That means, is dismissed. However, on the one occasion an Asian had been caught misusing the toilets he had been dismissed but allowed to return to work two weeks later. The Labour Officer added that the provision of Asiatic toilets had not got round the milk bottle problem. However, the use of bottles had been prohibited and the Asians now used cubes and 'squeezy' jars for oiling purposes.

[2] Firms 2, 6, 7, 8, 12, and 13.

[3] Firm 14.

surveys were carried out. With the exception of Edge Tools Ltd. (see above), this solution had met with a large measure of success. In two firms, however, management were opposed to the provision of Asian toilets. The Personnel Officer of Grange Graphite Co. said that they had been advised by a race relations body to provide Asian toilets, but had refused to do so. Instead they had threatened firing if the toilets were not used properly, which had worked to some extent. In Sovereign Steel Works the Personnel Manager stated:

We haven't provided Asian toilets and we have no intention of doing so. They must adjust to our standards, just as we would have to adjust to theirs if we visited their country. To be blunt about the matter, we did not ask them to come here and so if they do come, they must use our standards. It's not too much to ask is it? They can't expect us to provide facilities to fit in with them.

Surprisingly enough, the above respondent was, in other respects, most sympathetic towards coloured workers and the problems they faced.

Although misuse of toilets was the most common objection to coloured workers, the question of hygiene also gave rise to other complaints. These included body odour,[1] breath odour,[2] spitting,[3] bringing disease into the country,[4] and so on. Whilst these complaints may be justified in some cases, there also appears to be a tendency for a high standard of cleanliness to be expected of coloured workers. In Precision Engineers Ltd., for example, supervisors had objected to the coloured workers because they urinated in one of the yards instead of going to the toilets. The Personnel Director pointed out to them that this was not applicable only to the coloured workers because there had been complaints about the white workers doing the same thing before coloured workers had been employed by the firm. Similarly, it was pointed out in several firms[5] that misuse of toilets was not confined to coloured workers. One respondent (Personnel Manager, Sterling Metal Co.) went so far as to say that Asian workers 'couldn't be any filthier than British workers'.

---

[1] Mentioned by five managers and two white workers.
[2] Mentioned by one manager and one white worker.
[3] Mentioned by two managers and three white workers.
[4] Mentioned by one manager and five white workers.
[5] Firms 8, 15, 16, 24, and 30.

Moreover, seven managers in the interview surveys stated that the coloured workers used the bathing facilities of the firms more than the white workers.[1] In Westwood Foundry, for example, the Labour Officer stated: 'Whereas the British workers rush off home in their dirt, the Indians take advantage of the ablutions and get washed and changed before going home.'

Apart from the question of hygiene, there were a variety of other complaints concerning coloured workers reported by management and workers. However, none of these occurred very frequently. Three managers in the questionnaire survey stated that the slow working pace of coloured workers (West Indians in two cases and Pakistanis in the other) had caused resentment. In one of these firms, the difficulty arose because West Indian workers did not take poorly paid piece work operations in their stride and thus caused work study investigations. However, only one of the white workers interviewed complained about the working pace of coloured workers.

With regard to the Asian workers, there were complaints that their inability to speak English gave rise to difficulties (six white workers), that they 'grabbed' components before anyone else when working on piece work (three white workers) and that they were a danger to other workers (two white workers). Three white workers complained that they would work for low wages and thus take the white man's job or ruin his bargaining position. In two cases (both in Omega Metals Ltd.) there would seem to be some justification for these accusations (see pages 145–7), but the third white worker admitted that under-cutting did not take place in his firm (Edge Tools Ltd.). Finally, a worker in Steel Bars Ltd. complained that Arab workers did not have to pay income tax. He stated:

These Arabs don't pay any tax. They all claim for seven or eight kids back in Aden. It's not right you know. They are living and working in this country and working alongside people who have to pay tax, so why shouldn't they pay tax as well. They only have to put in a couple of 'double ones' and they get paid more than a man who is more skilled than what they are. It's worth while for them to do double shifts because they get all the money, so they'll do one anytime you ask. You ask a white bloke to do a double shift and

[1] Firms 7, 9, 12, 17, 24, 26, and 27.

he'll say, 'Not likely they'll only take it off me again in tax.' It's not fair you know, something out to be done about it.

Resentment concerning Asian workers not paying income tax was also mentioned by managers in four interview survey firms[1] and complaints concerning language difficulties were reported in two firms in the questionnaire survey.

Objections to coloured workers in general included taking white workers' jobs (four white workers), touchiness (two white workers[2]), and living off the dole (three white workers). In some cases, however, the white workers made an obvious attempt to see the coloured workers' point of view. One, for example, stated that with work slacking off they ought to go back to their own country, but added that of course it wasn't much use them going back if there was nothing to do there. Another, after complaining that coloured workers lived off the dole, stated: 'Of course, a lot of firms won't employ them. If I left here I could get a job straight away. I wouldn't have to go on the dole. But they probably wouldn't be able to get a job.'

Finally, there were some indications that attitudes towards the coloured immigrant as a worker were influenced by relations in the community setting. In three firms[3] managers claimed that the main objections to coloured workers arose not from relations at work but from resentment of their living conditions. One stated:

I should say that 75 per cent of white workers are against coloured workers. This is not the working environment but the domestic environment and naturally it percolates through to works attitudes. (Production Services Manager, Blackford Rolling Mills)

In the interviews with white workers, one respondent objected to coloured workers on the ground that they seemed to obtain council houses much more easily than white people and a further five respondents objected to the living conditions (noise, overcrowding, etc.) of coloured people.

In spite of the above complaints about coloured immigrants, however, there appeared to be relatively little overt friction between British and coloured workers in the firms under con-

---

[1] Firms 22, 27, 28 and 29.
[2] In both cases the coloured workers referred to were West Indians.
[3] Firms 1, 5, and 30.

sideration. In fourteen firms managers specifically stated that no friction had occurred and in a further eleven firms none was mentioned. In the remaining firms experience varied. In Major Castings Ltd. the Personnel Manager stated that there was occasional friction due to individual prejudice on the shop-floor, and in Brierley Metal Works and Components Ltd., there had been occasional fights but, according to the managers concerned, these had been on an individual rather than a racial basis. In Sovereign Steel Works, the Personnel Manager stated, there was a tendency for some white employees 'to take liberties with the coloured workers—to push them around'. On occasions, this had led to fights and management had sacked the white worker and kept the coloured man—despite objections from the white workers in general—when they had felt that the fight had been caused by someone picking on a coloured man.

In Westwood Foundry, on the other hand, where a number of fights had occurred when coloured workers had first been employed, there was a strict rule that any fighting would result in the dismissal of *both* parties. According to the Labour Officer:

> The causes of the fight are not judged and there is no question of whose fault it was—both are out. This is because any judgment of blame would result in people gathering on both sides, and you might get two countries, each blaming the other, which would be too unwieldy to handle.

However, there had been little recent friction in this firm. The Labour Officer stated: 'Apart from little irritations and one or two fights one needn't even mention, white and coloured get on well together and work well together.'

Finally, in Steel Bars Ltd. there had been a fight between a British worker and an Arab which had resulted in the British worker being taken to hospital to have stitches put in a cut. The Arab was sent home for the day to allow tempers to cool. However, before he left for the hospital, the British worker told management that he did not want the Arab sacked as the fight had been entirely his own fault, and the two men shook hands the next day.

3. *Social Relations Between White and Coloured Workers*
From the discussion thus far it will be apparent that—in spite

of various obstacles such as the reluctance of firms to employ them, language difficulties on the part of Asian immigrants, their generally lower level of skill and so on—-coloured workers had achieved a relatively high degree of work integration in the firms under consideration. Though to some extent confined to the lower jobs, they had fitted into and become established as part of the formal organization; they were in general accorded equal treatment by management and accepted as work-mates, albeit with some reservations, by the white employees. When we come to examine social relations, however, a quite different pattern emerges. Whilst there was some variation both between and within firms, the general level of social integration was comparatively low.

It was possible to obtain adequate data on the pattern of social relations between white and coloured workers in only twenty-six of the thirty-one survey firms. In sixteen of these firms,[1] managers stated that white and coloured workers tended to remain in separate social groups when not actually working together. Examples include:

Personal relations are non-existent. They will work together when necessary, but after that it's finished. (Personnel Manager, Muirhead Foundry)

They mix during work, but they tend to segregate during lunch-breaks. (Works Manager, Annerley Iron Foundry)

The Englishmen don't want the coloured workers and they don't want the Englishmen. . . . They certainly don't mix at all. You never see English and coloureds sitting together on the company 'bus. You don't see them walking down the yard together either. The situation hasn't changed at all since 1956, and it shows no sign of changing. (Personnel Manager, Grange Graphite Co.)

There's nothing said, but the coloured workers don't go in to eat with the white workers. They sit around a stove in the works. They use the showers whereas the whites don't. (Works Manager, Stainless Steel Ltd.)

In the remaining ten firms[2] some degree of social integration had taken place. Often, however, the level of integration varied

---

[1] Firms 2, 6, 7, 10, 12, 14, 15, 16, 17, 18, 21, 22, 23, 25, 26, and 30.
[2] Firms 1, 3, 5, 9, 19, 20, 24, 27, 29, and 31.

either between different coloured groups or between different social situations.

In Leigham Cannery, according to the Personnel Officer, there was 'very good integration' between the white and coloured women, but the men tended to remain in separate groups. In Precision Engineers Ltd. it was reported that West Indians were in general well liked, whereas the Pakistanis, most of whom could not speak English, were less popular. Similarly, the Personnel Manager of Sterling Metal Co. stated that the Pakistanis kept to themselves, whereas the other coloured workers, Arabs and Somalis, mixed quite well with the white workers. This was supported by a Departmental Manager in Polton Rolling Mills who claimed that Arab and British workers mixed very well and were very friendly, but the Pakistanis tended to keep apart. In both firms, however, all the coloured workers tended to remain in their own national groups at meal times.

In Steel Bars Ltd., on the other hand, white and coloured workers ate and played cards together at the same tables in the canteen. There was, according to the Works Director, 'a fair bond of friendship bet·veen them'. On one occasion there had been a fight between two British workers, and before anyone else could intervene, the coloured workers had separated them and were holding them back. This incident is highly significant in that it shows that the coloured workers were sufficiently sure of their status to 'interfere' in a private quarrel. In spite of the close relationship at work, however, the coloured workers did not, in general, join in the works social outings. The main reason was that, as Moslems, they neither smoked nor drank, and the latter, according to the Works Director, constituted a considerable social handicap on such occasions.

By contrast, quite a few of the West Indian workers employed in Drop Forgings Ltd. went on works outings, according to the Personnel Manager. In Ensign Spring Co., however, where the coloured workers were also West Indians, they participated in work social activities only to a limited extent. Although socially accepted within the works environment, coloured women took no part in any of the outside social activities and the coloured men participated only in out-door events such as cricket. Neither used the works social club. The Personnel Manager thought that this was a good thing; he did not like the idea of white and coloured people drinking at the same table because it 'might lead to trouble'. In City Transport, on the other hand, the coloured workers did use the social club. Here white and coloured played dominoes and snooker together and the relationship between them was said to be very good. In general, however, white and coloured workers tended to segregate when eating.

In Hamilton Engineering Co., according to the Labour Officer, there had been no difficulty in integrating white and coloured workers; they had mixed very well and in one case the white workers had bought a West Indian a leaving-present. The West Indians' passionate love of cricket, he claimed, had made a significant contribution to their integration, particularly during the West Indies Test Series.

> The West Indians take part in works sports matches, especially cricket. We don't have any who are good enough to play in the works team, but they do play in inter-departmental matches. This usually entails a night out in the pavilion afterwards and they have mixed very well. All this helps without a doubt. It causes social groupings when they have things in common.

The attitude here, it will be noted, differs considerably from that expressed in Ensign Spring Co. (see above).

Finally, in Pentland Alloys Ltd. coloured workers were socially integrated at work, but no data were obtained concerning their participation in works social activities, or whether indeed such activities were organized in this firm.

To summarize: in contrast to work integration, only a relatively small degree of social integration had taken place in the firms visited in the course of the interview surveys. Adequate data concerning social relations were obtained in twenty-six firms: in sixteen firms white and coloured workers tended to remain in separate social groups when not actually working together and whilst social integration had occurred to some extent in the remaining ten firms, this was often limited to certain coloured groups or to certain social situations.

How then are we to account for this situation? Part of the answer undoubtedly lies in the attitudes of the white workers. In the questionnaire survey, the evidence suggests that the level of social acceptance is lower than that of work acceptance.

Although there had been an initial resistance to the employment of coloured workers in some cases, they were accepted as workmates in 94 per cent of firms by the time the present research was carried out. By comparison, only in 57·5 per cent of firms (twenty-three out of forty) was it stated that coloured workers were accepted socially. Similarly, in the interview surveys, although attitudes towards immigrants ranged from highly favourable on the one hand to highly unfavourable on the other, white workers were in general less inclined to accept coloured workers in social as opposed to work relationships.

Even in the realm of social relationships, however, it is somewhat of an over-simplification to describe the situation in terms of a single level of acceptance or rejection. As with work acceptance, there were indications that the level of social acceptance varied under different circumstances. Firstly, West Indians tended to be accepted in social situations to a greater extent than Asian workers. The general level of social acceptance was considerably higher in firms such as Hamilton Engineering Co. and Pentland Alloys Ltd. where only West Indians were employed, while in firms where both West Indians and Asians were employed, white workers were, in general, more prepared to mix socially with West Indians. However, the evidence of the questionnaire survey is far from conclusive. Although white workers were more willing to accept West Indians in nine firms compared with only two in which Asians were preferred, it was stated in the remaining seventeen firms answering this question that there was no difference between the different coloured nationalities with respect to the level of social acceptance.

Secondly, social acceptance appeared to be higher the fewer coloured workers there were. In Precision Engineers Ltd. a Personnel Officer stated that when only a few coloured workers had been employed, they had been great favourites and had almost been 'adopted' by the white workers. Later, when the number of coloured workers had increased, relations between white and coloured workers had tended to become less close. In several firms, it was found that when there was only one coloured worker in a department or work group, he tended to be accepted to a much greater extent than when there were even, say, four or five. In Pentland Alloys Ltd., for example, a white worker stated that the one coloured worker in his shop mixed socially with the white workers, but on other shifts, where there were more of them, they tended to 'mix more with each other rather than with whites'. Similarly, in Torrington Cutlers, a West Indian, again the only coloured worker in the shop, was accepted by the white workers whereas the others tended to remain in their own social group.

Finally, there were indications that the degree of social acceptance varied in different situations. We noted in the previous section that in several firms white and coloured workers mixed during work, but tended to separate on other occasions. In other firms, where in general little social integration had occurred, a similar pattern could still be found. In Annerley Iron Foundry a white worker stated: 'They're sociable. I wouldn't say they mix, but they will talk to one another while they're working.' Similarly, in Ridgeway Steel Co., where the majority of coloured workers were employed in work groups under a white supervisor, a shop manager said that white and coloured workers never ate together and never sat together, but they did laugh and joke together sometimes when their work brought them into proximity with each other.

However, one coloured worker in this firm, a boiler firer who was employed in a team with white workers, was said to have 'very cordial relations' with his white work-mates. Of course, this may partly be due to the fact that the coloured worker in question was more prepared to mix socially with white workers because there were no other coloured workers in the group. Nevertheless, there did seem to be a tendency for coloured workers to be accepted to a much greater extent, both socially and as workers, where they worked with white workers on the same job, either as the mate to a skilled man as in Pentland Alloys Ltd. and Stainless Steel Ltd., or as members of the same work group as in the rolling teams in Steel Bars Ltd. and Sovereign Steel Works.

However, the most noticeable difference in the level of social acceptance was between the work and the community environment. One manager[1] went so far as to say: 'Any friendship between white and coloured ends at the works gate.' As a generalization this appears to hold true for the majority of white workers interviewed during the present research. Even

[1] Personnel Director, Precision Engineers Ltd.

those white workers who were willing to accept coloured immigrants as friends at work were, in the main, unwilling to do so outside.

> I wouldn't go out of my way to avoid them—I do talk to them when I see them out—but I prefer my own countrymen as personal friends. (White worker, Leigham Cannery)

> No I wouldn't really accept a coloured worker as a friend outside the works. If I saw my mate, I would acknowledge him but. . . . (White worker, Pentland Alloys Ltd.)

In some cases white workers had mixed socially with their coloured work-mates outside the works, but this tended to be seen as an exception to a general rule.

> I would accept a coloured man as a friend inside the works but not outside. I have taken my mate to a boxing match in Manchester and things like that, but I don't mix with them in general. (White worker, Pentland Alloys Ltd.)

> I shouldn't really pal with them. Well we have done on occasions —we have taken one or two on works trips—but not usually. But these we have here are exceptional. (White worker, Steel Bars Ltd.)

Where coloured workers were not accepted socially at work, rejection of them in the community environment tended to be much more vehement.

> I wouldn't live beside them. Once my day's work's done, I don't want anything to do with them. I wouldn't want to make friends with one outside the job. (White worker, Omega Metals Ltd.)

> A Jamaican has moved in near my house. A neighbour has moved out and I shall have to move soon. It will become a slum area— radios going all the time. If I had the money, I would go to Australia or New Zealand where they're not permitted. (White worker, Omega Metals Ltd.)

Nevertheless, one exception should be noted. A white worker in Leigham Cannery who was unwilling to accept coloured immigrants at work—mainly on the grounds that they were taking jobs from white people—was much more willing to accept them in the community environment. 'I should be friendly outside, but I don't want one working with me. Outside is different from working with them.' The respondent did, in fact, have one coloured friend outside the works. He stated: 'There's a West Indian that I have a drink with in the —— Hotel. He's a real nice chap—a grand fellow in every respect. But he's the only one I come into contact with.'

The existence of these variations in the level of social acceptance leaves us with two problems. Firstly, to explain why it was, in general, relatively low; and secondly, to explain why it varied under different circumstances.

Amongst white workers, the main reason given for the relatively low level of social integration at work was the fact that coloured workers came from a different cultural background and thus had, to a greater or lesser extent, different customs, values, and interests. The question of differences in values occurs in Richmond's[1] theory of race relations and also that of Carey.[2] However, both place much emphasis upon the beliefs of white people concerning the different *sexual* values of Negroes. Richmond states, for example, that insecurity amongst whites who are uncertain how to behave towards Negroes is 'aggravated by the belief that coloured people have different values especially with regard to sex'. Similarly, Carey suggests that the stereotype of the Negro as a sexually uninhibited and highly potent being, constitutes a threat to British values in matters of sex. Whilst such beliefs may have some relevance in the community environment, in the present research there was little to suggest that they influenced attitudes towards coloured immigrants at work. Only rarely did the question of sex arise, and even in these cases the evidence was inconclusive.

In only one of the interview survey firms was it suggested that matters relating to sex had influenced the British workers' attitude towards coloured immigrants. The Production Services Manager of Blackford Rolling Mills stated:

There seems to be more resentment against the Pakistanis than the others. They appear to have worse living conditions and appear to get away with more things. The Pakistanis are notorious for their relations with girls. Our workers have high average age and have daughters of their own and therefore there is resentment. And in one or two cases the daughters have been involved with Pakistanis.

---

[1] 'The Study of Race Relations', *Man.*
[2] A. D. Carey, op. cit.

Unfortunately, it was not possible to interview the white workers in this firm and therefore confirmation of this statement could not be obtained. However, it will be noted that whereas the theories of both Carey and Richmond are concerned with beliefs about the sexual values of Negroes, the resentment in this case was directed against Pakistanis.

Amongst the white workers interviewed, only one mentioned the matter of sex in relation to coloured workers. A white worker in Pentland Alloys Ltd. stated:

> I can't stand talking smut with coloured chaps about white women. Some of them (other white workers) delight in it, but I don't think it redounds to anybody's credit. Their sense of humour is different and I don't think it is a good idea to talk that way with them. My mate is all right. He doesn't talk smut.

Even here, however, the respondent's concern over this matter did not appear to influence his attitude towards coloured workers unduly. He was, in fact, quite favourably disposed towards coloured immigrants; he stated that he would not prefer to work where only white people were employed, spoke very highly of his West Indian mate, and was one of the few white workers who was not in favour of immigration restriction. The question of sex received no more emphasis than many other topics he talked about during the interview and the stereotype —that the coloured worker's sense of humour in relation to sex was different—was in any case relatively mild. He did not, for example, suggest that their sexual *behaviour* was different or even that all coloured workers 'talked smut'. Moreover, he blamed the white workers for encouraging their coloured work-mates to 'talk smut' about white women as much as he blamed the coloured workers themselves.[1]

During the management interviews, however, there was one case in which a highly unfavourable attitude towards coloured workers occurred in conjunction with stereotyped beliefs concerning coloured people and extreme prejudice in matters of sex. The respondent in question was the Departmental Manager in Sovereign Steel Works whose views we have already discussed

---

[1] The further point arises that if, as the respondent claimed, the coloured workers were encouraged to 'talk smut' then it would appear that at least some of the white workers did not object to the coloured workers discussing their experiences with white women.

in Chapter Six. This respondent, it will be remembered, stated that coloured people were dirty and uncivilized in their own countries and that he could not stand the idea of white women going out with coloured men. He also claimed that coloured workers were 'an idle set of black bastards' and yet later denied that he had said that they were not good workers. It seems likely, therefore, that the respondent's adverse assessment of coloured workers was motivated by prejudice, in which sexual rivalry was a major factor, rather than any objective appraisal of their work performance. By contrast, a foreman in Sovereign Steel Works who was also unfavourably disposed towards coloured workers, appeared to have a quite tolerant attitude towards mixed marriages. The respondent stated that 80 per cent of coloured workers were no good and yet spoke with considerable sympathy of one particular man, a Somali, whose white wife had left him. He was highly critical of the woman concerned who had, he stated, deserted the Somali although he had provided her with 'a good home and everything a girl could ask for'.

Thus it would appear that beliefs concerning the sexual values of coloured people do not play a major role in determining attitudes towards coloured immigrants at work. The vast majority of respondents did not mention the subject and amongst those who did the evidence was contradictory.

More important than beliefs concerning particular values seems to have been the image of the coloured man as a stranger —someone unacquainted with British norms and values in general. This seems to have been at the root of much of the initial resistance to coloured workers reported in several firms.

We had quite a lot of difficulty getting coloured workers accepted at first. At that time it was something new. . . . It was just the fact that they were a different nationality. (Shop steward, Major Castings Ltd.)

In the early days, there was a certain amount of natural resentment at the chargehand level. This was probably just because they were different. Over time, particularly when they got to know them as individuals, this began to break down. (Personnel Officer, Leigham Cannery)

When the blacks first came, they (the white workers) were afraid of them. There wasn't any trouble between them, but they were afraid of them—some of them were hot-heads. (White worker, Steel Bars Ltd.)

Actually, when they first came, I didn't fancy the idea, but it's turned out all right. It was just that strangeness you know. (White worker, Pentland Alloys Ltd.)

As we have already noted, and as the above examples indicate, this initial resistance to coloured workers tended to diminish in time. The white workers became accustomed to the coloured immigrants, sufficiently at least to accept them as workers, and in some cases friendships developed. The last respondent above, for example, in spite of his initial misgivings over the employment of coloured workers, said of his West Indian mate during the interview: 'He's one of the nicest personalities I've ever met. He takes everything in his stride. You can't help but like him.' More often, however, the white workers' image of the coloured immigrant as a stranger seems to have inhibited the growth of close social relationships.

This was particularly so in the case of Asian workers, where the desire to maintain social distance was often attributed directly to differences in cultural background.

It's not a matter of colour—it's their way of life. (White worker, Omega Metals Ltd., with respect to Pakistanis)

Myself, I can tolerate them, but I can't be friendly towards them. If you're friendly they take advantage of the fact. If they would change their ways and habits, there would be no difference. (Chargehand, Edge Tools Ltd., with respect to Indians and Pakistanis)

They're different. They had different habits, different religion, different hygiene. (Shop steward, Major Castings Ltd. with respect to Pakistanis)

West Indians, on the other hand, tended to be regarded as being less different from British people and therefore easier to get on with and easier to understand, both in terms of language and motivation. This seems to have been the main reason for the somewhat higher level of social acceptance of West Indians noted above.

I would rather have the Jamaican. He has the same way of life. He eats the same way as you do. He speaks the same language. When in Rome do as the Romans do—if you want to get on with him. (White worker, Omega Metals Ltd.)

They're too sly and oily for me. You can see it when they look at you, in their eyes. It isn't the Jamaicans I'm against—there are some decent chaps amongst the Jamaicans—it's these Indians. (White worker, Edge Tools Ltd.)

West Indians are all right—they do know our language. I would prefer them to Arabs or Pakistanis. The West Indians, they understand. The Arabs and Pakistanis, maybe they understand—when they want to. They're not out in the open like the West Indians. (White worker, Leigham Cannery)

The Jamaicans seem to be the easiest going. Some Pakistanis seem a bit moody. (White worker, Leigham Cannery)

Nevertheless, there was still a tendency for West Indians to be regarded as being, to some extent at least, strangers. A supervisor in Omega Metals Ltd., for example, stated that he preferred West Indians because their way of life was more similar to his own *up to a point*. In Pentland Alloys Ltd. a white worker spoke of some West Indians appearing to have come 'straight from the jungle'. He stated:

They come over here with remarkable ideas. One of them was a voodoo worshipper—he went off the rails eventually. . . . One thing I get on to them about is the way that they jabber when they get excited. I have to tell them to slow down so that I can understand what they're talking about.

Another white worker, in Leigham Cannery, was under the impression that English was not the West Indians' native language. He thought that they were taught it in the schools. Similarly two West Indians in Hamilton Engineering Co. commented, somewhat ruefully, that some English people were surprised that they could speak English so well.

Apart from the fact that white workers tended to regard coloured immigrants as being strangers, however, there is also evidence to suggest that they regarded them as being of lower status. One indication is the greater reluctance to accept coloured workers in the higher status jobs and particularly as supervisors.[1] Another is the reluctance, noted in Drop Forgings Ltd., to work for a firm which has acquired the reputation of being a coloured works.[2] A third is to be found in a report of one of the questionnaire firms that 'The white workers expect higher earnings than the coloured man despite the fact that they may be doing the same job.'

Furthermore, there was a tendency amongst white workers to regard themselves as being better workmen than the coloured immigrants. Among the twenty-five white workers interviewed, twelve thought that coloured workers were slower to learn than British workers, eighteen that they showed little initiative, ten that they were less intelligent than British workers,[3] and sixteen that they required more supervision. After the first eleven interviews, a further question was asked regarding the skill level of coloured workers. Ten respondents stated that they were less skilled than British workers, three that they were 'about the same' and one gave a non-committal answer.

This is not to say that these respondents had a uniformly low opinion of coloured immigrants as workmen. There was a considerable range of opinion and some of the answers were quite favourable. Nevertheless, all but two of the twenty-five respondents stated that coloured workers were inferior to white workers in at least one of the factors we have considered—skill, speed of learning, initiative, intelligence, and supervisory requirements—and none said that they were superior.

Some further comments made during the interviews also suggested that the white workers felt that they had superior status.

[1] In this context, it is interesting to note that one of the respondents in Edge Tools stated that he would accept a coloured university student in a superior job, but not a coloured worker from the shop-floor. As he obviously would not have required such high qualifications in the case of a white worker, this provides an apt illustration of the thesis that the coloured man has to go one better in order to obtain an equal position.

[2] Both the above points are also made by Sheila Patterson, op. cit.; see page 21 above.

[3] It is doubtful, however, whether some of the respondents clearly distinguished between intelligence *per se* and other factors such as education, cultural background, or merely ability to cope with working in British industry. One, for example, stated that some coloured workers had become more intelligent since joining the firm, but most of them still couldn't speak English; another stated that West Indians were more intelligent than Asians, having been taught English at school; whilst a third said that coloured workers who had lived in towns and been to school would be more intelligent than those who had been in agriculture.

These blokes here, cheap labour that's all it is. They have a low standard of living in their own country. . . . The boss would like to bring us down to their level if he could. (Omega Metals Ltd.)

Some of the coloured workers on night duty work very hard. Mind you, when you've finished, they're only doing woman's work. Women do their jobs in the day time. (Leigham Cannery)

I don't think a white man would come and do the kind of jobs they get. . . . There isn't so many white labourers now; they are mainly black men. (Hamilton Engineering Co.)

Some of the Arabs are pretty docile—a bit like little kids. (Steel Bars Ltd.)

You've got to use your patience to teach them because coming to work over here must be a terrible jolt to these kids. (Pentland Alloys Ltd.)

However, it is not sufficient merely to show that the white workers believed that coloured immigrants were of a lower social status, we must also demonstrate that these beliefs affected the level of social acceptance. The evidence here is mainly of an indirect nature. As we noted in Chapter Two, Banton[1] suggested that British people were not sure of the correct norms of conduct concerning coloured immigrants, mainly because the latter refused to enter into relationships in the role of a social inferior. There were several indications in the present research that the white workers experienced some difficulty in achieving a pattern of behaviour in relation to coloured immigrants which was acceptable to both parties.

In Major Castings Ltd. a shop steward stated:

I've always found it best to lean over backwards to be fair. They've had preferential treatment. We have always been very careful not to give them the chance to claim that they were not getting fair treatment because of their colour.

Similarly, in Torrington Cutlers, the Works Director said of the white workers:

They will sometimes be particularly nice to the coloured workers. More so than they would be to their own colleagues under the same circumstances. . . . This would appear to be a special attempt not to be condescending to the coloured people.

[1] *White and Coloured.*

In the same firm a white worker stated:

We always have the difficulty that when we try to tell them any-thing, they think we are trying to impose on them. . . . The chap in our department has come with a chip on his shoulder. His attitude is that, when we are trying to teach him anything, we are trying to take advantage of him.

Nevertheless, the respondent stated that, in a way, he got on very well with the coloured worker concerned. 'He resents being pushed around, but looks upon me as a father confessor in a way. Anything he doesn't understand, he'll come and ask me.'

This suggests that as long as the coloured worker was pre-pared to accept the role of a social inferior, asking for advice, he was accepted, but resentment arose when he refused to accept this kind of relationship. Further evidence to this effect was found in other firms. In Precision Engineers Ltd., it was stated that West Indians were very popular because they could be kidded, for instance, on how many wives or children they had, the coloured workers accepting such kidding with good humour. However, the fact that West Indians were sometimes able to buy a car (a symbol of status) by clubbing together, caused resent-ment amongst the white workers who could not afford one. In one of the questionnaire firms, where Indian workers were not socially accepted, it was said that resentment arose because they 'aped superiority' over the white workers. On the other hand, in Steel Bars Ltd., where the Arab workers were accepted socially, a white worker stated: 'I'll say this for them; if you do them an act of kindness of any kind, they do appreciate it.'

Finally, there were two cases in which white respondents were very favourably disposed towards particular coloured workers because they accepted the role of a coloured man. In Pentland Alloys Ltd. a white worker stated:

We have had incidents—one in particular is very touchy—if you snap at them, they say it's because they're coloured. My mate knows he's coloured. We had seen something on television about coloured Americans, and he said, 'Well, I'm a coloured Englishman' and I said 'Of course you are.' . . . He's a great kid, my mate, but we've had some funny ones. He doesn't interfere. I like him.

And in Sovereign Steel Works a foreman stated with respect to a Somali:

You couldn't hope to meet a nicer bloke. We know 80 per cent of them's no good, but he's a real good bloke. One thing about him, he *knows* he's coloured. You can say to him: 'Why don't you come in early one morning and we'll take a scrubbing brush and see if it will come off,' and he sees the joke and laughs with you.

Thus far, we have been concerned mainly with the attitudes of the white workers. As the above examples indicate, however, the attitudes of the coloured workers are also of vital importance in determining the pattern of inter-group relations at work. In the questionnaire survey respondents were asked whether the coloured workers showed willingness to mix socially with white workers or seemed to prefer to keep to themselves. The answers obtained are presented in Table 12.

TABLE 12   *Coloured Workers' Orientations towards Social Relationships with White Workers*

	No. of firms replying for each group	No. stating prefer to keep to themselves	%
West Indians	36	24	67
Indians	13	10	77
Africans	11	9	82
Arabs	12	11	92
Pakistanis	31	29	94

In one firm, employing West Indians, Arabs, and Pakistanis, the following additional comment was made:

Socially, the coloured workers tend to keep to themselves. This is in no way as a result of a 'cold shoulder' by the whites, and is more a voluntary situation. In other words, segregation is as much the choice of the coloureds as the whites. We have a social club, membership of which is open to all employees, coloured and white, but the coloured population are not interested.

It will be noted, however, that in general the tendency to remain in separate social groups was more marked in the case of

Asian workers, particularly Pakistanis.[1] The main reason for this would seem to be radical cultural differences between Asian and British workers. Of primary importance, of course, is the language barrier; the Asian workers do not speak English as their native language and relatively few have learned it. Nevertheless, this does not provide the whole explanation. Unlike the West Indians, Asian workers have their own distinct culture with customs, habits, and religious beliefs which differ markedly from those of the British workers. In the firms studied during the present research, Asian workers were in general willing to make only those adjustments to the British way of life which were necessary in order to achieve a minimum degree of integration into the work organization. Apart from this, they retained as many of their own cultural traits as possible and therefore tended to remain in their own social groups where little or no adaptation to British ways would be required. In two firms, for example, the Asian workers' eating habits led to voluntary segregation at meal times. The situation in Bradfield Foundry has already been described in the introduction to the present chapter. Similarly, in Omega Metals Ltd., the British workers and the one West Indian employed by the firm ate in the works canteen whereas the Pakistanis remained on the shop-floor and 'ate curry out of pans with chapatis'.

In the latter firm, there were also indications that the Pakistanis kept apart from the white workers as a means of avoiding friction. When asked how the British and the Pakistani workers got on together, the Pakistani chargehand stated that they were, '. . . not friendly, but not unfriendly. They (the Pakistanis) can't speak English so nobody quarrels. They don't argue, they just keep working.'

The greater willingness of the West Indians to mix socially may be attributed to the fact that, not only is their cultural background more similar to that of the white workers, but also, due to the 'mother country' image of Britain in the West Indies, they are much more willing to seek full acceptance into British society. Nevertheless, the fact remains that in a high proportion

[1] There were indications that Indians (see questionnaire survey results) and Arabs (see interview survey firms, Sterling Metal Co., Polton Rolling Mills and Steel Bars Ltd., page 181) were more willing to mix socially with the white workers than the Pakistanis, but the number of firms involved in each case is too small to permit firm conclusions to be drawn.

of firms, they tended to remain in their own social groups. Part of the explanation may be that, although there were no radical cultural differences, as in the case of Asian workers, there still existed differences in interests and topics of conversation sufficient to make the West Indians feel more at ease in the company of their fellow countrymen. One white worker stated that West Indians remained in their own social groups because they had 'their own things to talk about' and another stated: 'It's just the ordinary talk of everyday things they can't get into.' It is quite possible, of course, that the white workers merely assumed that the West Indians had different interests and therefore made no effort to associate with them. However, a similar point was made by a West Indian in Torrington Cutlers who stated:

I've got on all right with white workers because I like sports—football, racing, cricket—so we talk about it. But if I didn't have this, I wouldn't get on so well.

On the other hand, it would seem that the West Indians' tendency to remain with their own social groups resulted, to some extent at least, from the lack of social acceptance on the part of the white workers. When asked why the coloured workers tended to keep to themselves, a white worker in Quality Steel Co. stated: 'It's not language—Jamaicans speak good English. There's some of them think and others know that they are not wanted here.' Similarly, in Sovereign Steel Works, the Personnel Manager stated:

You tend to see them sitting having a meal in a corner rather than mixing in a group. They tend to have a chip on their shoulder. . . . There is a tendency to carry a constant concern about their relations with white people and it will be many years before they lose this. They carry their own colour bar about with them and tend to view our approaches a little suspiciously. They tend to meet people who do not treat them well—the odd one or two—so you can't blame them.

In its extreme form, this attitude was rarely encountered amongst the West Indians interviewed during the present research. In only two cases was any marked resentment of white workers expressed. In Torrington Cutlers a West Indian worker stated:

I'll tell you one thing I don't like. The reason why some of us have a chip on our shoulder is because people say: 'Why you come here?' They think that we come here to steal their jobs. But the world owes everyone a living. If they came to Jamaica we would welcome them. We would not ask why they come.

And in Omega Metals Ltd. a West Indian was extremely bitter about his relations with white workers. He stated:

Well I'll be frank with you . . . you get some of them—they're educated, but they're ignorant—they've got a chip on their shoulder. In the canteen the other day, one of them said: 'If there was another war, I bet you would go back to Jamaica.' I said, yes I would. If you live in a country, you ought to fight for it, but what's the point if you are just a 'wog' or a 'black' after the fighting has finished. The way things are going, if you were in the trenches, one of them would kill you instead of the enemy.

However, twenty-six of the twenty-seven West Indians interviewed, including the first respondent above, stated that they got on all right with the British workers. Sixteen respondents stated that they had found white workers friendly, and in two cases highly favourable attitudes towards white workers were encountered.

Well I'll tell you, I'm finding it all right. People have treated me very well. You couldn't have expected them to be any better. Whilst I have been in this country there has been no-one who hasn't been good. We are all living just the same and working just the same. (West Indian, Hamilton Engineering Co.)

I get on very well with the white workers. They are very friendly. It's better than with my own people. (West Indian, Pentland Alloys Ltd.)

In six cases it was said that whilst the majority of white workers were friendly, there were some who were not. However, little resentment was expressed and the general attitude seemed to be that it was best to ignore any unpleasantness which occurred.

I get on all right. You will find a few who are awkward, but if you don't take any notice, it don't go far. (West Indian, Annerley Iron Foundry)

I get along all right with them and they get along all right with me. There's a few of course that's nasty, but there's good and bad in every nation. . . . You haven't got to take any notice. You might hear people say bad things, but the best thing to do is to take no notice. (West Indian, Edge Tools Ltd.)

In only one case, however, was there any evidence that the West Indians kept apart from white workers as a result of the white workers' behaviour. A respondent in Torrington Cutlers stated: 'I don't put it in their way to make any fuss. If you're working here and you don't talk to me, I just don't talk.'

Thus in general, the interviews with West Indian workers suggest that relations with white workers were much closer and more friendly than appeared to be the case in the interviews with British respondents, both managers and workers. This inconsistency, the writer would suggest, results from a tendency on the part of the West Indians to present a more favourable account of inter-group relations at work than was actually justified. This may be attributed to two factors. Firstly, the West Indians were hurt and disappointed by the fact that the level of social acceptance was lower than they had expected and therefore tended to ignore as much as possible the incidence of unfriendliness or antagonism on the part of white workers. In Edge Tools Ltd., for example, a West Indian worker stated: 'I would like to say that they are friendly because they haven't treated me bad. Until they do, I would like to say that they are friendly.' And in the same firm, another West Indian said: 'I would have to say that they have treated me well. I haven't had any fuss—I just get along. If somebody else have difference, that's not my business.' Thus in both cases, the respondents stated that the white workers had treated them well or had been friendly simply because they had not been actively unfriendly. Under these circumstances it seems likely that the West Indians would remain within their own groups as a means of avoiding overt social rejection on the part of the white workers.

Secondly, the writer gained the impression during the interviews with coloured workers that the fact that the interviews were carried out within the works environment with the approval of management tended to make respondents reluctant to be critical either of working conditions or of their relations with white workers. An attempt was therefore made to arrange interviews outside work, but with little success. Ironically enough, at a meeting of a West Indian society visited for this purpose, one of the workers interviewed in Hamilton Engineering Co. approached the writer and said that he had not given an accurate account of the situation at his firm because it was impossible to do so at work. However, he refused to provide any further information, and none of the other West Indians present were willing to be interviewed.

We may now summarize our data and conclusions with regard to social relations between white and coloured workers. The relatively low level of social as opposed to work integration may be attributed both to a lower level of social acceptance on the part of the white workers and to a tendency for the coloured workers to remain with their own social groups. In the case of the white workers, avoidance of coloured immigrants in social situations seems to result from two main factors. Firstly, coloured immigrants tend to be regarded as strangers—people unused to British ways. This is most marked in the case of Asian workers, where fundamental differences in cultural background exist. However, West Indians are also regarded as strangers to some extent; they are thought to have different interests and in some cases erroneous beliefs concerning their cultural background were encountered. Secondly, coloured immigrants were regarded as being of lower social status. There was little evidence to suggest that this was a direct cause of avoidance of immigrants in social situations, although this may well be the case in view of the fact that the question of status seems to be an important factor in the avoidance of coloured immigrants in certain work relationships. However, there was evidence that ambiguities in the status of coloured immigrants did affect the pattern of inter-group relations. Richmond[1] suggests avoidance of coloured people arises not because they have low status, but because they do not fit into the British system of social stratification at all. The evidence of the present research, on the other hand, suggests that if the coloured immigrant does not have a status in the British hierarchy, it is because he is unwilling to accept the one available to him, that of a coloured man who 'knows' he is coloured and is willing to accept a lower status role.

In the case of coloured workers, the tendency of Asian workers

[1] 'The Study of Race Relations', *Man*.

to remain within their own social groups was attributed to the fact that their cultural background differed radically from that of the white workers and they wished to make as little adjustment to the British way of life as possible. The West Indians' way of life is much more similar to that of the white workers and in general they were much more willing to mix socially with them. Nevertheless, they still tended to remain in separate social groups in a high proportion of firms and this was attributed to two factors: firstly, differences in interests and topics of conversation; and, secondly, a reluctance to risk social rejection by the white workers. However, owing to the inconclusive results obtained from the interviews with West Indian workers, it is impossible to judge the relative importance of these two factors on the basis of the present data.

We now turn to the variations in the level of social integration found in different firms during the interview survey. The relatively low social integration of Asian workers, particularly Pakistanis, would seem to result from the fact that their cultural background differed so radically from that of the white workers. For this reason, not only were white workers less prepared to accept them socially, but also the Asian workers themselves were less willing to mix socially with the white workers. In general, the writer gained the impression that the Pakistanis were even more unfamiliar with British ways than either the Indians or the Arabs, most of whom were Adenese, which may account for the slightly higher level of social integration of the latter two groups.

The greater social integration in work groups or departments where there were few coloured immigrants may be explained in terms of a number of factors we have already discussed. Where there are relatively few coloured immigrants it follows that:

(1) The actual or ascribed cultural differences will constitute less of a threat to the values of the group, as the immigrants will not be in a position to dictate the form these values will take.

(2) The presence of the immigrants is less likely to constitute a threat to the prestige of the group.

(3) The immigrants are more likely to be perceived as individuals rather than simply as members of a stranger group and there is therefore a greater likelihood that common ground for social relationships will be found.

(4) There will be less opportunity for the coloured immigrants to withdraw into their own social group, either because of cultural differences or because they fear social rejection.

Finally, there were the situational variations in the level of social integration. These seemed to follow a definite pattern. Social acceptance of coloured workers was higher, the more the relationship occurred within the realm of the work organization. In general, white workers were less prepared to accept coloured immigrants socially than as workers; less prepared to mix socially with coloured workers during lunch and tea breaks than whilst actually working with them; less prepared to mix socially with them when they did not work on the same job; and were still less willing to mix socially with coloured immigrants outside the works than within.

The most tenable explanation of this occurrence would seem to be that of Banton.[1] Firstly, the British worker will tend to be less concerned about loss of prestige when his association with coloured workers is legitimized by the work relationship. As one white worker put it, when asked how he felt about working in a firm which employed coloured immigrants: 'That's up to the firm; that's the firm's business.' (Quality Steel Co.)

Similarly, being friendly towards coloured immigrants during the course of work does not have the same connotations as being friendly during tea and lunch breaks or outside the works environment. Contact in the first case results from factors largely beyond the control of the white worker—managerial decisions concerning the placing of employees—whereas in the latter it results from a deliberate choice on the part of the white worker concerned. Where there is a close, formal work relationship, then mixing socially with coloured workers during tea and lunch breaks may be justified by the fact that the white worker concerned is not associating with simply any coloured worker but rather with a member of his team or work group. Such considerations do not apply, however, outside the works environment where the existence of such a formal relationship would not be known to anyone observing the association.

Secondly, the more the association is based upon a work relationship, the less important will be differences in norms and values because the work relationship restricts the range of social

[1] *White and Coloured.*

interaction. If, for example, the association merely consists of friendly words exchanged in passing during work, then it is possible to discuss only trivial matters which are unlikely to involve underlying differences in values. Furthermore, this provides the white worker with a greater control over the nature of the relationship. Being friendly with coloured workers in one situation does not necessarily imply willingness to extend the relationship to other situations such as tea-breaks or outside work. Thus, differences in norms and values which might make the white worker reluctant to accept coloured immigrants in unstructured situations are less likely to inhibit friendship based on a work relationship because the white worker can employ the norms governing work-relationships to control the extent of social interaction.

4. *Social Relations Between Different Coloured Nationalities*

In the previous section, we saw that although white and coloured workers, in general, worked amicably together, the level of social integration was relatively low. A similar pattern emerged with respect to the different coloured groups where more than one coloured nationality was employed by the same firm. In the questionnaire survey, respondents were asked whether the different coloured nationalities:

(1) readily accepted each other as work-mates; and

(2) mixed socially with each other (e.g. during tea and lunch breaks) or tended to remain within their own national groups. The answers received (see Tables 13 and 14) indicate that the different coloured nationalities were, in most cases, prepared to accept each other as work-mates, but tended to remain separate in the realm of social relationships.

TABLE 13   *Work Relations between different Coloured Nationalities*

	No.	%
Accept each other as work-mates	25	81
Do not accept each other as work-mates	6	19
Total	31	100

TABLE 14   *Social Relations between different Coloured Nationalities*

	No.	%
Mix socially	9	28
Mix socially to a certain extent	3	9
Remain in national groups	20	63
Total	32	100

Data concerning social relations between the different coloured nationalities were obtained in fifteen of the interview survey firms,[1] and in each case it was stated that they tended to remain in separate social groups. This applied not only to relations between West Indian and Asian workers, but also with respect to the different Asian nationalities. Some comments of the managers concerned were as follows:

There is a fair degree of mutual segregation between the Pakistanis and the West Indians. I get the impression that there is more mixing between white and Pakistani and between white and Jamaican. On the night shift, the Pakistanis and West Indians tend to work in separate teams. They seem to like it that way so we leave them to it. (Personnel Officer, Leigham Cannery)

They tend to circumscribe themselves within their own groups. Although we (i.e. management) classify Arabs and Pakistanis together, they themselves keep apart. Although of the same faith, they do not appear to get on very well together. . . . We have never had any real trouble, physical violence or anything like that. They just tend to ignore one another. (Production Services Manager, Blackford Rolling Mills)

They keep to themselves. Naturally it is a question of language. You tend to see the Pakistanis grouped together in the canteen and you see the Arabs grouped together. They don't mix—they couldn't understand one another so there wouldn't be much point. They work amicably together though; we have never had any trouble. (Labour Officer, Polton Rolling Mills)

In eight firms altogether it was specifically stated that no friction between the different coloured groups had occurred,[2]

[1] Firms 1, 2, 6, 7, 14, 15, 16, 19, 20, 22, 23, 24, 26, 27, and 30.
[2] Firms 1, 8, 13, 16, 21, 22, 27, and 30.

and in a further eight firms employing more than one coloured nationality none was mentioned by the managers interviewed.[1] In seven firms, however, some friction had occurred.[2] In two cases, this had largely died out by the time the interview survey was carried out. In Sovereign Steel Works, where the majority of coloured workers were Arabs and Pakistanis, the Personnel Manager stated:

> We used to have trouble over religion in the early days. They have sorted this out themselves. The Works Manager got them all together and told them that if there was any more trouble, they would all be dismissed.

Similarly, in Westwood Foundry there had been some friction between Indians and Pakistanis on political and religious grounds when they were first employed. According to the Labour Manager, drastic action had put an end to it. The Indians and Pakistanis were told that they were on trial and that if there was any more trouble they would be dismissed.

In Westwood Foundry there had also been friction between Indian and West Indian workers. When they were first employed, the West Indians were split into two groups. On one shift, they were spread out amongst the other workers, and on the other they were put in two 'pockets' on their own. Where they were in 'pockets', according to the Labour Manager, the Indians did much more work than the West Indians and made fun of them for this reason. For example, they suggested to a supervisor that a conveyor-belt should be built to the toilet because the West Indians were going there so often. Where they were spread out amongst the other workers, the Labour Manager stated, a fight arose because a West Indian called an Indian a 'black bastard' although he was himself several shades darker.

In Bradfield Foundry, as we have already noted, there had also been friction between Indians and Pakistanis, but in this case it seems to have been mainly on a verbal level.[3] Moreover, there had been no friction between the Indian and West Indian workers, who tended to ignore each other. In Tool Steel Ltd., where the majority of coloured workers were Arabs and Paki-

[1] Firms 3, 12, 15, 18, 19, 24, 26, and 28.
[2] Firms 2, 6, 7, 14, 17, 20, and 23.
[3] See page 164.

stanis, there had been some friction between the different coloured groups, but again this seems to have been of a relatively minor nature. The Personnel Manager stated:

There have been isolated instances of trouble between the races, about four in ten to fifteen years. In general, we haven't had much cause for complaint. I have known foremen complain of the difficulty of putting one coloured worker with another of a different race, but it has not caused us any worry.

The Labour Officer of Brierley Metal Works, on the other hand, thought that conflict was inevitable if members of different coloured nationalities worked together. He stated that the firm used to have 'a fair amount of trouble due to the mixing of races, creeds, and religions'. The firm had therefore placed the different nationalities in separate, closely knit groups. The respondent claimed that this was the only way to preserve peaceful race relations. He stated that firms who tried to keep the different nationalities together ran into trouble and that firms were coming round to the point of view that it was best to employ only one race or to keep them separate if more than one was employed.

In the questionnaire survey, an attempt was made to obtain quantitative evidence concerning this question. Respondents were asked whether they thought the best policy with regard to the employment of different coloured nationalities was to employ only one nationality, to keep the different nationalities separate (such as, on different shifts or in different departments) or to employ and place them irrespective of nationality. The following answers were received:

	No.	%
Employ only one nationality	16	37
Keep separate	1	2
Employ and place irrespective of nationality	26	61
Total	43	100

It will be seen that over half the respondents thought that coloured workers should be employed and placed irrespective of nationality, whilst only one thought it necessary to keep the different national groups separate. However, a substantial minority believed that the best policy was to employ only one coloured group.

In only one of the interview survey firms had the number of coloured nationalities been limited because interracial friction had occurred. Omega Metals had at one time employed Arab workers but had ceased to do so because they 'did not get on with' the Pakistanis. In Steel Bars Ltd., however, Arab workers had been the first coloured immigrants to be employed, and the firm had made it a policy not to employ any other coloured groups because it was thought that this *might* lead to racial friction.

In three further firms, more than one coloured nationality had been employed, but had been placed in separate work groups. The Personnel Manager of Sterling Metal Co. stated that Arabs and Pakistanis had been kept apart; the firm had 'never tried mixing Arabs and Pakistanis in the same shop'. In Major Casting Ltd., a firm employing West Indians and Pakistanis, the Personnel Manager stated:

From my observation they don't mix. They confine themselves to their own people. They don't get much opportunity to mix. There had been some deliberate placing. We never put one coloured man alone in a department, and if there's two of them, they are of the same race.

Similarly, the Labour Officer of Hamilton Engineering Co. stated:

They tend to keep to themselves. It doesn't pay to mix them too much. We found that it was best to keep Pakistanis in one shop and West Indians in another. We have had as much of a clash between coloured and coloured as with white and coloured.

On the other hand, as we have already pointed out, in other firms in the interview survey different coloured nationalities had worked together without conflict arising. In Components Ltd., which, it is interesting to note, was situated on the same street as Brierley Metal Works, West Indians, Indians, and Pakistanis were employed in roughly equal numbers. According to the Personnel Officer, the different coloured nationalities were not kept separate as a matter of policy—the furnace group, for example, consisted of Indians, Pakistanis, and British workers—and yet no friction had occurred. In another firm, Indians and Pakistanis had been employed in the same work groups without management realizing it. The Labour Manager of Edge Tools Ltd. stated that when coloured workers had first been employed, it was thought that they were all Indians. It was not until an official visitor came to the firm to talk to their 'Indian' workers, that they discovered that the majority were Pakistanis. Nevertheless, some of them were Indians and the firm also employed West Indians and Arabs, yet here again there had been no interracial friction.

Amongst the coloured workers interviewed, only one expressed any hostility towards other coloured groups. The single West Indian worker employed in Omega Metals Ltd. stated:

I would work with Englishmen or West Indians, but not Indians or Pakistanis. I don't come into contact with the Pakistanis here, but they're the people who cause all the trouble. It makes your stomach sick, they're so ignorant. Before the Pakistanis came over here, a coloured chap could get a job, but they work for nothing, so it's quite likely that they (the employers) will have him. They'll do anything for less money.

In Edge Tools Ltd. one West Indian respondent said that he would prefer to work with other West Indians or British workers because he did not understand the Pakistanis very much. Another stated:

Naturally everybody would like to work with his own people. But if you get a factory where they are all mixed—Pakistanis, Indians, English—me I can get on with everybody so it doesn't make any difference.

All the remaining coloured workers, both West Indian and Asian, stated either that they had no preferences regarding with whom they worked or that they had not come across any of the other coloured groups at work.

To summarize: the available data suggests that the views of the Labour Officer of Brierley Metal Works concerning the inevitability of friction amongst the different coloured groups seem largely to be unjustified. In the majority of questionnaire survey firms, the different nationalities were prepared to accept each other as workers and in over half the firms it was the policy to employ and place coloured workers irrespective of nationality. Similarly, there had been no friction in many of the interview survey firms and only in a few cases was it the policy to employ only one coloured nationality or to place them in separate work groups.

Nevertheless, in the majority of firms, both in the questionnaire and interview surveys, the different coloured nationalities tended to remain in separate *social* groups. Here again, the most important factor seems to be that of cultural background— differences in values, religion, language, and so on. However, the somewhat limited data obtained in the interviews with coloured workers make it impossible to come to any firm conclusions with regard to this question.

5. *Summary*

We suggested in the introduction to this chapter that to view the pattern of inter-group relations at work in terms of a white-coloured dichotomy and even to examine the attitudes of the white workers in terms of simple acceptance or rejection was to over-simplify the situation to an unwarrantable degree. The data of both the interview and the questionnaire surveys lend considerable support to this contention.

1. The level of social integration between the different coloured groups was equally as low as between white and coloured workers, and conflict, although comparatively rare, had occurred in both cases.

2. The relatively low level of social integration in the case of white and coloured workers was due not only to a lack of social acceptance on the part of the white workers, but also in part to a tendency for the coloured workers to remain in their own social groups.

3. In the case of the white workers, the level of acceptance of coloured immigrants varied considerably under different circumstances. A major distinction was made between work and social acceptance, but the level of acceptance also varied within these categories in respect of a number of factors such as the

nationality of the coloured workers concerned, the numbers involved, and so on.

Thus any explanation of this situation must take into account not only the attitudes of the white workers, but also those of the coloured workers, both towards the white workers and the other coloured groups. A major factor, we suggested, was the question of cultural background—differences in values, language, religion, customs, and so on—which led each group to prefer the company of their fellows rather than the members of other groups with whom they had relatively little in common. However, this cannot provide a complete explanation. There existed considerable *similarities* in background between British and West Indian workers and, although the level of social integration was somewhat higher in this case, there was still a tendency to remain in separate social groups. Other factors must therefore be involved.

Apart from the minor differences in interests and topics of conversation which would result from having been born and brought up in different societies, we would suggest that three main considerations are relevant here. Firstly, there was evidence that avoidance of coloured workers resulted in part from a belief that they were of lower social status. This applied to Asian as well as West Indian workers, but is of greater importance in the latter case because differences in cultural background alone were sufficient to inhibit the social integration of the Asian group. Secondly, there existed erroneous beliefs amongst white workers which led them to believe that the cultural background of the West Indians was more different than was actually the case. And finally, although the West Indians wished to achieve full integration into British society, the possibility of rebuff from the white workers gave rise to a tendency to remain within their own social groups.

CHAPTER EIGHT

Summary and Conclusions

We suggested in Chapter One that the process of integration could be regarded as the outcome of an interaction between two sets of factors—the characteristics of the migrant groups and those of the receiving situation. In the industrial sphere, the characteristics which are of primary importance are respectively:
1. the skills and capabilities of the migrant group and their expectations towards the role which they are to play in the industrial system of the receiving country; and,
2. the vacancies available within this industrial system and the expectations of its members towards the migrant group.

It was further suggested that the process of adjustment between immigrant and host would proceed smoothly and without friction to the extent that these two sets of factors were complementary. Finally, we distinguished between four main spheres within which industrial integration may be said to take place; namely, employment level, occupational level, the treatment which the immigrants receive from managers, and supervisors, and inter-group relations at the shop floor level. Having examined the available data, both from the literature and the present research, we are now in a position to assess within the above framework the degree of industrial integration achieved by coloured immigrants to Britain.

Although precise data concerning the skill level of the immigrants are not available, it would appear that they have, in general, tended to be less skilled than British workers. Amongst the different coloured groups, however, West Indians have tended to be more skilled than Asian immigrants, with respect to both industrial sophistication and their ability to speak English as well as formal industrial training. Although less skilled according to British standards, skilled workers have, in fact, been over represented amongst West Indian migrants, in relation to the skill level of the general West Indian population.

During the greater part of the 1950s and early 1960s, there was a considerable shortage of labour in Britain, particularly in unskilled jobs. To this extent, then, the characteristics of the migrant population and those of the receiving situation were largely complementary. The immigrants were less skilled than British workers and wished to obtain jobs in British industry, and there were large numbers of unskilled vacancies which British firms desperately needed to fill. Undoubtedly, it was this state of affairs which stimulated the large-scale immigration from the Commonwealth in the post-war years. As we have already noted, however, the course of the integration process is not determined by objective factors alone. The respective orientations of migrant and host towards each other must also be taken into account.

Of particular importance are the attitudes of employers in the receiving country. Berry states that in the process of assimilation one society 'sets the pattern'.[1] The same may be said of the industrial sphere, where employers are in a position radically to affect the degree of industrial integration achieved by an immigrant group, simply because they have the power to grant or withhold the jobs which its members wish to obtain. Moreover, the decisions which the employers make will be based not so much on the actual attributes of the immigrant population as upon what they believe these attributes to be. In the present research cases were found in which erroneous beliefs affected employment opportunities for coloured workers. There was, for example, Ensign Springs where the Personnel Manager gave three reasons for the small number of coloured workers employed: (a) they lacked the necessary skill; (b) they had a high rate of labour turnover; and (c) the white employees would not accept a 'preponderence' of coloured workers. In fact, many of the jobs required little or no skill, labour turnover amongst the coloured workers was almost non-existent, and so few were employed that the danger of having a preponderance of them was negligible. In other cases, different managers expressed contradictory beliefs concerning coloured workers. One example was particularly striking. The Labour Officer of Brierley Metal Works claimed that Pakistanis were more educated than Indians

[1] B. Berry, op. cit.

whilst in Components Ltd., an adjacent firm, the Personnel Officer claimed that Indians were more educated than Pakistanis, and both firms preferred to employ the nationality believed to be *less* educated. To make such sweeping generalizations about the relative educational standards of Indians and Pakistanis seems highly dubious, but even if they were justified, it is impossible for both managers to be right.

In Chapter Three, we suggested that there are two main ways in which firms limit employment prospects for coloured immigrants. Firstly, there are the firms which will employ no coloured workers whatsoever. Considerable initial resistance to the employment of coloured workers was found in the firms studied during the present research. In general, firms would begin to employ coloured labour only when the shortage of British or foreign white workers became so severe that there was no other alternative. In firms where no coloured workers were employed, the usual reason given was the fact that there was an adequate supply of white labour. Secondly, there are the firms which do employ coloured workers, but still restrict the jobs available to them; for example by employing them only when white workers cannot be obtained; by limiting their numbers to a certain proportion of the labour force (the quota system), or by employing coloured workers only in certain departments or on certain jobs.

One effect of such policies has been to limit the actual number of jobs available to coloured workers. On the basis of a survey carried out by the Institute of Race Relations, Wood[1] concluded that coloured unemployment was at least twice as high as that of white workers. This view is supported by official statistics which have been released from time to time, and even greater disparities have been reported in particular areas. On the other hand, except during trade recessions when there is little demand for unskilled labour, the majority of coloured workers have been able to find work of some kind. Thus, perhaps a more important effect has been to limit the range of jobs available to coloured workers to those in industries most severely hit by labour shortage, and within these industries, initially at least, to the rough, heavy, less well paid labouring jobs which white workers prefer to avoid.

The question still remains, of course, as to whether such limi-

[1] D. Wood, op. cit.

tation of employment opportunities results from discrimination or simply from legitimate rejection of less skilled or less able workers. On the basis of the present evidence, it is impossible to assess with any degree of accuracy the relative importance of these two factors, but it would appear that both are involved. The available data in the literature suggests that coloured workers are, in general, less skilled than their British counterparts, but the evidence of the present study demonstrates that discrimination—whether as a deliberate policy or as a result of erroneous but genuinely held beliefs—also plays an important part.

It should be noted, however, that in the firms which do employ coloured labour, the reluctance of managers to accept coloured workers is to some extent only an initial phenomenon. With experience of their employment, managerial attitudes towards coloured workers often change considerably. As we have seen, the jobs available to coloured workers may still be limited in a number of ways, but in most firms in the present sample they had come to be accepted as a more or less normal part of the labour force. In only a few cases were their numbers restricted to an absolute minimum. In the majority of firms, coloured immigrants (or at least those of the nationality employed) were thought to be reasonably good workers and in some cases they were very highly regarded. In general, they were not used merely as 'stop-gap' labour; although the number of new coloured workers employed tended to decrease during trade recessions, existing coloured employees were, on the whole, fairly treated with respect to redundancy.

Moreover, whilst coloured workers were usually employed only as labourers at first, at least some coloured employees had later obtained semi-skilled jobs in the majority of firms, and in some cases they had progressed to skilled work. The occupational levels of coloured workers found in the questionnaire survey were lower than those of British and foreign white workers, but comparison with the available data concerning the skill levels of coloured immigrants to Britain, suggests that relatively few had experienced occupational downgrading, and many, in fact, had achieved considerable upgrading.

On the other hand, data obtained during the interview surveys indicate that British workers are often reluctant to accept coloured workers in positions directly above themselves in the status hierarchy. In general, the semi-skilled jobs obtained by coloured workers were of the differentiated type; that is, they either did not entail authority over other workers, or, if they did, the other workers were also coloured. Although the occupational levels of coloured workers were relatively high, therefore, it would appear that they could have been even higher had the British workers been more prepared to accept them in higher status jobs.

Thus far we have been concerned with the level of industrial integration achieved by coloured immigrants in general. In view of the higher skill level of the West Indian group, however, it might be expected that their employment and occupational levels would also be higher. Evidence that there is more unemployment amongst Pakistanis than West Indians was found by Davison.[1] On the other hand, the unemployment level was *lower* amongst Indians than West Indians, and the higher unemployment amongst Pakistanis can partially be explained in terms of geographical factors.

In the present research, no overall preference for West Indian workers was found amongst the managers interviewed. There was a tendency for firms to employ either West Indian or Asian immigrants, but the number of firms employing a preponderance of either group was approximately the same. Furthermore, the occupational level of Pakistani workers was only fractionally lower than that of the West Indians and those of Indians and Arabs, although admittedly based on a very small sample, were actually higher.

One of the main reasons for this somewhat surprising result, it is suggested, lies in the differing expectations of managers towards coloured immigrants. Although opinions often varied, the main advantage of employing West Indian immigrants was generally regarded to be the fact that, owing to their greater industrial sophistication and their ability to speak English, they were easier to train and supervise. On the other hand, the main advantages of employing Asian workers were said to be their greater diligence and amenability to discipline. Whether a firm employed one group or the other, therefore, depended to a considerable extent upon which set of characteristics were regarded

[1] *Commonwealth Immigrants.*

as being more desirable. In the firms studied during the present research, it would appear that there were sufficient managers who felt that the Asian workers' greater diligence and amenability to discipline more than compensated for their language difficulties and lack of industrial sophistication to ensure them relatively high employment and occupational levels.

To some extent, the attitudes of managers towards West Indian and Asian immigrants seem to have been based on the actual behaviour of these groups. The present data suggest that Asian workers are more prepared to comply unquestioningly with managerial instructions than West Indians, and accept much more willingly the menial jobs which coloured workers often obtain in British industry. These different patterns of behaviour in the industrial sphere, it is suggested, reflect the differing orientations of Asian and West Indian immigrants towards life in British society. In general, Asian immigrants do not wish to become fully integrated, but prefer to make only those adaptations to the British way of life which are necessary to achieve a minimum degree of accommodation into the receiving society's social and economic structure. Thus they tend to regard working in British industry merely as a means of making money and are little concerned with their status or even the treatment they receive in the firms in which they work. The West Indians, on the other hand, expect to obtain full integration into British society, and moreover many regard themselves, quite rightly in terms of West Indian standards, as being skilled workers. Often, therefore, they are quicker to object to what they consider to be unequal treatment or uncivil instructions, and are less willing to accept and work diligently at what they regard as being menial tasks, unworthy of their skills.

However, it would also appear that some managers[1] made considerably exaggerated claims concerning the lack of diligence and amenability to discipline of the West Indian workers they had employed. In these cases, it seems likely that the respondents expected a high level of diligence and amenability to discipline on the part of coloured workers, and formed an unfavourable opinion of West Indian workers in these respects, not because they were so much more 'lazy' or 'touchy' than British

[1] For example, those in Bradfield Foundry, Westwood Foundry and Omega Metals Ltd.

workers, but because, unlike Asian workers, they did not come up to the respondents' high level of expectation. In Edge Tools, an initially adverse assessment of West Indian workers eventually gave way, with continued experience of their employment, to a more favourable attitude towards them, which lends some support to this conclusion.

In the majority of interview firms, it appeared that coloured workers received reasonably fair treatment from managers and supervisors, but no firm conclusions can be drawn on the basis of the limited data available. In view of the above discussion, however, it may be significant that the few cases where discriminatory treatment was known or suspected to have occurred almost invariably involved Asian workers. Thus, to a certain extent, the differing skill levels of Asian and West Indian workers and their differing orientations towards the host society may be said to have cancelled each other out. In spite of their initially lower level of skill, the Asian workers' employment and occupational levels were remarkably similar to those of the West Indians, but they had achieved this at the expense of being more diligent, more amenable to discipline, and, occasionally, more prepared to accept discriminatory treatment.

A similar situation arises with respect to inter-group relations at the shop floor level. In the firms studied during the present research, there was a marked tendency for both West Indian and Asian workers to remain within their own social groups. However, it would appear that they did so for different reasons. In the social sphere, we again find that West Indian immigrants are more 'skilled', in the sense that they speak English as their native language and are much more conversant with British norms and values. Moreover, the West Indians wish to achieve full social acceptance, whilst the Asian immigrants, in general, prefer to remain socially separate, mainly because this enables them to retain their own distinct way of life, but perhaps also as a means of avoiding possible social conflict. As with work integration, however, the attitudes of members of the host society play a decisive role in determing the form of adjustment achieved by the immigrants. British workers, we suggested, are prepared to accept coloured immigrants as fellow workers, but are much less prepared to accept them in the realm of social relationships. On the other hand, despite the generally low level of social acceptance, there were indications that British workers were more prepared to accept coloured workers socially when their cultural background was similar to their own and when they were prepared to conform with the British workers' expectations towards coloured people by accepting a lower status role.

It will be seen that the respective orientations of West Indian and British workers are largely incompatible. They coincide to the extent that the West Indians desire social acceptance and the British workers are more prepared to accept them because of the greater similarities in cultural background. This, it is suggested, explains the higher degree of social integration achieved by West Indian workers in certain of the firms studied during the present research. For the most part, however, this is counterbalanced by the fact that the British workers are, in general, not prepared to accept coloured immigrants socially, irrespective of their cultural background, and West Indians are not prepared to accept the lower status role expected of them. In the case of the Asian workers, on the other hand, both groups have similar expectations towards each other; neither desires social integration. Thus, whereas the Asian workers remained in their own social groups from choice, the West Indians did so mainly because they were not accepted by the white workers or because they wished to avoid the possibility of rejection.

It might be expected, therefore, that relations between West Indian and British workers would involve greater social conflict than in the case of Asian workers. Several writers, such as Richmond,[1] Banton,[2] and Burt,[3] have noted the existence of considerable resentment amongst West Indian immigrants concerning their lack of social acceptance. In the present research, few of the coloured respondents expressed any bitterness towards white workers with respect to this question, but those who did so were West Indians. Similarly, in cases where white workers complained of difficulties in achieving an acceptable pattern of relationships with coloured workers, the workers concerned were usually West Indian. In other respects, however, greater resentment was expressed against Asian immigrants. Such resentment arose mainly because of differences in cultural

[1] *Colour Prejudice in Britain.*
[2] *Coloured Quarter.*
[3] R. Burt, op. cit.

background—the Asian workers' language difficulties, their different customs, and so on. This suggests that the Asian immigrants' desire to remain separate from the British workers was not entirely successful in avoiding social conflict. Although both groups wished to keep to themselves, this is possible only to a limited extent in a restricted environment such as that of the industrial concern, and the present research indicates that the presence of the Asian workers, in spite of their desire to remain separate, still impinged sufficiently upon the working life of British employees to give rise to resentment and friction.

Thus far we have been discussing industrial integration in the context of an immigration situation in which, as Burt puts it, 'race is a complicating, but not defining factor'.[1] In relation to the process of integration in the longer term, however, the present situation must be seen as no more than a period of transition. In the future, the characteristics of the migrant population and also the vacancies available in the receiving situation will become less and less important as factors determining the form of adjustment achieved by coloured workers in British industry. The children of the present generation of migrants, brought up and educated in this country, may retain some aspects of their parents' cultural background, especially in the case of Asian children, but the main difference between them and native British children will simply be a matter of colour. Similarly, as they will begin to look for jobs at the same time as British school leavers, the 'objective' vacancies available in industry will be the same for both groups. The main factor determining their level of industrial integration will, therefore, be the attitudes of British people in industry towards them.

Writing in 1960, Burt[2] stated '. . . we are not discussing a static situation. It is conceivable—though hopefully not probable—that a clear and identifiable "race problem" is *evolving* in Great Britain.' He concluded, however, that the situation was 'relatively stable and perhaps improving'. As far as the industrial situation is concerned, the present writer would tend to take a rather more pessimistic view. As we have seen, the present generation of migrants have made considerable progress to-

[1] See page 25 above.
[2] Op. cit.

wards work integration, at least when judged in terms of their skills, cultural background, and so on. Nevertheless, the range of jobs available to them is still restricted owing to the large number of firms still employing no coloured workers, and their opportunities for advancement are limited, partly by their lack of adequate apprenticeship training and partly by the reluctance of British workers, and also management, to accept them in higher status jobs. The danger for the future, and it is a very real one, lies in the possibility that the next generation of coloured workers will not maintain the progress made by their parents and may, in certain spheres, even have to begin again at the bottom of the industrial ladder.

As we noted in Chapter Three, one of the main factors limiting the number of jobs available to coloured workers is sheer inertia. Firms which have not been compelled by a shortage of white workers, seriously to consider the employment of coloured labour seem to prefer to 'leave well alone' rather than to take a chance on the unknown. Similarly, there are indications that managers are reluctant to give apprenticeships to coloured school leavers because they fear that the white workers may not accept them in skilled jobs. We have seen that, once the initial resistance to coloured workers has been overcome, most firms find that they are satisfactory workers, and that although resistance to coloured workers in higher status jobs does exist, this can be overcome and, in fact, has been overcome in a number of firms. In the writer's view, however, there is a strong possibility that firms not already employing coloured workers will not begin to do so and that in the firms in which they are employed, coloured school leavers will not be given apprenticeship jobs, simply because, although the risks involved may be relatively slight, the material benefits to the firm will be negligible. Providing sufficient white workers of an adequate standard can be obtained, firms will not lose anything by not employing coloured workers. Thus the only reasons for doing so are considerations such as the desire to avoid a possible future social problem or a belief in social equality, and it seems unlikely that this will be enough. Even if the social consequences of not employing coloured workers are recognized, it is all too easy for individual firms to argue that their own special problems make it too difficult for them to do so in their particular case, and to leave the employment of coloured labour to other firms who will, most probably, have the same attitudes as themselves.

In this case, the range of jobs available to the next generation of coloured workers is likely to be restricted largely to those available in firms which are already employing coloured immigrants at the present time. Moreover, as far as employment levels are concerned, coloured school leavers are likely to be in a worse position than their parents. Although the adult immigrant may have found it difficult to obtain a skilled or semi-skilled job at first, he at least had the opportunity of taking an unskilled job and perhaps later working his way up the job hierarchy. For the coloured school leaver at the age of fifteen, even this avenue for advancement is not available until he is old enough to be employed as a labourer. In the meantime, he may have to bide his time in a dead-end job, with the result that, when he does enter industry, he has no qualifications or training, and must accept the most menial of labouring work.

If future progress towards work integration is likely to be restricted, what then of social integration? We have seen that, in the realm of social relationships, the present generation of migrants has made relatively little progress towards industrial integration. However, the present research suggests that close social relationships are more likely to arise (a) when the immigrants' cultural background is similar to that of the British workers; (b) when there are few coloured workers in the firm or department concerned; and (c) when social contact occurs within the context of a close, formal work relationship. In the future, cultural differences between white and coloured workers may be expected to decrease considerably. This is not to say that they will disappear completely. As we have already noted, Asian children are likely to retain certain aspects of their parents' culture and similarly, in the case of West Indian children, some allegiance to and interest in the West Indies may remain. Nevertheless, the Asian children will at least learn English and gain much more knowledge of the British way of life than their parents, and as far as West Indian children are concerned, the minor differences in interests and topics of conversation which arise through being born and brought up in a different country from their British work-mates will largely disappear. One might expect, therefore, that they will become more integrated into the social structure of the firms in which they work than the present generation of migrants.

On the other hand, lack of work integration may to a considerable extent inhibit progress towards social integration at work. If firms continue to be reluctant to begin employing coloured workers, they will continue to be employed in relatively large numbers by those already doing so. Restriction of the range of jobs available to coloured workers within these firms will result in their concentration in particular departments and on particular jobs; and restriction of coloured workers to labouring jobs or the 'differentiated' type of skilled and semi-skilled job will tend to prevent the development of social relations based on formal work relationships. All this will encourage the white workers to regard coloured workers as a separate group within the firm, with their own group characteristics, instead of regarding each coloured worker as an individual. Thus coloured workers may still be thought of as strangers, even though cultural differences are in fact minimal. Furthermore, the restriction of coloured workers to lower status jobs may be expected to reinforce beliefs concerning the low *social* status of coloured people. On balance, therefore, there seems to be a strong possibility that the next generation of coloured workers will make little more progress toward social integration at work than their parents.

Thus, within the present immigration situation, there are the seeds of a future race problem in British industry; a situation in which coloured workers will become the 'second class citizens' of the industrial world, confined to certain industries which the white workers prefer to avoid, confined to the least desirable jobs within these industries and socially segregated from the remainder of the labour force. Perhaps this is an over-pessimistic view of the situation, but it is a possibility which must be faced now whilst there is still time to avert it. The measures suggested in the 1965 White Paper on immigration[1] seem unlikely to be sufficient to achieve this end. The prevention of discrimination in Employment Exchanges may be a necessary step, but it must be remembered that firms are no longer required by law to fill vacancies through an Employment Exchange, and as we have seen, many firms prefer to contact prospective coloured workers

[1] *Immigration from the Commonwealth*, London: H.M.S.O. Cmnd. 2739, August 1965.

through existing workers rather than to use official channels. The White Paper states that the efforts of the Youth Employment Service to help Commonwealth immigrant school leavers to obtain employment and training 'have met with a welcome measure of success'. Against this, there is the evidence of the present research and the statement of a Youth Employment Officer (quoted on page 58) that she would like to refuse to send anyone else to employers who discriminated against coloured people, but they were 'so numerous that this would be impossible to carry out'.[1]

If these measures are unlikely to be successful, or at least are unlikely to be successful enough, what further measures then are called for? The main necessity, the writer would suggest, is the extension of the present Race Relations Act[2] to include legislation against discrimination in employment in addition to discrimination in public places. At the time of writing, there are indications that this step may well be taken in the near future. In late 1966, a Private Member's Bill was introduced in Parliament which would have redefined 'places of public resort' to include such spheres as employment and housing. The Bill was later withdrawn, but on the understanding that the Government would itself introduce such legislation in the next session of Parliament should a survey then being carried out on behalf of the Race Relations Board and National Committee for Commonwealth Immigrants confirm that it was necessary. On the other hand, both the T.U.C. and the Confederation of British Industry have stated that they are opposed to Government legislation against discrimination in employment. After a meeting of the two groups held in January 1967, a joint statement was issued informing the Government that, in their view, neither an

---

[1] Newspaper reports suggest that coloured youths may experience considerable difficulty in obtaining apprenticeships and white collar jobs. The first, 'Insurance firms have race bar', *The Observer*, 28 November 1965, states: 'The C.A.R.D. (Campaign Against Racial Discrimination) action group hopes to send carefully matched pairs of applicants—one coloured, one white—to be interviewed for jobs. A preliminary test with several firms showed that they were prepared to reject a West Indian youth of good appearance and university entrance standard in favour of a less qualified English youth.' The second, 'Immigrant group alleges promotion barrier', *The Guardian*, 1 December 1965, states that, according to the Indian Workers Association of Great Britain, 'immigrant children leaving school are finding it almost impossible to obtain apprenticeships or to join training schemes.'

[2] *Race Relations Act 1965*, London: H.M.S.O.

extension of the Race Relations Act nor a clause denying Government contracts to discriminators was likely to succeed.[1]

American experience of anti-discrimination legislation does not support this view. According to Norgren and Hill, analysis of the effects of Fair Employment Practices commissions and their work provides 'strong evidence that F.E.P. legislation of the type now in effect in more than a third of the states can, if effectively administered, be a potent instrument in combating discrimination in employment'. They state:

Follow-up reviews of compliance actions conducted by the long-established commissions in New York, New Jersey, Philadelphia, and other jurisdictions provided the most direct indications of progress in overcoming racial bias in the allocation of jobs. The reviews and other studies conducted by the New York State Commission, in particular, revealed major breakthroughs and subsequent sustained improvement in employment of Negroes in banking, insurance, retail trade, and public utilities and in numerous traditionally 'all white' occupations in other industries. These evidences of substantial positive results from commission compliance efforts are borne out by the Census statistics on employment by occupation and colour for 1950 and 1960. A 1950–60 comparison of non-white representation in fourteen middle- and upper-level occupational categories in New York State revealed striking increases in nine categories and significant improvements in the other five. Moreover, on the average, the gains in non-white representation in New York were more than double, and in several instances more than triple, the corresponding increases in the total for three Midwestern states that had non-enforceable laws[2] during 1950–60.[3]

Furthermore, Norgren and Hill show that, providing that enforceable legislation against discrimination in employment exists, compliance can often be achieved without resorting to enforcement through legal channels. Most American Fair Employment Practices laws provide for a 'conciliation stage' after sufficient evidence has been obtained to support an allegation of discrimination. Norgren and Hill state:

In F.E.P. law parlance, the term 'conciliation' denotes conference approaches and techniques that utilize a combination of persuasion

[1] Quoted *The Guardian*, 18 January 1967.
[2] That is, laws which prohibit discrimination, but do not provide effective machinery for their enforcement.
[3] P. H. Norgren and S. E. Hill, *Toward Fair Employment*, Columbia, 1964.

16

and coercion. The commissioner meets with the non-complying employer and endeavours to persuade him to correct his practices voluntarily, while as an aid to the persuasion process, keeping him reminded that his non-compliance is illegal and may, if persisted in, result in unfavourable publicity or even legal sanctions.[1]

They conclude: 'The great majority of complaint cases handled by the New York Commission have been satisfactorily concluded through conciliation, both with respect to adjustment of individual grievances and revision of general policies and practices.'[2]

In Britain, the necessary machinery for the operation of legislation against discrimination in employment has already been devised in relation to the question of discrimination in public places. The 1965 Race Relations Act provides for a Race Relations Board and local conciliation committees in such areas as the Board considers necessary. It is the duty of the local conciliation committees to receive and consider any complaint concerning discrimination in places of public resort; to make such enquiries as they think necessary with respect to the facts alleged in any such complaint; and, where appropriate, to use their best endeavours by communication with the parties concerned or otherwise to secure the settlement of any difference between them and a satisfactory assurance against further discrimination. In any case where the local conciliation committee is unable to secure such a settlement, or such a settlement and assurance, or it appears that such an assurance is not being complied with, the committee makes a report to the Race Relations Board, who will, if it appears that an offence has taken place and is likely to continue, report the matter to the Attorney General or the Lord Advocate, as the case may be. In essence, these procedures are remarkably similar to those employed by American Fair Employment Practices commissions, and there would seem to be little difficulty involved in the extension of the

[1] Ibid.

[2] It may even be that, in some cases, compliance with anti-discrimination laws could be obtained without the necessity of going through any official channels whatsoever. Already coloured immigrant organizations are testing the probable effectiveness of the approaching legislation against discrimination in public places by patronizing public houses where landlords are said to practice a total colour bar or segregation (see 'Smethwick opens up to the "freedom drinkers"', *The Guardian*, 15 November 1965, page 5). It seems likely that many landlords will cease to discriminate of their own accord simply because they wish to avoid the possible inconvenience and adverse publicity of an official enquiry.

provisions of the Race Relations Act to cover legislation against discrimination in employment.

However, American experience indicates that these provisions alone are unlikely to be sufficiently effective. Norgren and Hill[1] suggest that, in addition to examining specific complaints of discriminations, F.E.P. commissions should attempt to eliminate all-over patterns of discriminatory practices pervading entire firms and should plan and programme these efforts over a number of years; should deal with complaints of discriminatory practices filed by minority-group organizations as well as by aggrieved individuals; and should initiate their own investigations when information suggesting the existence of discriminatory practices comes to their knowledge and, if the evidence warrants it, attempt to correct the discriminatory situation. The extension of the powers of local conciliation committees to include these procedures would, in the writer's view, greatly increase their effectiveness in the field of employment. It would transform their role from that of merely responding to specific allegations of discrimination to that of an organization working in a much more positive manner to secure the industrial integration of coloured people in Great Britain.

If, as we have suggested, one of the main factors limiting the range of jobs available to coloured workers is simple inertia rather than any deep-rooted opposition to their employment, then there is little doubt that, by means of the powers and procedures outlined above, local conciliation committees could make a very significant contribution towards overcoming discriminatory practices in industry, often without the necessity of resorting to legal sanctions. On the other hand, mere exhortation of employers to discontinue such practices, in the absence of any effective legislation to enforce compliance, is unlikely to produce the desired change in employment policies. Norgren and Hill[2] state that, in the United States, 'Neither non-enforceable F.E.P. laws nor voluntary F.E.P. programmes have had any appreciable effect in reducing employment discrimination'. Moreover, the existence of laws against discrimination in employment provides a powerful weapon for employers who wish to initiate non-discriminatory employment practices, but who meet with resistance from the white workers. According to Norgren and Hill,

[1] Op. cit.   [2] Ibid.

'Several company representatives stated that objections from white employees to the use of Negroes in non-traditional jobs could be effectively countered by citing state F.E.P. laws as a reason for changes in company policy.' It must be admitted, of course, that it is often dangerous to extrapolate directly from American experience in race relations to the British situation, but in the case of the examples cited above, the writer is strongly of the opinion that British reaction to legislation against discrimination in employment would not differ markedly from that already encountered in the United States.

This is not to say that the writer believes that effective legislation can provide a panacea which will immediately eliminate discrimination in employment or that such legislation alone can ensure the full industrial integration of coloured workers even in the longer term. For this to occur, far reaching changes in the attitudes and behaviour of both employers and British workers are also necessary. For these changes to take place, however dispersal of coloured workers throughout industry and throughout the different status levels within industry would seem to be a necessary prerequisite, and this does not seem likely to occur without the type of legislation outlined above. Furthermore, the time for such legislation is now, whilst the coloured school leavers are beginning to enter the labour market. We are at a cross-roads. If these children continue the progress made by their parents then there is the possibility that full industrial integration may be achieved in the foreseeable future. If they do not, then the present inequalities of employment and occupational levels will be perpetuated, perhaps becoming entrenched in the industrial system and thus more resistant to effective action in the future. The introduction of legislation against discrimination in employment may cause inconvenience or even hardship amongst employers who are unjustly accused of discriminatory practices; it may cause friction, either between workers and management or between white and coloured workers, where white employees are reluctant to accept coloured workers in skilled jobs or in apprenticeships, but this is a small price to pay for the avoidance of a future social problem of very serious magnitude.

APPENDIX

Firms[1] Visited During the Interview Surveys

Non-directive Survey

1. Precision Engineers Ltd.
Out of a total of 3,633 male manual workers, 381 were West Indian and 118 Indians and Pakistanis. The coloured workers were mainly employed in unskilled and semi-skilled jobs on the production side.
Respondents: Personnel Director, Personnel Officer, Training Officer, Union official and Works Council representative.

2. Bradfield Foundry
The male manual workers consisted of 77 Indians and Pakistanis, 37 British workers, 12 Italians, 4 West Indians, and 4 Arabs. 19 British and 4 West Indian women were also employed. Coloured workers were employed in skilled, semi- and unskilled jobs.
Respondents: Works Superintendent, Technical Controller, Production Manager, Fettling Shop Foreman.

3. City Transport
Out of 4,088 employees, 334 were coloured, including 238 West Indians, 83 Pakistanis, 10 Indians, 1 West African, 1 Somali, and 1 Arab. The coloured workers were mainly conductors, but there were 24 drivers, most of whom had been recruited from amongst the conductors.
Respondents: Personnel Manager, Assistant Personnel Manager.

4. Regal Manufacturing Co.
Forty coloured workers were employed out of a total of 1,650 employees. All the coloured workers were West Indian apart from the two 'East Indian youths'.
Respondent: Personnel Manager.

[1] As throughout the text, the firms have been given fictional names.

5. Ensign Spring Co.

A light manufacturing company employing 20 to 25 West Indians out of a total 800 to 900 employees. All the coloured workers were in unskilled jobs.

Respondent: Personnel Manager.

6. Brierley Metal Works

A foundry employing 700 coloured workers out of a total of 2,300 employees. The majority were Indians, but there were also some Pakistanis, about 6 West Indians and 1 or 2 Arabs and West Africans. Coloured workers were employed in skilled, semi-skilled and unskilled jobs.

Respondent: Labour Officer.

7. Westwood Foundry

Out of approximately 500 employees, 45 per cent were Indian, 40 per cent British, 8 per cent Pakistani, and 3 per cent West Indian. Coloured workers were employed in skilled, semi-skilled and unskilled jobs.

Respondents: Labour Officer, Assistant Labour Officer.

8. Components Ltd.

A foundry employing approximately 500 workers; 4 per cent were Indians, 4 per cent Pakistanis and 4 per cent were West Indians. Some coloured workers had obtained skilled jobs, but the majority were labourers.

Respondent: Personnel Officer.

9. Drop Forgings Ltd.

This firm had employed Indians during the Second World War, but only West Indians were employed at the time the present study was carried out. There were 55 West Indian workers out of a total labour force of 450 manual workers and they were employed mainly on the production side in skilled, semi-skilled and unskilled jobs.

Respondent: Personnel Manager.

10. Trafford Iron & Steel Co.

West Indians were the only coloured workers employed and they constituted 10 per cent to 12·5 per cent of the labour force. They did semi-skilled and labouring jobs.

Respondent: Personnel Officer.

11. Central Glass Works
All the coloured workers were West Indian. They constituted some 12 per cent of the labour force and were mainly employed in unskilled jobs on the production side.
Respondent: Personnel Manager.

12. Muirhead Foundry
Seventy-five per cent of the labour force was coloured, the majority being Indians, but there were also a few Pakistanis and West Indians. Coloured workers were employed 'on every operation in the foundry except fitting'.
Respondent: Personnel Manager.

13. Edge Tools Ltd.
The firm employed 81 coloured workers, including 70 Pakistanis, Indians and Arabs, 9 or 10 West Indians, and 1 or 2 Africans, out of a total labour force of 218. The coloured workers were in labouring and semi-skilled jobs.
Respondents: Labour Manager; 2 Chargehands, 6 British workers, 6 West Indians, 5 Pakistanis, and 1 Indian (formal interviews).

14. Omega Metals Ltd.
A small heavy engineering company. The manual workers consisted of 53 Pakistanis, 9 British workers, and 1 West Indian. The coloured workers were employed on skilled, semi-skilled and labouring jobs. One of the Pakistanis was a Chargehand.
Respondents: Works Manager; Foreman, Works Engineer, 11 Pakistanis (including the Chargehand), 6 British workers, and 1 West Indian (formal interviews).

Directive Interview Survey

15. Major Castings Ltd.
A foundry employing 44 coloured workers, including 29 West Indians, 12 Pakistanis, 2 West Africans, and 1 Indian, out of a total labour force of 3,200. In the main the coloured workers were labourers, but a small proportion had obtained semi-skilled jobs.
Respondents: Personnel Manager, Assistant Personnel Manager; Convener of the Shop Stewards Committee, 1 Pakistani worker (formal interviews); 1 British worker and 1 West African (informal interviews).

16. Quality Steel Co.

A steel works employing about 6 Arabs and Pakistanis out of a total labour force of 700. The coloured workers were mainly employed in labouring jobs.

Respondents: Personnel Officer; British worker (formal interview).

17. Tool Steel Ltd.

A heavy engineering company, employing 40 to 50 coloured workers, mainly Pakistanis and Arabs out of a total labour force of 1,200. Coloured workers were mainly employed in unskilled jobs.

Respondents: Personnel Manager, Assistant Personnel Manager.

18. Annerley Iron Foundry

Ironfounders and engineers. Nine coloured workers were employed (6 Arabs, 2 West Indians and 1 Pakistani) out of a total of 50 employees. All were in unskilled jobs, except for 1 Arab semi-skilled worker.

Respondents: Works Manager; 1 West Indian, 1 Arab and 1 British worker (formal interviews).

19. Leigham Cannery

A food canning and packing factory. About 1,000 workers were employed, 10 per cent of whom were coloured. These were mainly Pakistanis and West Indians, in about equal numbers, but there were also 'a few Indians and 1 or 2 Somalis'. The coloured workers were in labouring and semi-skilled jobs.

Respondents: Personnel Officer; 3 British workers, 2 West Indians, 1 Somali (formal interviews).

20. Hamilton Engineering Co.

Fourteen coloured workers were employed out of a total of 2,400 manual workers. All were West Indian, but Pakistanis had been employed in the past. Coloured workers were employed in unskilled and semi-skilled jobs in about equal numbers.

Respondents: Labour Officer; 6 West Indians, 1 British worker (formal interviews); 2 West Indians (informal interviews).

21. Torrington Cutlers Ltd.

Goldsmiths, silversmiths and cutlers. Five coloured workers were employed, all West Indians, out of a total of 300 workers. All were in unskilled jobs, mainly services to production.

Respondents: Works Director; 2 British workers, 5 West Indians (formal interviews).

22. Grange Graphite Co.
Seventy-five coloured workers were employed out of a total of 632
employees. About 60 per cent of the coloured workers were Pakistanis
and Arabs, the remainder being West Indians. Almost all were in
unskilled jobs.
Respondent: Personnel Officer.

23. Sovereign Steel Works
A steel works and engineering company, this firm employed 200
coloured workers out of a total labour force of 2,600. The majority
were Arabs and Pakistanis, but 'quite a few' were West Indians and
there were also Somalis, East Africans, and South Africans in smaller
numbers. They were mainly in unskilled jobs, but some had obtained
semi-skilled posts.
Respondents: Personnel Manager; Labour Manager, Assistant
Labour Manager, a foreman, 6 British workers, 3 Arabs, 2 Somalis,
1 Pakistani, 1 West Indian, and 1 East African (informal interviews).

24. Sterling Metal Co.
Stainless steel manufacturers. Eighty-nine coloured workers (Somalis,
Arabs, and Pakistanis) were employed, mainly in semi-skilled and
unskilled jobs, but a small number had obtained skilled jobs and one
was a Chargehand.
Respondents: Personnel Manager; 2 Departmental Managers, a foreman, a shop steward, 1 British worker, and 4 Somalis (informal
interviews).

25. Ridgeway Steel Co.
Manufacturers of steel strip, steel bars, and wire. Fourteen Pakistanis
were employed out of a total of 2,500 employees. Ten were labourers
and the remainder were in semi-skilled jobs.
Respondents: Personnel Manager; Assistant Personnel Manager, a
foreman, and 2 Pakistanis (informal interviews).

26. Stainless Steel Ltd.
A stainless steel foundry, this firm employed 3 coloured workers, 2
Pakistanis and an Arab, out of a total of 109 manual workers. All
were in unskilled jobs.
Respondents: General Manager; 1 British worker and 1 Pakistani
(informal interviews).

27. Polton Rolling Mills
Eighty to 100 coloured workers, mainly Arabs and Pakistanis, were

employed out of a total of 550 to 600 employees. The majority were labourers, but some had obtained semi-skilled jobs.

Respondents: Labour Officer; 1 British supervisor and 1 Pakistani (formal interviews); 2 Departmental Managers (informal interviews).

28. Castle Iron Co.

An iron and steel works employing 20 coloured workers, mainly Pakistanis, out of a total of 190 to 200 employees. The coloured workers were in unskilled and semi-skilled jobs.

Respondent: Personnel Manager.

29. Steel Bars Ltd.

A rolling mill, employing 8 coloured workers, all Arabs, out of a total of 62 employees. The coloured workers were employed in semi-skilled and unskilled jobs.

Respondents: Works Director; a foreman, 1 British worker, and 1 Arab (formal interviews).

30. Blackford Rolling Mills

This firm had previously employed Arab and Pakistani workers on a full time basis, but at the time of the present study they were employed only as casual labourers during the yearly 'shut down'.

Respondent: Production Services Manager.

31. Pentland Alloys Ltd.

A heavy engineering company. Thirty-five West Indians were employed out of a total of 4,000 employees. They were in semi-skilled and unskilled jobs.

Respondents: Personnel Manager; 4 British workers, 4 West Indians (formal interviews).

BIBLIOGRAPHY

H. A. Alavi, 'Pakistanis in Britain', London Council of Social Service: Extract from a report prepared for the Overseas Socialist Fellowship, 1963.

G. W. Allport, 'Prejudice: A Problem in Psychological and Sociological Causation' in *Towards a General Theory of Action*, T. Parsons and E. Shils (eds.), Harvard University Press, 1951.

G. W. Allport, *The Nature of Prejudice*, New York: Doubleday, 1958.

G. W. Allport, 'Prejudice: Is it Societal or Personal?' in *Journal of Social Issues*, Vol. 18, 1962.

M. Argyle, *Psychology and Social Problems*, London: Methuen, 1964.

M. P. Banton, *Coloured Quarter*, London: Jonathan Cape, 1955.

M. P. Banton, *White and Coloured*, London: Jonathan Cape, 1959.

M. P. Banton, 'Social Distance: A New Appreciation' in *The Sociological Review*, Vol. 8, 1960.

Ruth Benedict, *Race and Racism*, London: Scientific Book Club, 1943.

Jessie Bernard, 'Where is the Modern Sociology of Conflict' in *American Journal of Sociology*, Vol. 56, 1950.

B. Berry, *Race Relations*, Boston: Houghton Mifflin, 1951.

J. Biesanz and L. M. Smith, 'Race Relations in Panama and the Canal Zone' in *American Journal of Sociology*, Vol. 57, 1951.

H. Blumer, 'Recent Research into Race Relations: United States of America' in *International Social Science Bulletin*, Vol. 10, 1958.

W. D. Borrie, *The Cultural Integration of Immigrants*, Paris: Unesco, 1959.

H. Brunle, 'The Cultural Assimilation of Immigrants' in *Cultural Assimilation of Immigrants*; *Population Studies Supplement*, March 1950.

R. Burt, *Colour Prejudice in Britain*, unpublished Senior Thesis, Princeton University, 1960.

E. Butterworth, 'Aspects of Race Relations in Bradford' in *Race*, Vol. 6, 1964.

A. T. Carey, *Colonial Students*, London: Secker and Warburg, 1956.

S. Chase, *Roads to Agreement*, London: Phoenix House, 1952.

S. Collins, *Coloured Minorities in Britain*, London: Lutterworth Press, 1957.

L. A. Coser, *The Function of Social Conflict*, London: Routledge and Kegan Paul, 1956.

G. E. Cumper, 'Working Class Migrants to the U.K., October 1955' in *Social and Economic Studies*, Vol. 6, 1957.

R. B. Davison, *West Indian Migrants*, Oxford University Press, 1962.

R. B. Davison, *Commonwealth Immigrants*, Oxford University Press, 1964.

R. Desai, *Indian Immigrants in Britain*, Oxford University Press, 1963.

Economist Intelligence Unit, *Studies on Immigration from the Commonwealth*, 4. *The Employment of Immigrants*, London, 1962.

S. N. Eisenstadt, *The Absorption of Immigrants*, London: Routledge and Kegan Paul, 1954.

H. P. Fairchild, *Immigration*, New York: MacMillan, 1924.

E. L. Faris, 'Development of the Small Group Research Movement' in *Group Relations at the Crossroads*, M. Sherif and M. O. Wilson (eds.), New York: Harper, 1953.

Ruth Glass, *Newcomers*, London: Allen and Unwin, 1960.

D. V. Glass, 'Introduction' to *Cultural Assimilation of Immigrants*; *Population Studies Supplement*, March 1950.

F. M. Hankins, 'Social Discrimination' in *Encyclopaedia of the Social Sciences*, London: MacMillan, 1934.

J. Harding and R. Hogrefe, 'Attitudes of Department Store Employees towards Negro Co-workers' in *Journal of Social Issues*, Vol. 8, 1952.

Judith Henderson, 'A Sociological Report' in *Coloured Immigrants in Britain*, Oxford University Press, 1960.

C. S. Hill, *West Indian Migrants and the London Churches*, Oxford University Press, 1963.

M. Hill, 'Some Problems of Social Distance in Intergroup Relations' in *Group Relations at the Crossroads*, M. Sherif and M. O. Wilson (eds.), New York: Harper, 1953.

Kathleen Hunter, *History of Pakistanis in Britain*, Norwich: Page Bros., 1963.

A. Hyndman, 'The West Indian in London' in *The West Indian Comes to Britain*, S. K. Ruik (ed.), London: Routledge and Kegan Paul, 1960.

D. P. Irish, 'Reactions of Caucasian Residents to Japanese-American Neighbours' in *Journal of Social Issues*, Vol. 8, 1952.

C. Kondapi, *Indians Overseas*, New Delhi: Indian Council of World Affairs, 1949.

D. Krech and D. S. Crutchfield, *Theories and Problems of Social Psychology*, New York: McGraw-Hill, 1948.

Ruth Landes, 'A Preliminary Statement of a Survey of Negro-White Relationships in Great Britain', unpublished communication, Royal Anthropological Institute, 6 May 1952.

F. F. Lee, 'Racial Patterns in a British City: An Institutional Approach' in *Phylon*, 1st Quarter 1960.

R. Lewis, 'Americanization' in *Encyclopaedia of the Social Sciences*, London: MacMillan, 1930.

S. Lieberson, 'A Societal Theory of Race and Ethnic Relations' in *American Sociological Review*, Vol. 26, 1961.

K. L. Little, *Negroes in Britain*, London: Kegan Paul, 1948.

K. L. Little, 'Race and Society' in *The Race Question in Modern Science*, London: Sidgwick and Jackson, 1956.

G. A. Lundburg, *Foundations of Sociology*, New York: MacMillan, 1939.

Barbara G. McKenzie, 'The Importance of Contact in Determining Attitudes towards Negroes' in *Journal of Abnormal and Social Psychology*, Vol. 43, 1948.

G. Mauco, 'The Assimilation of Foreigners in France' in *Cultural Assimilation of Immigrants*; *Population Studies Supplement*, March 1950.

W. F. Maunder, 'The New Jamaican Migration' in *Social and Economic Studies*, Vol. 4, No. 1, 1955.

R. D. Minard, 'Race Relations in the Pocahontas Coal Field' in *Journal of Social Issues*, Vol. 8, 1952.

G. Myrdal, *An American Dilemma*, New York: Harper, 1944.

P. H. Norgren and S. E. Hill, *Toward Fair Employment*, Columbia University Press, 1964.

R. E. Park, 'Our Racial Frontier on the Pacific' in *Survey Graphic*, Vol. 9, May 1926. Reprinted in R. E. Park, *Race and Culture*, Glencoe Ill., Free Press, 1926.

R. E. Park, 'Assimilation, Social' in *Encyclopaedia of the Social Sciences*, London: MacMillan, 1930.

R. E. Park and E. Burgess, *Introduction to the Science of Sociology*, Chicago: University Press, 1924.

Sheila Patterson, *Dark Strangers*, London: Tavistock Publications, 1963.

Nadine Peppard, 'The Co-ordination of Social Sciences for Migrant Workers' in *Institute of Race Relations Newsletter*; *Supplement*, May 1963.

T. F. Pettigrew, 'Regional Differences in Anti-Negro Prejudice' in *Journal of Abnormal and Social Psychology*, Vol. 59, 1959.

T. F. Pettigrew, 'Social Psychology and Desegregation Research' in *American Psychologist*, Vol. 16, 1961.

E. Raab and S. M. Lipset, *Prejudice and Society*, New York: Anti-Defamation League, 1959.

Janet Reid, 'Employment of Negroes in Manchester' in *The Sociological Review*, Vol. 4, 1956.

D. C. Reitzes, 'The Role of Organizational Structures' in *Journal of Social Issues*, Vol. 9, 1953.

D. C. Reitzes, 'Institutional Structure and Race Relations' in *Phylon*, 1st Quarter 1959.

J. Rex, 'Integration: the Reality' in *New Society*, 12 August 1965.

A. H. Richmond, *Colour Prejudice in Britain*, London: Routledge and Kegan Paul, 1954.

A. H. Richmond, 'The Study of Race Relations' in *Man*, Vol. 57, 1957.

A. H. Richmond, 'Recent Research in Race Relations: Great Britain' in *International Social Science Bulletin*, Vol. 10, 1958.

A. H. Richmond, 'Applied Social Science and Public Policy Concerning Race Relations' in *Race*, Vol. 1, 1960.

A. H. Richmond, *The Colour Problem*, Harmondsworth: Penguin Books, 1961.

G. W. Roberts and D. O. Mills, 'Study of External Migration Affecting Jamaica: 1953–1955' in *Social and Economic Studies*, Vol. 7, 1958.

A. M. Rose, 'The Roots of Prejudice' in *The Race Question in Modern Science*, Paris: Unesco, 1956.

A. M. Rose, 'Intergroup Relations vs. Prejudice: Pertinent Theory for the Study of Social Change' in *Social Problems*, Vol. 4, 1956.

A. M. Rose, 'The Causes of Prejudice' in *American Minorities*, M. L. Barron (ed.), New York: Alfred A. Knopf, 1957.

C. Senior and D. Manley, *A Report on Jamaican Migration to Great Britain*, Kingston, Jamaica: Government Publications, 1955.

C. Senior, 'Race Relations and Labour Supply in Great Britain', paper for the American Sociological Society, Race Relations Section, Detroit, 1956. Published with minor alterations in *Social Problems*, Vol. 4, 1957.

S. Salvon, 'The West Indians in our Midst' in *The Times*, 27 August 1961.

G. Simmel, 'The Stranger' in *The Sociology of George Simmel*, K. H. Wolff (ed. and translator), Glencoe, Ill.: Free Press, 1950.

L. Stephens, 'Employment of Coloured Workers in the Birmingham Area', London: Institute of Personnel Management Occasional Paper, 1956.

S. A. Stouffer, E. A. Suchman, L. C. Devinney, Shirley A. Star, R. M. Williams, Jnr., *Studies in Social Psychology in World War II*, Vol. 1. *The American Soldier: Adjustment During Army Life*, Princeton: University Press, 1949.

H. C. Triandis and L. M. Triandis, 'Race, Social Class, Religion and Nationality as Determinants of Social Distance' in *Journal of Abnormal and Social Psychology*, Vol. 61, 1961.

R. H. Turner, 'The Relative Position of the Negro Male in the Labour Force of large American Cities' in *American Sociological Review*, Vol. 16, 1951.

O. C. Useem and Ruth H. Useem, 'Minority Group Pattern in Prairie Society' in *American Journal of Sociology*, Vol. 50, 1945.

V. Waughray, 'Race Relations in Britain' in *Peace News*, pamphlet, 1961.

J. Wickenden, *Colour in Britain*, Oxford University Press, 1958.

R. M. Williams, Jnr., 'Basic Assumptions and Principle Techniques in Intergroup Action Programs' in *American Minorities*, M. L. Barron (ed.), New York: Alfred A. Knopf, 1957.

D. Wood, 'A General Survey' in *Coloured Immigrants in Britain*, Oxford University Press, 1960.

B. Zawadski, 'The Limitations of the Scapegoat Theory of Prejudice' in *Journal of Abnormal aud Social Psychology*, Vol. 43, 1948.

Index

QUEEN MARY COLL

WITHDRAWN
FROM STOCK
QMUL LIBRARY